SOTHEBY, WILKINSON & HODGE,
WELLINGTON STREET, STRAND, LONDON.

CATALOGUE

OF VALUABLE

Illuminated and other Manuscripts

AND

EARLY PRINTED & MODERN BOOKS.

Days of Sale.

FIRST DAY	Monday, 16th March	LOTS	1 to 280
SECOND DAY	Tuesday, 17th March	LOTS	281 to 504
THIRD DAY	Wednesday, 18th March	LOTS	505 to 715
FOURTH DAY	Thursday, 19th March	LOTS	716 to 978
FIFTH DAY	Friday, 20th March	LOTS	979 to 1255
SIXTH DAY	Saturday, 21st March	LOTS	1256 to 1433

1903

CATALOGUE

OF VALUABLE

Illuminated & other Manuscripts

AND

EARLY PRINTED & MODERN BOOKS,

COMPRISING A NUMBER OF

Manuscript Hours, Offices, Psalters, Missals, Antiphonaries,

AND OTHER ANCIENT SERVICE BOOKS,

A VERY FINE ILLUMINATED WYCLIFFE NEW TESTAMENT,
Written in 1425;

CODEXES OF THE NEW TESTAMENT;

Ancient Historical and Theological Manuscripts;

AN IMPORTANT SERIES OF RARE EDITIONS OF SHAKESPEARE,
AND WORKS RELATING TO HIM;

VALUABLE AND RARE WORKS ON AMERICA,

A SERIES OF SCARCE FIRST AND EARLY EDITIONS OF JOHN BUNYAN'S
WRITINGS,

ROMAN CATHOLIC BOOKS PRINTED ABROAD,

VERY NUMEROUS & RARE EARLY PRINTED ENGLISH & FOREIGN BOOKS,

BOOKS ILLUSTRATED BY CRUIKSHANK, ROWLANDSON, AND OTHERS;

Fine Art, Architectural and Topographical Works,

FIRST EDITIONS OF AUTHORS OF THE XVIIITH AND XIXTH CENTURIES,

AN IMPORTANT SERIES OF THE

Publications of Famous Modern Presses.

WHICH WILL BE SOLD BY AUCTION

BY MESSRS.

SOTHEBY, WILKINSON & HODGE,

Auctioneers of Literary Property & Works illustrative of the Fine Arts,

AT THEIR HOUSE, No. 13, WELLINGTON STREET, STRAND, W.C.

On MONDAY, 16th day of MARCH, 1903, and Five following Days,

AT ONE O'CLOCK PRECISELY.

MAY BE VIEWED TWO DAYS PRIOR. CATALOGUES MAY BE HAD.

DRYDEN PRESS: J. DAVY & SONS, 137, LONG ACRE, W.C.

CONDITIONS OF SALE.

I. The highest bidder to be the buyer; and if any dispute arise between bidders, the lot so disputed shall be immediately put up again, provided the Auctioneer cannot decide the said dispute.

II. No person to advance less than 1*s*.; above five pounds, 2*s*. 6*d*.; and so on in proportion.

III. In the case of lots upon which there is a reserve, the Auctioneer shall have the right to bid on behalf of the Seller.

IV. The purchasers to give in their names and places of abode, and to pay down 10*s*. in the pound, if required, in part payment of the purchase-money; in default of which the lot or lots purchased to be immediately put up again and re-sold.

V. The lots to be taken away at the buyer's expense immediately after the conclusion of the sale; in default of which Messrs. SOTHEBY, WILKINSON & HODGE, will not hold themselves responsible, if lost, stolen, damaged, or otherwise destroyed, but they will be left at the sole risk of the purchaser. If, at the expiration of ONE WEEK after the conclusion of the sale, the books or other property are not cleared or paid for, they will then be catalogued for immediate sale, and the expenses (the same as if re-sold) will be added to the amount at which the books were bought. Messrs. SOTHEBY, WILKINSON & HODGE will have the option of re-selling the lots uncleared, either by public or private sale, without any notice being given to the defaulter.

VI. All the books are presumed to be perfect unless otherwise expressed; but if, upon collating, any should prove defective, the purchaser will be at liberty to take or reject them, provided they are returned within ONE WEEK after the conclusion of the sale, when the purchase-money will be returned.

VII. The sale of any book or books is not to be set aside on account of any worm-holes, stained or short leaves of text or plates, want of list of plates, or blank leaves, or on account of the publication of any subsequent volume, supplement, appendix or plates. All the manuscripts, autographs, all magazines and reviews, all books in lots, and all tracts in lots or volumes, will be sold with all faults, imperfections, and errors of description. The sale of any illustrated book, lot of prints or drawings, is not to be set aside on account of any error in the enumeration of the numbers stated, or error of description.

VIII. No IMPERFECT BOOK will be taken back, unless a note accompanies each book, stating its imperfections, with the number of lot and date of the sale at which the same was purchased.

IX. To prevent inaccuracy in the delivery, and inconvenience in the settlement of the purchases, no lot can on any account be removed during the time of sale.

X. Upon failure of complying with the above Conditions, the money required and deposited in part of payment shall be forfeited; and *if any loss is sustained in the re-selling of such lots as are not cleared or paid for, all charges on such re-sale shall be made good by the defaulters at this sale.*

Gentlemen who cannot attend the Sale may have their Commissions faithfully executed by their humble servants,

SOTHEBY, WILKINSON & HODGE,

13, Wellington Street, Strand, London.

CATALOGUE

OF

𝕺𝖆𝖑𝖚𝖆𝖇𝖑𝖊 𝕭𝖔𝖔𝖐𝖘 & 𝕸𝖆𝖓𝖚𝖘𝖈𝖗𝖎𝖕𝖙𝖘.

FIRST DAY'S SALE.

OCTAVO ET INFRA.

LOT 1

1   BRIEF TREATISE concerning the Burnynge of Bucer and Phagius at Cambrydge......translated into English by ARTHUR GOLDYNG, *portions of text in facsimile*, black letter, *mottled calf, g. e. Thomas Marshe, 1562*—CLARK (Sa.) A Mirror or Looking Glasse for Saints, *portrait by* GAYWOOD, *and frontispiece in compartments, calf gilt, 1654*; and another (3)

2   A'Beckett. Comic History of England, *coloured plates and wood-cuts by John Leech*, FIRST EDITION, 2 vol. *half calf (broken)* 1847-8

3   Across Country, by "Wanderer," *numerous coloured plates by G. Bowers*, FIRST EDITION, *cloth gilt, uncut* 1882

4   Acton (Harriet and Rose) Poems, FIRST EDITION, *with long list of subscribers' names, for the Authors*, 1846—Toulmin (Camilla) Poems, FIRST EDITION, *Orr & Co.* 1846   *2 vol.*

5   Addison (J.) Poems on several Occasions, with a Dissertation upon the Roman Poets, FIRST EDITION, *portrait (usually wanting) and plates, original calf*   *E. Curll,* 1719

6   Address to Persons of Fashion, relating to Balls, with some occasional hints concerning Play Houses, Card Tables, &c. *old calf*, 1771—A New Dictionary of the Fashionable World, *frontispiece, calf gilt*, 1820—A Suit of Armour for Youth, *plates, calf gilt*, 1824 (3)

7   Æsop. Æsopi Phrygis Fabulæ, Gr. et Lat. cum aliis Opusculis, *ancient MS. notes in the margins, old calf (rebacked), with an allegorical figure of Faith stamped on each side of the binding*   *Basil.* 1541

B

8   Ainsworth (W. H.) The Tower of London, FIRST EDITION, *plates
    by George Cruikshank, purple morocco extra gilt, t. e. g. uncut, by
    Rivière*   1840

9   Ainsworth (W. H.) The Miser's Daughter, 3 vol. FIRST EDITION,
    *numerous plates by George Cruikshank, crushed levant morocco
    extra gilt, t. e. g. uncut*   1842

    *** Special copy with the plates in two states, plain and coloured ;
    scarce.

10 Ainsworth (W. H.) Saint James's : or the Court of Queen Anne,
    3 vol. FIRST EDITION, *with illustrations by Geo. Cruikshank, half
    bound*   1844

11 Ainsworth (W. H.) The Flitch of Bacon, FIRST EDITION, *with the
    illustrations by John Gilbert, half morocco, t. e. g. uncut (illustrated
    cover and back bound up at end)*   1854

12 A'Kempis (Thos.) Viator Christianus Recta ac Regia in Coelum
    Via tendens (Imitatio Christi, &c.) nova cura recensuit J. M.
    Horstius, *copperplate engravings*, 2 vol. in 1, *old boarded black
    morocco, with clasps*, 16mo, *Col. Agr.* 1643—S. Pufendorfii de
    Officio Hominis et Civis, *Traj.* 1728—H. Grotii de Jure Belli
    ac Pacio, *Amst.* 1712   (3)

13 Almack (Edw.) The Cavalier Soldier's Vade-Mecum, reproduced
    in facsimile from the unique copy, with Introduction and
    Notes, *plates, one of 50 copies on hand-made paper (No. 47), half
    bound, uncut*   *Blades,* 1900

14 America. Aikin (Dr.) Letters from a Father to his Son, on
    various topics, *original calf*   *Philadelphia, M. Carey,* 1796

15 America. Benzoni (G.) Novæ Novi orbis Historiæ, id est Rerum
    ab Hispanis in India Occidentali hactenus gestarum, et acerbo
    illorum in eas gentes dominatu his adjuncta est de Gallorum
    in Floridam expeditione, *limp vellum*
                                          Genevæ apud E. Vignon, 1578

16 America. Byron (Lord) English Bards and Scotch Reviewers,
    FIRST AMERICAN EDITION, *original boards, uncut*
                                                      New York, 1817

17 America. Collection of Memorials concerning the Quakers in
    Pennsylvania, New Jersey, &c. *original binding*   1788

18 America. Examination of Lord Sheffield's Observations on the
    Commerce of the United States, and Notes on American
    Manufactures, *Philadelphia*, 1791—Letter from a West-India
    Merchant concerning that part of the French Proposals which
    relates to North America, 1712, *unbound*   (2)

19 America. Franklin (Dr. B.) Information to those who would
    remove to America, and Remarks on the Savages of N.
    America, 1784—A Circular Letter from George Washington
    to Wm. Greene, Governor of Rhode Island, 1783 —Wolfe
    (Gen.) Instructions to Young Officers......a Placart to the
    Canadians, &c. 1780, *unbound and original sheep binding*   (3)

20 America. Johnson (Dr. Samuel) Elementa Philosophica; containing chiefly Noetica, or Things relating to the Mind and
Understanding : and Ethica, or Things relating to the Moral
behaviour, *fine copy, original calf*
Philadelphia, printed by B. FRANKLIN *and* D. HALL, 1752
**** ONE OF THE RAREST WORKS PRINTED BY B. FRANKLIN.
Not in the British Museum or in Mr. Stevens' list of works
printed by Franklin. The work is divided into two parts,
each bearing Franklin's imprint with the above general
title.

21 America. Lynch (Dean) Sermon preached before the Incorporated Society for the Propagation of the Gospel in Foreign
Parts, 1736—Browne (A.) Sermon preached at Portsmouth,
New Hampshire, 1748, *presentation copy from the author, Portsmouth, n. d.* — Sermon preached at Portsmouth, N. H.
presentation copy from the author, ib. 1757 ; *calf gilt, uncut,
t. e. g. uniform*   (3)

22 America. Mably (Abbé de) On the Government and Laws of the
United States, *calf*, 1785—Price (R.) On the War with
America, *calf*, 1776 ; and others   (5)

23 America. Memorial, &c. of the Commonwealth of Virginia, 1786
—Carroll (Dr.) Address to the Roman Catholics of the U. S.
of America, *imperfect at end*, 1785—Volney, The Law of
Nature, *Philad.* 1797 ; and others, *all unbound*   (5)

24 America. Monardes (Nic.) Delle Cose che vengono portate dall'
Indie Occidentali pertinenti all' vso della Medicina, 2 parts
in 1 vol. *cuts of plants, &c. old vellum, Venetia*, 1575—Nouvelle
de l'Amérique ou le Mercure Amériquain, *old calf, Rouen*,
1688—Dutch Edition of OLIVER VAN NOORT'S Voyage to
Magellan's Straits, 1598, *head lines and fore edges shaved,
copperplates, unbound, t' Utrecht*, 1652   (3)
**** Monardes was the first physician to write a treatise on the
medicines of the New World.

25 America. Murphy (H.) The Conquest of Quebec : an Epic Poem,
original binding, Dublin, 1790—Grassi (G.) Notizie sullo
stato presente della Republica degli Stati Uniti, *uncut, Roma*,
1818   (2)

26 America. The Unfortunate Englishman, or a Faithful Narrative
of the Distress and Adventures of John Cockburn and Five
other English Mariners who were taken by a Spanish Guarda
Costa, and set on shore at Porte-Cavallo naked and wounded ;
containing a Journey overland from the Gulf of Honduras to
the Great South Sea, wherein is some new and useful Discoveries of the Inland of those almost unknown parts of
America, &c. *frontispiece (pp.* 164), *sewed, uncut*
J. Lever, 1773

27 America. Volney (C. F.) The Law of Nature, *Philadelphia*, 1797
—Paine (Thos.) Letter to the Abbé Raynal on the Affairs of
North America, *Philad. printed, Dublin reprinted*, 1782—
Common Sense, addressed to the Inhabitants of America,
Philadelphia, 1791, *unbound*   (3)

28 AMERICAN REVOLUTIONARY ATLAS. The American Military Pocket Atlas ; being an approved collection of correct maps, both general and particular, of the British Colonies, especially those which now are, or probably may be, the theatre of war, &c. *original half calf, uncut* 1776

₄ The maps are in fine preservation.

29 Analysis of the Hunting Field, FIRST EDITION, *with numerous beautifully coloured plates by H. Alken, and woodcuts, several leaves soiled, original cloth, g. e. (loose in cover) R. Ackermann,* 1846

30 Anecdotes on the Origin and Antiquity of Horse-racing, from the earliest times, *plate,* FIRST EDITION, *calf extra, with symbolical tooling on sides by T. Gosden, g. e. scarce T. Gosden,* 1825

32 Angling. Brown (Moses) Angling Sports, in nine Piscatory Eclogues, *frontispiece, half calf* 1772

₄ PRESENTATION COPY, with inscription on half title : "The gift of the Author, Rev. Mr. M. Browne, to Robert Pickersgill."

33 ANNALS OF SPORTING and Fancy Gazette, a Magazine entirely appropriated to Sporting Subjects and Fancy Pursuits, complete in 13 vol. *coloured plates by Alken and Cruikshank, and numerous plates by Landseer, Herring, and others, red levant morocco extra by Riviere & Son, g. t. uncut, a specimen monthly wrapper bound up with each vol.* 1822—May, 1828

34 Anselmus Archiep. Cantuariensis. Liber qui Elucidarius dicitur, *MS. on vellum, finely written in neat* gothic letters, *in red and black, double columns, vellum* 4to. SÆC. XIV

35 Apology for the Protestants (*no title*), commences with the dedication to Henry II, King of Navarre, black letter, "The Author of this Apology his Song," *four seven-line stanzas, and also* "The Author to his Booke," *nine lines in verse, old calf*
at end of epistle, 1578

₄ This vol. appears to be undescribed.

36 APPERLEY (C. J.) The Life of a Sportsman, by "Nimrod," *with 36 coloured illustrations by Henry Alken (some plates mounted as usual),* FIRST EDITION, *calf extra, rich symbolical tooling by T. Gosden, with his bookplate, g. e.* 1842

37 Arabian Nights, translated by E. Forster, 4 vol. *calf gilt, m. e.*
1810

38 Armorial. Emblazoned Arms of English and Irish Barons, *carefully drawn, with MS. descriptions, 105 coats of arms, with the crests, vellum in 1 vol.*

39 Authentic Records of the Court of England for the last Seventy Years, *large coloured coat of arms as frontispiece, original boards, uncut J. Phillips,* 1832

₄ Rigidly suppressed and very scarce.

40 AUTOGRAPH LETTER. Cobbett (W.) A. L. s. 1¼ pp. 4to, dated *Pall Mall,* 14 *Feb.* 1802, to Rev. J. Boucher (1)

41 AUTOGRAPH LETTER. Colman (G.) A. L. s. 1 p. 4to, dated *Theatre,* 31 *July,* 1805, to "Dear Elliston" relative to his benefit, &c.
(1)

42 AUTOGRAPH LETTER.   Elliston (R. W.) A. L. s. 1½ pp. 8vo, dated *Temple Place, 22 Jan.* 1826, to J. Winston, Esq.   (1)

43 AUTOGRAPH LETTER.   Ruskin (J.) A. L. s. 2 pp. 8vo, dated *Brantwood, Coniston, Lancashire, 9 May,* '81, to "My dear Wright"   (1)

44 AUTOGRAPH LETTER.   Southey (R.) A. L. s. 1 p. 4*to*, dated *Keswick, 2 Sept.* 1828, advising an aspiring poet not to appear before the public   (1)

45 AUTOGRAPH LETTER.   Wellington (Duke of) A. L. s. 2¼ pp. 4*to*, dated *Paris, Jan.* 19, 1815, *fine specimen*   (1)

46 Aytoun and Sir T. Martin.   The Book of Ballads, edited by Bon Gualtier, FIRST EDITION, *portrait, illuminated title, and illustrations by Crowquill, original cloth, g. e.*
12mo.   S. Orr & Co. 1845

47 Aytoun and Sir T. Martin.   The Book of Ballads, edited by Bon Gualtier, *illustrated by Crowquill, Leech and Doyle, original cloth, g. e.*   *Blackwood, n. d.*

48 Bacon (Lord) The Wisdome of the Ancients, done into English, FIRST EDITION, *tall copy, morocco extra, g. e. by Riviere*
London, imprinted by John Bill, 1619

49 Ballooning.   Lunardi (V.) An Account of the first Ærial Voyage in England, *fine portrait after Cosway, by Bartolozzi, and 2 plates (wants false title), printed for the author,* 1784 ; Another copy, *without portrait or plates, but having false title with Lunardi's signature, ib.*—Walker (Thos.) A Treatise on Ærostation ; or the Art of Travelling through the Air by Mechanical Means alone, *frontispiece, Bristol,* 1831—Sadler and Clayfield, an Authentic Account of the Ærial Voyage at Bristol, Sept. 24, 1810, *chart of journey,* 1810 ; *all unbound*   (4)

50 Bath Memoirs ; or, Observations in three and forty years Practice, at the Bath, what cures have been there wrought on the direction of Robert Pierce a constant inhabitant in Bath from 1653 to 1697, *old calf*
Bristol, printed for H. Hammond, Bookseller at Bath, 1697

51 Beattie (James) Original Poems and Translations, FIRST EDITION, *printed on thick paper, original calf*   1770
*** Presentation copy, with author's signed autograph inscription.

52 [Beckford (W. *Author of Vathek*)] Modern Anecdotes of the Ancient Family of the Kinkvervankotsdarsprakengotchderns : a Tale for Christmas, 1779, dedicated to the Hon. Horace Walpole, Esq. FIRST EDITION, *for the author, n. d.*—Les Dernières Aventures du jeune d'Olban ; Fragment des Amours Alsaciennes, *no name or place,* 1779 ; *old calf*   *in 1 vol.*

53 Beckford (W.) An Arabian Tale (Vathek), from an unpublished MS. with Notes critical and explanatory, FIRST EDITION IN ENGLISH, LARGE PAPER, *original calf*   *J. Johnson,* 1786
*** Excessively rare on large paper, only 25 copies having been printed.   Beckford's copy sold in his sale for £24.

54 Beckford. Gordon (John, *of Glencat, Aberdeenshire*) Memoirs, 2 vol. in 1, *frontispieces, William Beckford's copy, with 2 pages of MS. notes in his autograph, original calf*   1733
*** Some of Beckford's notes are very curious.

55 Bede (Cuthbert) Photographic Pleasures, FIRST EDITION, *in the
    original cloth gilt*   1855
    *** The author's own copy before the plates were inserted, he
    having the space interleaved with blanks, which he has partly
    filled up with his autograph manuscript, mainly copying
    reviews from the Press relating to his work.   There is also a
    slip pasted inside cover containing his manuscript copy of a
    criticism from the " Wolverhampton Chronicle." Furthermore
    " Extract from Literary Gazette, March, 1855," consisting of
    10 pages written by Mr. Cuthbert Bede is loosely inserted in
    the volume.   UNIQUE.

56 Bellamy (George Anne) Apology for her Life, written by herself,
    with original letters to J. Calcraft, Esq. 6 vol. in 3, *clean copy,
    in old calf, with ex-libris of Mary Robinson for the author,* 1785

57 BERMONDSEY. A Document on Parchment signed by Robert,
    Abbot of St. Saviour's Monastery, Southwark, "*Monasterii
    Scti Salvatoris de Barmondsey,*" connected with the Will of a
    certain Henry Baker, Goldsmith of London, dated August 16,
    Anno Regis Henrici VIII, 16, "*Per me Robtt. Abbat De Bar-
    mondesey,*" *countersigned* "*J. Carkeke*"   (1524)

58 Bewick. Select Fables, with a Memoir and a Descriptive Cata-
    logue of the Works of Messrs. Bewick, *portrait on india paper,
    and woodcuts by T. and J. Bewick,* FIRST EDITION, *old marble
    calf gilt*   *Newcastle,* 1820

59 Bible (Holy) containing the Old and New Testament, *engraved title
    in compartments, R. Barker,* 1634 — The Way to True Happi-
    nesse, *R. Young,* 1633—The Whole Book of Psalmes in Eng-
    lish Meeter by Sternhold, Hopkins, &c. *G. M. for the Companie
    of Stationers,* 1635 ; *fine copies but a few headlines shaved, old
    calf, rebacked, with initials* A.T. *on sides*   *in 1 vol.*

60 Bible (The Holy) containing the Old Testament and the New newly
    translated out of the original Tongues, and with the former
    Translations diligently compared and revised by his Majesties
    speciall command, *thick velvet*   *J. Field,* 1658
    *** An exceedingly rare edition.   At the foot of the title-page
    will be found a finely-engraved view of Old London with
    SHAKESPEARE'S GLOBE THEATRE in a prominent position.

61 Bible (Holy) containing the Old Testament and the New appointed
    to be read in Churches, 2 vol. in 1, *engraved title, very fine
    copy, old blue morocco extra, full gilt back, gold borders on the sides,
    g. e. very scarce, in fine condition, with ex-libris of Scott of Bal-
    comie   sm. 8vo.   Edinburgh, printed by James Watson,* 1722
    *** Mr. Horne pronounced this one of the most valuable of the
    earlier pocket editions.

62 BIBLIOTHÈQUE DE CARABAS SERIES, published by David Nutt;
    viz. : (I) The Marriage of Cupid and Psyche, done into Eng-
    lish by Wm. Adlington, with a Discourse on the Fable by A.
    Lang, 1887 ; (II) Euterpe, the Second Book of Herodotus
    Englished by B. R. 1584, edited by A. Lang, 1888 ; (III) The
    Fables of Bidpai, the earliest English Version by Sir T.
    North, now again edited by Jos. Jacobs, 1888 ; (IV-V) Fables
    of Æsop, as first printed by Wm. Caxton in 1484, &c. now

LOT 62—BIBLIOTHÈQUE DE CARABAS SERIES, *continued.*

again edited by Jos. Jacobs, 2 vol. 1889 ; (VI) The Attis of C. V. Catullus, translated into English Verse, with dissertations, &c. by Grant Allen, 1892 ; (VII) Plutarch's Romane Questions, translated by Ph. Holland, 1603, now again edited by F. B. Jevons, 1892 ; (VIII) Kirk (Rob.) The Secret Commonwealth of Elves, Fauns and Fairies (1691), with Comment by A. Lang, 1893 ; (IX) Tyson (Edw.) Philological Essay concerning the Pygmies of the Ancients, 1699, now edited by B. C. A. Windel, 1894 ; (X) Barlaam and Josaphat, English Lives of Buddha, edited by Joseph Jacobs, 1896 ; *together* 10 *vol.* LARGE HAND-MADE PAPER EDITION, *with duplicates of the plates, only 60 copies printed, boards, half vellum, uncut*

imp. 8vo

*** The "Cupid and Psyche" in this set is an unique copy, containing the dedicatory lines to Andrew Lang by R. L. Stevenson which were cancelled at the last moment. The "Euterpe" is one of three copies with cancelled sheet G.

63* Biblical Cuts, Thirty-four early (artists unknown), including a Series of Twenty-six " Passion " Subjects, *mounted on 8vo leaves of drawing-paper* (151—)

63 BINDING. AN EMBROIDERED BOOK COVER OF THE 17TH CENTURY, *very richly worked in woollen threads and beads of various colours, interspersed with spangles on a white silk ground, with full-length figures of Fortune on the sides, with dragon, lion, flowers, &c. a hound coursing a hare, &c. in a very excellent state of preservation*

64 Binding. An old Pocket Card Case, &c. *fitted with ivory tablets with engraved headings of the days of the week, the sides of beautifully chased metal work (believed to be silver-gilt) in scrolls with flowers, shipping, views, &c.* (1)

65 Biographia Curiosa, or Memoirs of Remarkable Characters of the Reign of George the Third, *portraits, calf gilt*   *Robins,* 1822

66 Boaden (James) An Inquiry into the Authenticity of various Pictures and Prints, which, from the decease of the Poet to our own times, have been offered to the Public as Portraits of Shakespeare, containing a careful examination of the evidence on which they claim to be received, by which the pretended portraits have been rejected, &c. *fine portraits of Shakespeare, after Cornelius Jansen (open-letter proof), Droeshout, the Stratford bust, the Chandos portrait, and Will. Marshall, uncut* 1824

*** Boaden's own copy, annotated, corrected and amplified throughout in his autograph, doubtless for the purpose of a new edition. Boaden's notes at page 59 are of considerable interest as regards the painting of the famous Chandos portrait. An extremely interesting volume.

67 Boaysteau (P.) Le Theatre du Monde, ou il est faist ung ample discours des Miseres Humaines, avec ung brieff discours de l'excellence & dignité de l'homme . . . . . nouvellement traduict en Aleman, tres utile pour apprendre tant Aleman que Francoises, *title also in German, calf extra, g. e.*   *Wirtzeburgi,* 1588

*** Refer to Mr. Hazlitt's Shakespeare's Library " First part of the whole contention."

68   Boccaccio (Giovanni) L'Amorosa Fiametta, *tooled calf*
                                   Vinegia, Giolito, 1545

69   Boccaccio. The Modell of Wit, Mirth, Eloquence and Conversa-
     tion, framed in ten Dayes, of a hundred curious pieces, by
     seven Honourable Ladies and three Noble Gentlemen, now
     translated into English, third edition, 2 vol. in 1, *contemporary
     calf*   *T. Cotes for B. Allen,* 1634
     ⁎ An exceedingly rare edition (not in the British Museum) much
     more so than the folio. The present copy is remarkably fine
     and its interest is enhanced by having the autograph of Nar-
     cissus Luttrell inside, and his initials in gold on covers, the
     latter a singularly rare circumstance.

70   Boccaccio. The Modell of Wit, Mirth, Eloquence and Conversa-
     tion, framed in ten Dayes, of a hundred curious Pieces, by
     seven Honourable Ladies and three Noble Gentlemen, now
     translated into English, *numerous woodcuts,* 2 vol. *original calf*
                                                              1657
     ⁎ This copy contains an extra title-page not recorded by biblio-
     graphers. A very rare book in good condition.

71   Bodenham (John) Politeuphuia, Wits Commonwealth, newly cor-
     rected and amended, *fine copy, morocco extra, g. e. (circa* 1630)
     ⁎ Apparently the third edition. This collection of wise sayings,
     proverbs and pithy sentences (taken from Elizabethan and
     other authors) was extremely popular at the end of the 16th
     and beginning of the 17th centuries.

72   Bosworth (Rev. J.) Anglo-Saxon Grammar, *frontispiece, old russia,
     g. e.* 1823—[Mathias (T. S.)] The Pursuit of Literature, &c.
     3 in 1 vol. 1794-99, *calf (rubbed)*; and another   (3)

73   Brathwaite (Richard) The Arcadian Princesse : or the Triumph of
     Justice, *bright impression of the fine frontispiece by Marshall,*
     FIRST EDITION, *very clean and tall copy in original calf*   1635
     ⁎ A perfect copy, with the rare four leaves at end containing
     the Life of the Author, and the Errata.

74   Brathwaite (R.) A Comment upon Chaucer's Miller's Tale, and
     The Wife of Bath, FIRST EDITION, *morocco extra*   1665

75   Brathwaite (R.) Barnabæ Itinerarium, or Barnabees Journal, edited
     from the first edition by Joseph Haslewood, *portraits,* 2 vol.
     old green morocco extra, full gilt backs, g. e. only 125 *copies
     printed*   1820

76   Breviarium sive horæ alme Ecclesiæ Pataviensis, lít. goth. *two
     sizes, in red and black, double column, cut of* SS. STEPHEN *and*
     VALENTINE *on title,* 5 *large and numerous smaller cuts of New
     Testament incidents, some pages bordered by them, binding of
     stamped Niger morocco, by Douglas Cockerell*
                 *Venetiis, arte Petr. Liechtēstein Impēsa Leoni & Luce
                                          Allantse fratrū,* 1515
     ⁎ A RARE EDITION, UNKNOWN TO BRUNET. A number of
     interesting notes in a contemporary hand.

77   Breviarium Romanum ex Decreto Sacrosancti Tridentini restitutum, cum Calendario et PROPRIUM FESTORUM ORDINIS MINORUM, lit. goth. *in red and black, double columns, half-page cuts, old red morocco, elaborately gold tooled, sacred motto on side, gilt gauffré edges, back restored*   *Venetiis, J. B. Sessa,* 1585

78   Bridges (Robt.) Ode for Bicentenary Commemoration of Henry Purcell, FIRST EDITION, *original wrappers (two copies),* 1896— LITTLE (J. S.) What is Art? PRESENTATION COPY FROM THE AUTHOR TO WILLIAM MORRIS, 1884 ; and another   (4)

79   BRONTË (Anne) The Tenant of Wildfell Hall, by Acton Bell, FIRST EDITION, 3 vol. *original cloth, uncut*   1848

     *** ANNE BRONTË'S OWN COPY, with her autograph signature upon the fly-leaves of vol. I and III, dated July 6th, 1848, and very numerous corrections throughout also in her autograph.

80   BRONTË (Charlotte) MANUSCRIPT MISCELLANEOUS POEMS, 12 *pages,* ENTIRELY IN THE AUTOGRAPH OF CHARLOTTE BRONTË, *May* 31, 1830

81   BRONTË (Charlotte) A CLOSELY WRITTEN MANUSCRIPT, 12 *pages,* descriptive of an evening Service at Ebenezer Chapel, ENTIRELY IN THE AUTOGRAPH OF CHARLOTTE BRONTË

82   Brontë (Charlotte) The Adventures of Ernest Alembert, a Fairy Tale, now first printed from the Original Manuscript, edited by Thomas J. Wise, *one of* 30 *copies, printed for private circulation only, parchment, uncut*   1896

83   Brontë (Charlotte) The Professor, a Tale, by Currer Bell, 2 vol. FIRST EDITION, *original cloth*   1857

84   Brontë (P. B.) Laussane, a Tragedy, bye Young Soult, in 1 vol. 12 *pages,* in a small and neatly written character, entirely in the autograph of P. B. Brontë, 1829

85   Brontë (P. B.) An Historical Narrative of the War of Encroachment, from November first, A.D. 1833, by Sir John Flower, in 2 vol. 33 *pages,* in a small and neatly written character, entirely in the autograph of P. B. Brontë, dated *Dec.* 17, 1832-33

86   Brontë (P. B.) The Odes of Quintus Horatius Flaccus, translated by P. B. Brontë, 33 *pages,* entirely in his autograph, and dated " *Haworth, nr. Bradford, Yorks, June* 27, 1840 "

87   Browning (Mrs. E. B.) An Essay on Mind, and other Poems, FIRST EDITION, *original boards, with the printed label on back*   1826

88   BROWNING (ROBERT) Gold Hair : a Legend of Pornic, *the excessively rare* FIRST EDITION, PRIVATELY PRINTED, *calf extra, t. e. g.* 1864

89   Browning (Robert) The Inn Album, 1875—Fifine at the Fair, 1872 ; FIRST EDITIONS, *original cloth*   (2)

90   BUNYAN (JOHN) THE HOLY WAR, made by Shaddai upon Diabolus, for the Regaining of the Metropolis of the World, or the losing and taking again of the Town of Mansoul, *brilliant impression of the portrait by R. White " John Bunnyon," and plate*

LOT 90—*continued.*

of Mansoul (the outside margin of the latter defective), original calf sm. 8vo. Printed for Dorman Newman at the Kings Arms in the Poultry; and Benjamin Alsop at the Angel and Bible in the Poultry, 1682

*** THE EXCEEDINGLY RARE FIRST EDITION OF THIS CELEBRATED BOOK, perfect, except the defect in the plate, with the leaf of verses at end (Cc 8) by Bunyan referring to his authorship of the *Pilgrim's Progress.* A GENUINE COPY THROUGHOUT, with the marginal notes intact (measures 6¼ by 3¾ in.)

91 BUNYAN (JOHN) THE/ PILGRIM'S PROGRESS/ FROM/ THIS WORLD/ TO/ THAT WHICH IS TO COME/ The Second Part/ Delivered under the Similitude of a/ Dream/ Wherein is set forth/ The manner of the setting out of Christi/ stian's Wife and Children, their/ Dangerous Journey/ and/ Safe Arrival at the Desired Country./ By John Bunyan./ The third edition corrected :/ I have used Similitudes ; Hosea 12, 10/ Licensed and entred according to Order/, *a very few headlines cut into, sold not subject to return, original calf*

London/ Printed for Robert Ponder, and Sold by the/ Book-sellers of London, 1690

*** The only other copy of this volume it has been possible to trace is that in the British Museum, with which this compares favourably, being much larger; in neither copy is there a frontispiece. It is very probable that the author revised or corrected this edition immediately before his death. The second edition was published in 1686, which was followed by another issue in 1687. This third edition as will be seen was brought out in 1690. It may therefore be assumed that its publication was contemplated by the writer before he passed away. The very early editions of Bunyan's Pilgrim's Progress are exceedingly *rare,* and possess certain peculiarities which add greatly to their value and interest.

92 BUNYAN (JOHN) A COLLECTION OF HIS VARIOUS WRITINGS, INCLUDING MANY ORIGINAL EDITIONS, as under :—

THE PILGRIM'S PROGRESS [PART I] "Ninth Edition," *portrait and cuts (some ll. wanting),* N. *Ponder,* 1684 ; "The Tenth Edition," *cuts (wants portrait, leaf defective), ib.* 1685 ; "The Thirteenth Edition," *portrait (inlaid) and cuts, blue morocco extra, g. e. good copy, R. Ponder,* 1693 ; "The Sixth Edition," *cuts, Glasgow, R. Sanders,* 1717 ; "The Nineteenth Edition," *portrait and cuts, large copy, M. Boddington,* 1718 ; Another copy *(smaller), ib.* ; Another copy ? *(or earlier)* ; "The Three and Twentieth Edition," *portrait and cuts, J. Clarke,* 1731 ; "The Twenty-eighth Edition," *Dublin, J. Jackson,* 1751 ; "The Nine and Twentieth Edition," *portrait and cuts, W. Johnston,* 1755 ; "The Thirty-first Edition," *portrait and cuts, ib.* 1764 ; [The 32nd Edition], *wants all before A* 5 [*ib.* 1767]; Another Edition, *W. Oliver,* 1776

The Pilgrim's Progress [PART II] "The Ninth Edition," *cuts (imperfect), N. and M. Boddington,* 1712 ; "The Eleventh Edition," *portrait and cuts, ib.* 1719 ; "The Twenty-third Edition," *W. Johnston,* 1760

LOT 92—BUNYAN, *continued.*

The Pilgrim's Progress [PART III *spurious*], with the Life and Death of John Bunyan, "The Second Edition," *Glasgow, R. Sanders*, 1717; "The Twelfth Edition," *frontispiece, A. Bettesworth, &c.* 1733; "The Nineteenth Edition," *portrait, half morocco, C. Hitch, &c.* 1761

The Pilgrim's Progress, PARTS I AND II *together, portrait and copper plates, by Sturt* [Part I, "Two and Twentieth Edition," *J. Clarke*, 1728, part II, *ib.* 1727]; *Portrait and plates, ib.* 1741; *Portrait and plates*, 1794, *W. Johnston*, 1749; "The Twenty-eighth Edition," *portrait and plates by Sturt, calf gilt, y. e. ib.* 1751; "The Thirty-first Edition," *cuts, ib.* 1760; "The Thirty-first Edition," *plates, ib.* 1766; "New Edition," *plates, Wolverhampton, T. Smith*, 1769; "The Thirty-second Edition," *plates, Rivington, &c.* 1775; Another copy, *ib.*; Part I, "The Fifty-eighth Edition," 1789, Part II, Fifty-fifth Edition, 1776; New Edition, *plates, T. Axtell*, 1775; With Notes, *plates, Birm. R. Martin*, 1786; With Notes by Scott, *portrait and plates*, 1794; With Notes, *portrait*, 1795; Bath, 1796; and eight other later editions

The Pilgrim's Progress, PARTS I-III *together :* A COLLECTION OF 69 VARIOUS EDITIONS, *mostly with plates, published between* 1733 *and* 1813

The Pilgrim's Progress, in Foreign Translations: Dutch (FIRST EDITION), *Amst. Boehholt*, 1682; Another Edition, *ib.* 1687; Another Edition, *Gronigen*, 1747; Another, *Amst. n. d.*; Swedish, 1892; French, 2 vol. *Basle*, 1717; Another Edition, *Rotterd.* 1778; Gaelic, *Edinb.* 1892

THE HOLY WAR: FIRST EDITION ? [*imperfect*], *frontispiece* [*D. Newman*, 1682 ?]; "The Second Edition," *portrait and title, &c. mended, ib.* 1684; *Edinb. Jas. Watson*, 1703 [First Scotch Edition ?]; *N. Boddington*, 1707; *Edinb. Jas. Watson*, 1711; *ib. J. Moncur*, 1718; *ib. T. Lumisden*, 1742; *London, W. Johnston*, 1752; Another copy, *ib.*; *Glasgow*, 1752; Another copy, *ib.*; *W. Johnston*, 1759 (3 *copies*); *Birm. T. Holliwell*, 1770; *Glasgow, J. Robertson*, 1770; *Edinb. by the Booksellers*, 1776; *Glasgow, J. Robertson*, 1777; *Paisley, A. Weir*, 1777 (2 *copies*); *W. Beynes*, 1804; *Bungay, n. d.*; *A. Hogg*, 1782 *and n. d.*; Dutch, FIRST EDITION, *Amst. J. Boehholt*, 1685; *Edinb.* 1784; *Newcastle*, 1787; *London*, 1791 (2 *copies*), *and* 1795

SOLOMON'S TEMPLE SPIRITUALIZED: FIRST EDITION (*cut*), *G. Larkin*, 1688; Another copy, *larger* (*hole in title*), *ib.*; Third Edition, *J. Gwillim*, 1698; Fifth Edition, *J. Marshall*, 1706; Eighth Edition (3 *copies*), *ib.* 1727; and four other Editions, 1756, *Edinb.* 1760, 1762, *&c.*

VISIONS: *J. Gwillim and T. Norris on London Bridge, n. d.*; *Leeds, J. Binns*, 1786 (2 *copies*), *and* 1792; Three other Editions; 1789, '93, '98; The same in Gaelic, 1891; and another

SIGHS FROM HELL: "Tenth Edition," *A. & J. Churchill*, 1700; *Wren & Hodges* (2 *copies*), 1785; *Berwick*, 1760; *Leeds*, 1795; Gaelic Translation, 1890

Lot 92—BUNYAN, *continued.*

GRACE ABOUNDING to the Chief of Sinners: "Seventh Edition," *R. Ponder*, 1692; "Eighth Edition," *Edinb. Heirs of And. Anderson*, 1707; and eleven other Editions between 1726 and 1804; With translations in Dutch, *Groningen*, 1746; *Edinb.* 1891

COME AND WELCOME to Jesus Christ: "Third Edition," *B. Harris*, 1685 (*title defective*); "Seventh Edition," *John Harris*, 1694; and nine other Editions between 1719 and 1798; Dutch Versions, 1711 and 1753

THE DOCTRINE OF THE LAW AND GRACE UNFOLDED: Second Edition, *W. Marshall*, 1701; and five other Editions between 1751 and 1788

THE BARREN FIG-TREE: "The Fifth Edition," *Glasgow, R. Sanders*, 1697; "Fifth Edition" (*title backed*), *R. Janeway for J. Robinson*, 1698; "Sixth Edition," *J. Robinson*, 1709; *W. Johnston*, 1762; and two other Editions

THE HEAVENLY FOOTMAN: "Second Edition," *J. Marshall*, 1700; "Fourth Edition," *portrait, ib.* 1708; *A. Millar*, 1792; Gaelic Version, 1882; and two others

THE WORK OF JESUS CHRIST AS AN ADVOCATE: FIRST EDITION (*margins frayed*), *D. Newman*, 1688; *J. Marshall*, 1725, *portrait* (3 *copies*)

THE WATER OF LIFE: FIRST EDITION (*title mended*), *calf gilt, N. Ponder*, 1688; Another Edition, *portrait, Wren & Hodges*, 1785; Gaelic Version, *Edinb.* 1891; and another

Divine Emblems: "Tenth Edition," *E. Dilly*, 1757; *C. Dilly*, 1790; The same, 1793; *Coventry*, 1806, *all with cuts*

Relation of the Imprisonment of Mr. John Bunyan at Bedford in 1660, *J. Buckland*, 1765 (3 *copies*)

Life and Death of Mr. Badman (FIRST EDITION ?), *imperfect;* The same in Dutch, *copper-plate engravings, vellum, Amst.* 1702

The Acceptable Sacrifice: "Third Edition," *R. Janeway for J. Gwillim*, 1698 (3 *copies*); "Fourth and Fifth Editions," *portrait, J. Gwillim*, 1702, *and J. Marshall*, 1718

DISCOURSE UPON THE PHARISEE AND PUBLICAN: FIRST EDITION, *frontispiece*, FINE COPY, *Jo. Harris*, 1685; "Third Edition," *J. Marshall*, 1704; "Fifth Edition," *frontispiece, ib. n. d.;* "Twelfth Edition," *ib. n. d.* (2 *copies*)

Treatise of the Fear of God, FIRST EDITION (*wants frontispiece*), *N. Ponder*, 1679; The same, in Dutch, *vellum, Dordrecht*, 1738

The Jerusalem Sinner Saved (2 *copies*) *Glasgow, R. Calder*, 1765

Differences in Judgment about Water-Baptism no Bar to Communion, FIRST EDITION (2 *copies, one very large*) *J. Wilkins*, 1673

A Defence of the Doctrine of Justification by Faith in Jesus Christ, first and second (?) editions (against E. Fowler, Bp. of Gloucester)   *sm. 4to. Fr. Smith*, 1672-3

[Fowler (Edw. *Bp. of Gloucester*)] Dirt Wipt Off; against a Vile Pamphlet of One John Bunyan, lay-preacher in Bedford on *The Design of Christianity*   *sm. 4to. R. Royston*, 1672

Lot 92—BUNYAN, *continued*.

Hearts Ease in Heart-Trouble, by J. B. "Second Edition," *portrait (said to be the only copy known), J. Robinson*, 1691 ; Another Edition, 1814

Seasonable Counsel, or Advice to Sufferers, FIRST EDITION
B. Alsop, 1684

A Holy Life the Beauty of Christianity, FIRST EDITION
B. W. for B. Alsop, 1684

The Greatness of the Soul, second edition, *portrait*
J. Marshall, 1730

Good News for the Vilest of Men, FIRST EDITION, *unbound*
G. Larkin, 1688

A Discourse of Prayer, second edition, *printed for the author*, 1663 ; and another

"Minor Works": Visions, Barren Fig-tree, Sighs from Hell, Water of Life, Grace Abounding, The Heavenly Footman, &c.   *A. Millar, &c.* 1798

Whole Select Works, with Notes, &c. by Wm. Mason, *plates*, 6 vol.   *A. Hogg, n. d.*

Works, second edition, with Additions, *fine portrait by Sturt*, 2 vol.   *folio. E. Gardner, &c.* 1736

Works. The First Volume (all printed), collected and printed by the Procurement of his Church and Friends, &c. *title mounted*   *folio. W. Marshall*, 1692

Works, with recommendatory Preface by the Rev. Geo. Whitfield, *portrait and plates*, 2 vol.   *folio. W. Johnston*, 1767

⁎ The whole Collection comprises 277 volumes and contains MANY VERY RARE SEPARATE WORKS; they are generally in very good condition, mostly in their original bindings. It would take many years, much labour and money to form another similar Collection. The lot will be sold not subject to return.

93 Bunyan (J.) Come and Welcome to Jesus Christ, *frontispiece, some headlines shaved, calf, very early edition, with advertisement of books at the end*   *B. Harris*, 1707

94 Bunyan (J.) The Pilgrim's Progress from this World to that which is to come, *frontispiece, old calf*, 1760—A Kempis (Thomas) The Christian's Pattern, or a Treatise of the Imitation of Christ, *frontispiece, old calf*, 1706—A Spiritual and most Preciouse Perle teaching all men to love and embrace ye Crosse, *calf gilt*, 1530, *reprinted* 1812 ; and others   (5)

95 Burnet (Bishop) Some Passages of the Life and Death of the Right Hon. John Earl of Rochester, FIRST EDITION, *portrait by White, and Flatman's Pastoral Elegy in a contemporary hand on the fly-leaf, original calf, with ex-libris of John Williams Bishop of Chichester, dated* 1703   1680

96 Burney (Miss) Camilla: or a Picture of Youth, 5 vol. FIRST EDITION, *original calf (broken)*   1796

97 BURNS (ROBERT) AUTOGRAPH LOVE LETTER, 1 p. folio (21 lines), not signed, therefore probably written on behalf of a friend, *in an oak frame*

    *** This letter is described in Chambers' Life of Robert Burns, 1896, p. 181, and its genuineness is attested by his son, at the end, " Dumfries, 1836."

98 BURNS (ROBERT) TWO ORIGINAL HOLOGRAPH POEMS—(I) " On Captain Fr. Grose's Present Peregrination through Scotland collecting the Antiquities of that Kingdom." The well-known poem beginning :

> Hear Land o' Cakes and Brither Scots,
> Frae Maiden Kirk to Johnie Groats,
> Gif ther's a hole in a' your coats
>   I rede you tent it.
> A Chiel's amang you takin notes,
>   And faith he'll prent it.

10 *stanzas, comprising* 60 *lines with heading as above.*

(II) " THE KIRK'S ALARM—A Ballad. Tune, Push about the Brisk Bowl," beginning :

> Orthodox, Orthodox, who believe in John Knox,
> Let me sound an alarm to your conscience,
> There's a heretic blast has been blawn i' the West,
> That what is not sense must be nonsense, Orthodox,
> That what is not sense must be nonsense, etc.

17 *stanzas, comprising* 85 *lines, at end the following note :* " *Mr. Mitchel Dr. to Gilb. Burns for Cheese* "

    *** These VERY INTERESTING AUTOGRAPH POEMS were presented by the Poet himself to the Grandfather of the present owner, who was Minister of Keir in Dumfriesshire.

99 Burns (Robert) Poems, chiefly in the Scottish Dialect, FIRST EDINBURGH EDITION, *portrait by Beugo, margin of a leaf mended, original calf*   *Edinb.* 1787

100 Burns (Robert) Selected Poems, with an Introduction by Andrew Lang, LARGE PAPER, *one of* 50 *copies, uncut*   1891

101 Byron (Lord) Manfred, a Dramatic Poem, FIRST EDITION, *very clean copy, with half-title, in the original wrapper, uncut*   1817

102 Byron (Lord) Works, with his Letters, Journals and Life, by Thos. Moore, 17 vol. *frontispieces and vignettes, original cloth, uncut*   1832-33

103 Byron (Lord) Manfred, a Dramatic Poem, FIRST EDITION (*some ll. stained*), *original wrappers, uncut, J. Murray,* 1817—Letter to **** ****** (John Murray) On the Rev. W. L. Bowles' Strictures on the Life and Writings of Pope, FIRST EDITION, *unbound, J. Murray,* 1821   (2)

104 Callot (Jacques) Miseries of War, 18 *fine plates by L. Schenk, Dutch title and cover plate*   sm. obl. 4to. (*Amst.*) *n. d.*

105 CAMPBELL (T.) Author of " The Pleasures of Hope," etc. Valedictory Address to the Students of Glasgow University, May, 1827, 9 *quarto pages in his autograph, apparently edited for publication by another person, in a blue calf slip case*

106 Cantica Canticorum, and Liber Elucidarius, MANUSCRIPT *of the XIIth century on vellum, sm.* 4to, *old green morocco*   SÆC. XII

107   Carew (T.) Poems, Songs and Sonnets, together with a Masque, fourth edition, revised and enlarged, *one leaf slightly defective, and a few lines shaved, in the original calf*   H. Herringman, 1671

108   CAREY (DAVID) LIFE IN PARIS, comprising the Rambles, Sprees and Amours of Dick Wildfire, Squire Jenkins, etc. . . . . including Sketches of a Variety of other Eccentric Characters in the French Metropolis, FIRST EDITION, ROYAL PAPER, *with first impressions of the coloured plates, drawn and engraved by Geo. Cruikshank, and woodcuts,* complete in 21 parts, *original wrappers, wanting the wrapper to no. 1 (the wrapper to 8 substituted), and the front wrapper to no. 2, a fine copy, in a box*
         Fairburn, 1822

109   Carolina Poetarum Novem, Alcæus, Sappho, Anacreon, &c. *pigskin, dated 1575,* 16*mo (? Geneva)* 1566—Henricus Stephanus, editio secunda, with Latin translation, partly prose, partly verse

110   Caroline (Queen) Memoirs, by Adolphus, 2 vol. 1821—The Royal Exile, 1820—Trial of Queen Caroline, edited by Adolphus, 1820—Last Days, Death and Funeral Obsequies, &c. 1822; *together 5 vol. portraits and numerous plates, calf gilt* 1820-2

111   Carroll (Lewis) Alice's Adventures under Ground, FIRST EDITION, *with 37 illustrations by the author, original cloth, g. e.*   1866

112   Cartwright (Wm.) Comedies, Tragi-Comedies, with other Poems, FIRST EDITION (*with the hiatuses in sheet U*), *fine portrait by Lombard, some margins cut close, leaf with Stapleton's poem uncut, clean copy, half bound*   *H. Moseley,* 1651

QUARTO.

113   Abaelard et Heloisa. Opera, nunc primum edita ex Mss. codd. v. illus. Francisci Ambroesii, EDITIO PRINCEPS, *old calf gilt, arms on sides of Louis Henri Comte de Lomenie, Secretary of State to Louis XIV, g. e.*   *Parisiis,* 1616

114   ACKERMANN (R.) THE MICROCOSM OF LONDON, 3 vol. *with upwards of* 100 *beautifully coloured plates by Pugin and Rowlandson, of the interiors and exteriors of the Public Buildings, and of the Manners, Customs, etc. of London, a large and fine copy, in half crimson morocco, t. e. g.*   (1811)

115   Æneas Sylvius. Sompnium de Fortuna, sine nota, *stained, wants blank leaf at end*   *Rome (Bart. Guldiubuck), circa* 1475-80

116   Æneas Sylvius. De Miseria Curialium, sine nota, *in black* semi-gothic type, *circa* 1480, *probably German press, title on verso of last leaf*

117   AMERICA. Apian (P.) Cosmographia Petri Apiani per Gemmam Frisium, *with the very interesting map of the World, including America, and with the volvelles so rarely found, old limp vellum*
         Antverpiæ, 1564
    *** A rare edition and in exceptionally good state. Bound up with it is Frisius (G.) De Radis Astronomico et Geometrico *Antverpiæ,* 1545, *with numerous woodcuts.*

118 AMERICA. WHITE (JOHN) THE FIRST CENTURY OF SCANDALOUS
       MALIGNANT PRIESTS, made and admitted into Benefices by
       the Prelates, in whose hands the Ordination of Ministers and
       government of the Church hath been; or a Narration of the
       Causes for which the Parliament hath Ordered the Sequestra-
       tion of the Benefices of severall Ministers complained of before
       them, for vitiousnesse of Life, errors in Doctrine, contrary to
       the Articles of our Religion, and for practising and pressing
       superstitious Innovations against Law, and for Malignancy
       against the Parliament, *half calf*   1643

   ₊ A long account of this *excessively rare tract*, is given by the
       late Paul Leicester Ford, in *The Bibliographer* for March, 1902 :
       "What gives this volume peculiar interest to American col-
       lectors is a paragraph on page 4 concerning LAWRENCE
       WASHINGTON, whom recent research has shown to be the
       great-great-grandfather of our greatest American, which is
       herewith reproduced. As is well-known, the Washington
       family were strong Royalists, and in consequence of this were
       objects of dislike to the Puritans, this Lawrence Washington
       being the especial sufferer, for, as recorded here, he was re-
       moved from this good living, and from that time was rector
       at Brixted Parva, where the living was 'such a Poor and
       Miserable one that it was always with Difficulty that any one
       was persuaded to accept of it.' Yet no one can to-day regret
       this seeming misfortune, for the resulting poverty of the
       family drove LAWRENCE WASHINGTON'S son John to sea as a
       sailor, and led to his ultimate settling in Virginia. . . . . . .
       WHITE'S BOOK MUST TAKE RANK AS THE CORNER STONE
       OF A LIBRARY OF WASHINGTONIANA."

119 Anderson (Wm.) The Scottish Nation, or Surnames, Families,
       &c. and Family History of the People of Scotland, 3 vol.
       numerous portraits, morocco gilt, g. e.   1860

120 ANNE OF CLEVES. Repudio della Reina Maria (Anna) d'Inghil-
       terra, sorella del Duca di Cleves, et Difesa sua con molta
       Eloquentia inverso el Re tradotto da G. B. dei Gillandari,
       FINE COPY, *boards*   *Bologna*, 1558

   ₊ EXTREMELY RARE. Originally written in French, but never
       printed in that language, as Henry VIII objected to its pub-
       lication.

121 Antoninus (S.) Tractatus Notabilis de Excommunicationibus, sus-
       pensionibus, &c. lít. gotlj. *double columns, vellum*
                                      Venetiis. Joh. de Colonia, 1480

122 [ARMIN (Robert)] The Valiant Welshman, or the True Chronicle
       History of the Life and Valiant Deeds of Caradoc the Great,
       King of Cambria, now called Wales, as it hath been sundry
       times acted by the Prince of Wales, his servants (*wants frontis-
       piece*)   1663

123 Ascham (Roger) Toxophilus, the Schole of Shootinge, conteyned
       in two Bookes, FIRST EDITION, *with the rare engraved first leaf
       containing the arms of Henry VIII, russia gilt*
             sm. 4to. *London, in aedibus Edouardi Whytchurch*, 1545
   ₊ Very rare. A good tall copy, but 7 leaves have been margined.

124   Ainslie (Sir R.) A Series of Views Illustrative of the Holy Scriptures, selected from his Celebrated Collection of Drawings, 34 *coloured plates by J. Clarke, marbled calf gilt, Bowyer, n. d.*—Graphic Illustrations of the Life and Times of Samuel Johnson, 24 *plates, calf gilt*, 1837   (2)

125   Augustalis. "Libellus qui dicitur Augustalis, continens sub compendio brevem descriptionem omnium Augustorum ad illustrem Marchionem Estensem," MANUSCRIPT ON THIN VELLUM (114 *ll.* 8½ *by* 6 *in.*) *finely written in semi-gothic letters, long lines, 24 to a full page, by an Italian scribe, with rubrics, painted capitals in blue and red, and a few illuminated, half vellum* sm. 4to. [*at end*]: *Amen. Deo Gracias. Petrus Lomer* [SÆC XV]

126   BACON (LORD) THE TWO BOOKES OF FRANCIS BACON, of the proficience and advancement of Learning, divine and humane, to the King, FIRST EDITION, *morocco extra, g. e.*   1605

     *** AN EXCEEDINGLY LARGE COPY, measuring 7½ by 5¾ in. Perhaps one of the LARGE PAPER copies which are stated to have been printed. Every second page only is numbered, and the paging is extremely irregular throughout the volume.

127   Bacon (Lord) Considerations touching a Warre with Spaine, FIRST EDITION, *top of title shaved and lower margins in 4 last leaves slightly cut into, else a fine copy in morocco extra, g. e. by Rivière, rare*   sm. 4to.   *imprinted* 1629

128   Baskerville.   Juvenalis et Persius Satyræ, *calf*
            Birmingham, typis Baskerville, 1761

     *** A presentation copy from Baskerville to Wm. Shenstone, the Poet, with autograph inscription on fly-leaf.

129   Beaumont and Fletcher, The Knight of the Burning Pestle, full of Mirth and Delight, *red morocco extra, g. e.*   1635

     *** A portion of this edition was reprinted by Capel in his "School of Shakespeare."

130   BEDA (Ven.) HISTORIA ECCLESIASTICA GENTIS ANGLORUM : Cuthberti quædam Epistola de transitu Bedæ : Vita S. Mariae Egyptiacae : Bedae Epistolae de VI Ætatibus Sæculi : Beda contra Julianum, Bedae Epistola de Templo-Salamonis, MANUSCRIPT ON VELLUM (90 *ll.* 9½ *by* 6¾ *in.*) *written in small cursive characters, long lines, 34 to a full page, oak boards, modern leather*
            SÆC XIV

     *** An important MS. of our earliest English Historian. So many Works of Bede are seldom found together.

131   Benvenuto, Italian [*pseud.*], *Professor of his Native Tongue for these nine yeeres in London* : The Passenger, [7 Dialogues in Italian and English on opposite pp.] *old limp vellum gilt*, VERY RARE
            J. Stepneth, 1612

     *** There was a copy of this rare Shakespearean volume in Halliwell's sale, June, 1858. An early attempt to teach languages by means of familiar phrases and dialogues. They are adapted to contemporary Italian customs and manners, and as such are of no little interest as well as evidence of the common study of Italian by the educated Englishmen of Elizabethan and Jacobean times.

C

132   BEHN (Mrs. A.) The Emperor of the Moon, A Farce, As it is Acted by Their Majesties Servants, At the Queen's Theatre, FIRST EDITION   1687

   *** Refer to Mr. Hazlitt's " Shakespear," pages xx and xxi.

133   Bernardus (S.) Sermoni devotissimi del devotissimo Sancto Bernardo, a una sua Sorella Monacha, *fine outline woodcut on title in the style of the Savonarola tracts representing a monk preaching, ornamental initials, fine copy, morocco extra*
Venet. P. de Quarengi, 1508

   *** A rare edition undescribed by Brunet. The woodcut is mentioned by Kristeller, as being probably Florentine.

134   Beroaldus (Philippus, *the Elder*) Carmina aliquot, *Heidelberg, s. a. (rather after* 1500), *wants title-page, bound in part of a vellum MS. on the Canon Law*

135   Biblia cum summario, *stamped calf, Lugduni (Saccon),* 1522, *title in red and black, early writing on fly-leaves and title, including date* 1541, *small woodcut initials*

136   BIBLE. THE HOLIE BIBLE, faithfully translated into English out of the authentical Latin, with arguments, annotations, &c. BY THE ENGLISH COLLEGE OF DOWAY, 2 vol. *title to vol. II repaired, and a few marginal notes shaved by binder, sold not subject to return, old morocco, full gilt back, gold dentelle borders on the sides, g. e.*
Printed at Doway, by L. Kellam, 1609-10

   *** FIRST EDITION of the English Roman Catholic version of the Bible.

137   Bible of Every Land. History of the Sacred Scriptures in every language and Dialect into which translations have been made, *coloured maps, &c. half morocco, gilt edges, Bagster, n. d.*—The New Testament of our Lord and Saviour Jesvs Chist [*sic*], **black letter**, *uncut, Robert Barker,* 1631   (2)

138   Bituricus (G. T.) Cosmographia Pii Papae in Asiae et Europæ eleganta descriptione, *half vellum Parisiis, H. Stephanus,* 1509

139   Blake. Cumberland (George) Thoughts on Outline Sculpture, and the System that guided the ancient artists in composing their Figures and Groups, 24 *fine plates by W. Blake and Cumberland*, VERY FINE COPY, *calf super extra, t. e. g. uncut, by Riviere* 1796

140   Boccaccio (Giovanni) Il Decamerone, *Firenze (Giunta),* 1527, *the reprint executed by Pasinello in* 1729, *for Consul Smith of Venice*

141   Boccaccio (Giov.) Il Decameron, di nuovo ristampato, e riscontrato dal Cav. Lion. Salviati, *numerous fine woodcuts (title backed), half bound*   *sm. 4to. Venet. A. Vecchi,* 1602

142   Boetius. De Consolatione Philosophiae necnon de disciplina Scholarium cum Commento Sanctae Thomæ de Aquino, **lit. goth**. 2 *types, device on title containing initials* P. L. I. B. *plain margins damaged by damp, original Netherlands binding, oak boards, leather, stamped in rosettes and fabulous birds (rebacked)*
absque ulla nota

143 Boetius de disciplina Scholarim ab Ascensio compēdio se dilucide
que explanatus una cum Quintiliani de officio discipulorum
cōpendio, **gothic letter**, *curious woodcuts, two leaves defective,
head-lines cut into, a few ancient MS. notes at the end, J. de Platea,
s. a. (circa* 1500)—Boetius de Consolatione, cum triplici commento Thome Raymundi necnon et Ascensii, &c. **gothic letter**,
*curious woodcuts, some side-notes, and a few headlines cut into,
Symon Vincent, s. a. (circa* 1500), *calf extra, g. e. uniform*   (2)

144 Boissard (J. J.) Emblematum Liber, ipsa Emblemata ab Auctore
delineata, a THEODORA DE BRY, sculpta, et nunc recens in
lucem edita, *engraved title, portrait, coat of arms, and* 51 *fine
copper-plate emblems, original impressions, fine large copy, in the
original white vellum, g. e.*   *Francof.* 1593

145 Bonner (E. Bp. of London) A Profitable and necessarye Doctrine,
with certayne homelies adjoined thereunto set forth for the
instruction and enformation of the people beynge within his
Diocesse of London, **black letter**, *the blank margins of a few
leaves repaired, large copy, with very fine woodcut initial letters,*
FIRST EDITION (*the homilies not included*), *morocco extra, blind
tooled sides, g. e.*   *J. Cawood,* 1555

146 Book of Common Prayer and Administration of the Sacraments
and other parts of Divine Service for the use of the Church
of Scotland, **black letter**, *Edinburgh,* 1637—The Whole Booke
of Psalmes collected into English Meeter, by T. Sternhold and
J. Hopkins, *London,* 1604 ; in 1 vol. *calf gilt, m. e. the Psalms
imperfect, sold not subject to return*   *sm. folio*

147 Book of Common Prayer and Administration of the Sacraments
and other Rites and Ceremonies of the Church, *illuminated
and illustrated with engravings, purple morocco extra, g. e.*
Murray, 1845

148 Bossewell (John) Workes of Armorie, *some leaves torn and soiled,
and some missing,* FIRST EDITION, **black letter**, *cuts of arms,
sold not subject to return*   *Richard Tottell,* 1572

149 BOSWELL (James) LIFE OF DR. SAMUEL JOHNSON, a series of his
Correspondence, and various original pieces of his Composition, never before published, 2 vol. FIRST EDITION, *portrait,
after Sir Joshua Reynolds,* FINE CLEAN COPY, *in the original calf,
y. e.*   1791

150 Brant (S.) Stultifera Navis, Narragonice perfectionis nunquam
satis laudata Navis .... per Jacobum Locher in latinum
traducta eloquium et per Sebastianum Brant denuo revisa,
*numerous fine woodcuts, original stamped pigskin clasps, a
few headlines very slightly shaved, and one leaf of index wanting,
otherwise a* FINE COPY
Basil. J. Bergman de Olpe, 1498, *Kal. Martii*

151 Brooke (Henry, *author of Gustavus Vasa*) Redemption, a Poem,
FIRST EDITION, *fine clean copy,* UNCUT, *with the autograph of
the poet John Scott of Amwell on half-title*   1772

152 Buckler (J. C.) Views of the Cathedral Churches of England and
Wales, 32 *plates, tree-calf gilt,* 1822—Storer (J. and H. S.)
Delineations, Graphical and Descriptive, of Fountains Abbey,
15 *plates on india paper, n. d. ;* and another   (3)

153 Brydges (Rob.) Shorter Poems, *printed in black letter at the private press of H. Daniel, Oxford, only 150 copies printed (no. 16), crushed purple morocco extra, inside dentelles, t. e. g. uncut*
sm. 4to. *Oxford, H. Daniel,* 1894

154 Burger (G. A.) Leonora : a Tale, translated by J. T. Stanley, *with a beautiful frontispiece and vignette by William Blake, uncut* 1796

155 Burgmaier (Hans) Images de Saints et Saintes issus de la Famille de l'Empereur Maximilian I, 119 *fine large woodcuts by various German engravers of the 16th century, printed from the original blocks, half calf*   *Vienne, F. X. Stöckl,* 1799

156 Bury (T. T.) Six coloured Views on the Liverpool and Manchester Railway, with a plate of the Coaches, Machines, &c. *original half binding*   *R. Ackermann,* 1831

157 BURY (RICHARDUS DE) PHILOBIBLION ex optimis Codicibus recensuit Versione Anglica necnon et Prolegomensis Adnotationibusque auxit Andreas Fleming West, **gothic letter**, *printed in red and black, rubricated capitals, 3 vol. vellum gilt, uncut, limited to 297 copies by the Grolier Club*
Novi Eboraci, typis et impensis Societatis Grolierianæ, 1889

158 Byron (Lord) English Bards and Scotch Reviewers, a Satire, *a beautifully written transcript of the fourth edition of 1811, morocco gilt, g. e.*

159 C. (J.) A Pleasant Comedy, called the Two Merry Milkmaids, or The best Words wear the Garland, as it was Acted before the King, with general Approbation, by the Company of the Revels, *unbound*   1661

160 Camden (William) Britannia sive Florentissimorum Regnorum Angliæ, Scotiæ, Hiberniæ, &c. *woodcut coats-of-arms on title, with autograph of J. Somers and Johannnis Cox, vellum*
Londini, G. Bishop, 1594

161 Camden (W.) Britannia, *in Latin, title mended, woodcut initials*
ib. 1594

162 CARPENTER (Richard) A New Play Call'd The Pragmatical Jesuit New leven'd, a Comedy, *unbound*   *n. d.*
*** THE ONLY EDITION.

163 Catalogue of Egyptian Antiquities in possession of F. G. Hilton Price, *plates and numerous illustrations in the text, buckram* 1897

164 Caxton (William) The Game of the Chesse, edited by Vincent Figgins, with Remarks and Bibliography, *facsimile reprint* 1855

165 Centlivre (Mrs.) The Perjured Husband, or the Adventures of Venice, a Tragedy, FIRST EDITION, *unbound*   1700

166 Cervantes. The Life and Exploits of the ingenious gentleman Don Quixote, translated from the original Spanish by C. Jarvis, 2 vol. *frontispiece and 68 fine plates after Vanderbank, by Vander Gucht, old calf gilt*   *Tonson,* 1742

167 Charles I. Treason discovered from Holland, 1642—The Queen's Letter from Holland directed to the King's Most Excellent Majesty . . . Whereunto is added His Majesties late Speech (1642)—The King's Majesties Letter to the Queen, 1648—The King's Declaration to all his Subjects, 1648—The Devilish Conspiracy, Hellish Treason . . . committed and executed by the Jewes, against the Annointed of the Lord Christ their King, 1648-9 ; *all in half calf*   (5)

168   Chiromancy.   Ex divina philosophorum academia secundum
        nature vires ad extra; Chyromantitio, diligentissime col-
        lectum, gothic letter, 21 *woodcuts of palmistry, sewed, s. l. et a.*
      *** VERY RARE.   One of the earliest printed books relating to
        palmistry.

169   Chiromancy.   Della Chiromantia, *Italian manuscript, in cursive
        hand, on* 102 *pages of paper, illustrated with many diagrams, half
        morocco*   SÆC. XVI

170   CIVIL WAR.   Bond (J.) Ortus Occidentalis, or a Dawning in the
        West, 1645—Marshall (S.) A Sacred Record of God's Mercies
        to Zion, a Thankesgiving Sermon for the Victory of Sir
        Thos. Fairfax in Naseby-Field (1645)—Caryl (J.) Joy Out-
        joyed, a Sermon for reducing the City of Chester, 1646—
        Case (T.) A Sermon before the H. of Commons, for gaining the
        towns of Bath, Bridgewater, Scarborough Castle, and Sher-
        born Castle, and the Success in Pembrokeshire, 1645—Gib-
        son (S.) The Ruine of the Authors and Fomentors of Civill
        War, 1645—Woodcock (F.) Joseph Paralleled by the present
        Parliament . . . . in the reduction of the City of Chester,
        1646—White (J.) The Troubles of Jerusalem's Restauration,
        or the Churche's Reformation, 1646—Foxcroft, The Good of
        a Good Government and Well grounded Peace, 1645—
        Case (T.) A Model of True Spiritual Thankfulnesse . . . for
        the Surrender of the Citie of Chester, 1646 ; and 22 others,
        all fine and clean copies, in original calf binding   *in* 1 *vol.*

171   CIVIL WAR, A SIMILAR COLLECTION, viz. : Ley (J. *of Cheshire*)
        The Fury of Warre and the folly of Sinne, 1643—Calamy (E.)
        The Noble-Man's Patterne of True and reall Thankfulnesse
        for the Discovery of a dangerous, desperate and bloody de-
        signe, tending to the utter subversion of the Parliament and
        the famous City of London, 1643—Herle (C. *of Lancashire*) A
        Pair of Compasses for Church and State, *with autograph of
        Richard Hollinworth on title,* 1642 ; and 24 others, *all fine clean
        copies, in original calf binding*   *in* 1 *vol.*

172   Cocker (Edward, *author of the Arithmetick*), Cocker's Morals, or the
        Muse's Spring-Garden, adorned with many Sententious Dis-
        tichs and Poems, FIRST EDITION, *calf gilt*   *sm.* 4*to.*   1694

173   COLLIER (JOHN PAYNE) AN OLD MAN'S DIARY, forty years ago,
        for 1832 and 1833, *printed strictly for private circulation, the 4
        parts complete, heads on the titles, original covers bound up at end,
        presentation copy to E. F. Flower, Stratford-on-Avon, with pencil
        note in the autograph of J. P. Collier, half morocco, t. e. g.* 1871-72

174   Columbus Letter.   Epistola Cristoferi Colom (cui etas nostra
        multum debet, de Insulis in mari Indico nuper inventis), &c.
        woodcuts, unbound   *sm.* 4*to.*   1493, *reprint circa* 1860

175   Congreve (W.) Love for Love, a Comedy, Acted at the Theatre in
        Little Lincoln's-Inn Fields, by His Majesty's Servant, *William
        Dowton's copy, with numerous lines outscored in ink by him* 1695

176   Cooper's Chronicle, Contenynge the whole Discourse of the His-
        tories as well of thys realme, as all other Countries . . . cor-
        rected and augmented to the VII yere of the raigne of Queene
        Elizabeth that now is, black letter, *fine copy, but two or three
        headlines shaved, old red morocco, gold borders on the sides, g. e.*
                              no name or place, 1 *Aug.* 1565

177   CONTARENO (Cardinal) The Commonwealth and Government of
       Venice . . . . translated out of Italian into English by
       Lewis Lewkenor, Esquire. . . With sundry other Col-
       lections, annexed by the Translator for the more cleere and
       exact satisfaction of the Reader, with a short Chronicle in the
       end, of the lives and raynes of the Venetian Dukes, &c.
       original calf   1599
       ₊ Malone considered that this volume was one of the principal
       sources of Shakespeare's " Othello "

The Property of a Gentleman.

OCTAVO ET INFRA.

178   Alken (Henry) Sporting Scrap Book, containing 50 plates, de-
       signed and engraved by himself, *some of the engravings a little
       soiled, original boards*   *imp. 8vo. T. McLean* (1824)
179   EGAN (PIERCE) Life in London, or the Day and Night Scenes of
       Jerry Hawthorn, Corinthian Tom, etc. *with 36 coloured plates
       and numerous woodcuts by I. R. and G. Cruikshank, Virtue, n. d.*
       —Finish to the Adventures of Tom, Jerry and Logic, FIRST
       EDITION, *coloured plates and woodcuts by Robert Cruikshank, soiled
       copy, slightly defective, bound in 2 vol.* 1830 ; *half calf, not
       uniform*   (3)
180   Egan (Pierce) Real Life in London, . . . by an Amateur, vol. I,
       ORIGINAL EDITION, *plates by Alken, Dighton, Rowlandson, etc.
       coloured by hand, some of the text and plates soiled, calf (re-
       backed)*   1821
181   Goldsmith (Oliver) The Vicar of Wakefield : a Tale, *with designs
       (coloured) by Thomas Rowlandson, wants 2 plates, title soiled, last
       leaf soiled and margin mended, calf gilt, uncut, with all faults*
                                                                 1823

QUARTO.

182   ACKERMANN (R.) THE MICROCOSM OF LONDON, 3 vol. *with up-
       wards of 100 beautifully coloured plates by Pugin and Rowlandson,
       of the Interiors and Exteriors of the Public Buildings, etc.* vol.
       I and II *in crimson morocco gilt, g. e.* vol. III *in old russia
       (rebacked)*   (1808)
183   [Bunbury (Henry)] An Academy for Grown Horsemen, and
       Annals of Horsemanship, third edition, 29 *plates by Bunbury,
       water-stained, a nearly uncut copy in half morocco, t. e. g.*   1808
184   Lane (R.) Studies of Figures, selected from the Sketch-Books of
       Thos. Gainsborough, executed in lithography, Nos. I and II,
       original wrappers   *n. d.*
185   LAVATER (J. C.) Essays on Physiognomy, translated by Dr. H.
       Hunter, 5 vol. *numerous beautiful plates, executed by, or under
       the inspection of, Thomas Holloway, russia*   1789
186   Underhill (F. T.) Driving for Pleasure : or the Harness, Stable,
       and its Appointments, *numerous illustrations, half bound, t. e. g.*
                                                                 1897

FOLIO.

187 Cipriani (G. B.) A Collection of Prints, after his Sketches and Drawings, engraved by Richard Earlom, *portrait, engraved title, and* 49 *plates, fine impressions, a nearly uncut copy in half calf*   1789

188 Colebrook (R. H.) Twelve Views of Places in the Kingdom of Mysore, from the original drawings, engraved by J. W. Edy, *water-stained,* 1794 — Tennyson (Alfred, Lord) Idylls of the King, *illustrated by Gustave Doré, poor copy,* 1868; and others   (4)

189 Inskipp (James) Studies of Heads, 12 *beautiful plates, proofs on india paper, original cloth*   imp. 4to.   C. Tilt, 1838

190 Meyrick (Sir S. R.) and C. H. Smith, The Costume of the Original Inhabitants of the British Islands, from the Earliest Periods to the Sixth Century, *with* 24 *beautifully coloured plates, morocco gilt, g. e.*   imp. 4to. 1815

191 Pergolesi, Ornaments, 66 *fine plates* (wanting plates 7, 36, and 40) *of designs for the decoration of Ceilings, sides of Rooms, Furniture, etc. engraved by the authors, the last plate defective (no title), half bound, with all faults*   (1777-92)

192 Road Scrapings, by GＩＩƆ, 12 *large and finely coloured plates, in the original illustrated boards (no title)*   oblong. 1840

193 Scenes on the Road, 18 *large and beautifully coloured plates by C. B. Newhouse, of Coaching Scenes on the Bath, Brighton, Dover and other Roads (no title), cloth*   oblong. M'Lean, 1835

The Property of J. A. Winter, Esq.

OCTAVO ET INFRA.

194 Apperley (C. J.) Nimrod's Sporting Tour, with Anecdotes, etc. of Sporting Men, Notices of the principal Crack Riders of England, FIRST EDITION, *morocco gilt, g. e.*   1835

195 Apperley (C. J.) Nimrod's Northern Tour, 1838—Carleton (J.W.) The Sporting Sketch Book, *engravings, the front. and title stained,* 1842, FIRST EDITION, *original cloth, uncut*   (2)

196 Bindley (C.) The Pocket and the Stud, by " Harry Hieover," 1848—Youatt (W.) On the Horse, 1855—Rarey (J. S.) Art of Taming Horses, 1858; and another, *all illustrated, half bound*   (4)

197 Combe (William) The History of Johnny Quae Genus, the Little Foundling of the late Dr. Syntax, a Poem, *coloured plates by Rowlandson, original salmon coloured cloth*   1822

198 Combe (W.) The Tour of Dr. Syntax in Search of the Picturesque, new edition, *with* 80 *engravings, from original designs by Alfred Crowquill, original cloth, uncut,* 1844—James (G. P. R.) Last of the Fairies, *illustrated by Sir J. Gilbert, original cloth, n. d.*   (2)

199   Cruikshank. Life of Napoleon, a Hudibrastic Poem in fifteen
        Cantos, by Dr. Syntax, *with 30 engravings by Geo. Cruikshank,
        half morocco, fine copy*   1817

200   Dickens (C.) A Christmas Carol, *with the green end papers,* 1843—
        The Chimes, 1845—Cricket on the Hearth, 1846—Battle of
        Life, 1846—The Haunted Man, 1848 ; *all (with the exception
        of " The Chimes")* FIRST EDITIONS, *illustrated by Leech, Doyle,
        Tenniel, etc., original red cloth, g. e.*   (5)

201   D'Oyly (Sir C.) Tom Raw, the Griffin : a Burlesque Poem, *with
        25 finely coloured plates, original salmon coloured cloth, uncut,
        t. e. g.*   *R. Ackermann,* 1828

202   Hawker (Lieut.-Col. P.) Instructions to Young Sportsmen in all
        that relates to Guns and Shooting, seventh edition, enlarged,
        plates and woodcuts, original cloth, uncut   1833

203   Mills (John) Life of a Foxhound, FIRST EDITION, *plates slightly
        spotted, original cloth, uncut*   1848

204   Penn (R.) Maxims and Hints for an Angler, and Miseries of
        Fishing, *with woodcuts,* 1839—Hutchinson (Lieut.-Col.) Dog
        Breaking, *illustrated,* 1848—The New Sporting Almanack for
        1843 and 1845, *plates, R. Ackermann ; original cloth*   (4)

205   Rodwell (G. H.) Old London Bridge, *illustrated by Alfred Ashley,
        original cloth, n. d.*—Robinson (H. B.) Memoirs of Sir Thos.
        Picton, 2 vol. *portrait, half calf,* 1836   (3)

206   Ronalds (Alfred) The Fly-Fisher's Entomology, second edition,
        with 20 beautifully coloured plates, 1839—Fly-Fishing in Salt
        and Fresh Water, *with 6 coloured plates of artificial flies, etc.*
        1851 ; *original cloth, uncut*   (2)

207   South (T.) The Illustrated Fly-Fisher's Text-Book : a Guide to
        the Science of Fly-Fishing for Salmon, Trout, Grayling, etc.
        FIRST EDITION, *with 23 engravings, after Cooper, Newton, Field-
        ing, and others, slightly stained, original cloth, uncut*   1845

208   Surtees (R. S.) Jorrocks's Jaunts and Jollities, second edition,
        *with 12 illustrations by " Phiz," somewhat stained, original cloth,
        uncut*   1839

209   Surtees (R. S.) Mr. Sponge's Sporting Tour, FIRST EDITION, *with
        coloured illustrations and woodcuts by John Leech, original cloth*
                                                                         1853

210   Surtees (R. S.) Handley Cross : or Mr. Jorrocks's Hunt, FIRST
        EDITION, *with coloured illustrations and woodcuts by John Leech,
        original cloth*   1854

211   Surtees (R. S.) "Ask Mamma," or the Richest Commoner in
        England, FIRST EDITION, *with coloured illustrations and wood-
        cuts by John Leech, original cloth*   1858

212   Surtees (R. S.) "Plain or Ringlets?" FIRST EDITION, *with coloured
        illustrations and woodcuts by John Leech, original cloth*   1860

213 Cervantes Saavedra (M. de) Don Quichotte, traduit et annoté par L. Viardot, 2 vol. *numerous vignettes by Tony Johannot, calf gilt, m. e.*   *imp. 8vo.* 1836

214 Jesse (Edward) Anecdotes of Dogs, *with illustrations, original cloth, t. e. g.*   *sm. 4to.* 1846

215 London Gazette Extraordinary, various Nos. between 1803 and 1814, *half bound*   *sm. fol. in* 1 *vol.*

216 Milton (John) Paradise Lost, *with illustrations by John Martin, fine impressions, half morocco, t. e. g.*   *imp. 8vo.* 1849

Other Properties.

FOLIO.

217 ACKERMANN (R.) HISTORY OF THE UNIVERSITY OF CAMBRIDGE, its Colleges, Halls, and Public Buildings, 2 vol. complete in the original 20 parts, *engraved portrait of the Vice-Chancellor,* 64 *beautifully coloured aquatinta engravings by Pugin, Mackenzie, Nash, etc. and* 15 *coloured plates of Costumes (does not contain the portraits of the founders). The text of part I is stained and one of the margins is damaged, wants the front wrapper of part X, and a few of the wrappers are damaged and defective ; with these exceptions the copy is a fine one*   *imp. 4to.* 1815

218 Ainslie and Mayer, Views in Egypt, Palestine, the Ottoman Dominions, in Europe, in Asia, the Ottoman Empire, chiefly in Caramania, etc. *numerous beautifully coloured views from the original drawings, with Descriptive Text, half bound,* 1803-10 *in* 2 *vol.*

219 ALKEN (HENRY) Illustrations to Popular Songs, 43 *beautifully coloured plates in the original half binding, very scarce   obl.* 1825

220 Alken (H.) The Grand Leicestershire Steeple Chase on the 12th of March, 1829, most respectfully dedicated to Capt. Ross and the Gentlemen in the Quorn Hunt ; the complete set of eight large coloured plates by C. Bentley, after Henry Alken, *original impressions*   *folio. Ackermann,* 1830

221 America. DE SOLIS (Don Ant.) History of the Conquest of Mexico, done into English by THOS. TOWNSEND, *fine Portrait of Cortes by Vertue, after Titian, Maps, Views, etc. calf, fine copy*   1725

222 AMERICA. WALKER (JOHN) AN ATTEMPT TOWARDS RECOVERING AN ACCOUNT OF THE NUMBERS AND SUFFERINGS OF THE CLERGY OF THE CHURCH OF ENGLAND, Heads of Colleges, Fellows, Scholars, &c. who were Sequester'd, Harrass'd, &c. in the late Times of the Grand Rebellion : Occasion'd by the Ninth Chapter (now the Second Volume) of Dr. Calamy's Abridgment of the Life of Mr. Baxter, Together with an

Lot 222—*continued.*

Examination of that Chapter, *original half calf, uncut*   1714

₊ An account of the great Washington interest of this book is given by the late Paul Leicester Ford in *The Bibliographer* for March, 1902. " White's charges against Lawrence Washington were made the subject of a special notice in his reply to White by Walker, and his defence is as follows : *Purleigh,* R., one of the best Livings in these Parts : To which he had been admitted in March, 1632, and was Sequestered from in the Year 1643, which was not thought punishment enough for him, and therefore he was also put into the *Century,* to be transmitted to Posterity, as far as that Infamous Pamphlet could contribute to it, for a *Scandalous,* as well as a *Malignant Minister,* upon these weighty Considerations, That he had said ' the Parliament have more Papists belonging to them in their Armies, than the King had about him, or in his Army, and that the Parliament's Army did more Hurt than the Cavaliers, and that they did none at all, and had Published them to the Traytors, that lent to, or assisted the Parliament.' It is not to be supposed that such a Malignant could be less than a Drunkard, and accordingly he is charged with frequent Commissions of that Sin, and not only so, but with Encouraging others in that Beastly Vice. Altho' a Gentleman (a Justice of the Peace in this Country) who Personally knew him, assures me, that he took him to be a Worthy, Pious Man, that as often as he was in his Company, he always appeared a very Modest, Sober Person, and that he was Recommended as such, by several Gentlemen, who were acquainted with him before he himself was. Adding withal, that he was a Loyal Person, and had one of the best Benefices in these Parts, and this was the *only* cause of his Expulsion, as I verily believe. After which, he subjoyns that another Ancient Gentleman of his Neighbourhood, agrees with him in this Account. Mr. Washington was afterwards permitted to Have, and Continue upon a Living in these Parts, but it was such a Poor and Miserable one, that it was always with Difficulty that anyone was persuaded to Accept of it." An uncut copy of this rare volume is perhaps unique.

223 ANARCHISM. An Extraordinary Collection of Anarchist Documents (about 2,000) written in French, English, Russian, German, Italian, Polonese, Armenian, Tzechish, Flemish, Spanish, Portuguese, Dutch, Greek, Danish, Hebrew, etc. comprising Autographs of the most celebrated Anarchists : Prince Bakounine, Prince Kropotkine, Elisé Reclus, Louise Michel, Ravachol, Vaillant, Henry, Caserio Santo, etc. Anarchist Brochures and Books in different languages ; Anarchist Posters and single sheets (some of very large size) ; Anarchist Newspapers of every part of the Globe ; Anarchist Portraits, Photos ; Anarchist Manuscripts, etc. etc. *contained in 24 red Folio Cases of* 4½ *in. width, with inscription " Evolution libertaire since* 1871."

₊ A detailed list will be sold with the collection. It would be impossible now to form another similar collection.

224 APPERLEY (C. J.) Sporting : *embellished by large engravings and vignettes, illustrative of British Field Sports, from pictures by Gainsborough, Landseer, Cooper, &c.* edited by "Nimrod," *some plates loose, and a few slightly stained, original cloth*   1838

225 Armstrong (Sir Walter) Sir Joshua Reynolds, First President of the Royal Academy, *numerous plates and vignettes,* with a duplicate set of the illustrations, *on india paper, in a portfolio,* 1900   (2)

226 AYRER (J.) Opus Theatricum, Drietzig Auszbundtige schöne Komedien und Tragedien von allerhand Denckwürdigen alten Romischen Historien und andern Politischer geschichten und gedichten, &c. *fine copy, original sheep (title in facsimile)*
Nuremberg, 1618

   ⁎ "This extremely rare and curious work is especially interesting to the English student, as containing early German versions of plays derived from English sources, such as *Der schön Sidea,* the play founded on the same story as Shakespeare's *Tempest ; Der Schönen Phoenicia,* the comedy of *Much Ado about Nothing ;* the tragedy of *King Edward III, Valentine and Orson, &c.* The thirty-six Witsun plays at the end, although many of them are extremely broad, are of a high degree of literary interest, and include *The History of the English John Posset, Owleglas, &c.* These latter plays appear, from the second imprint, to have been originally printed in 1610, but no separate edition or title to them has yet been discovered ; the few copies of Ayrer's work known to exist having them added in continuation with a catch-word, as in the present copy. *This is believed to be the first exemplar of this work sold by auction in this country."—Halliwell's Sale Catalogue,* May 23rd, 1856.

227 BAKER (GEORGE) History and Antiquities of the County of Northampton, vol. I, and vol. II, part 1 (*all that was published), in 4 vol. portrait and plates, half calf, m. e.*   1822, *&c.*

228 Bacon (Francis) The Historie of the Raigne of King Henry the Seventh, *portrait of John Payne, and woodcut title-page, calf extra, g. e.*   1622

   ⁎ A very fine and large copy of the FIRST EDITION (see *Grolier Club's Catalogue of Early English Literature,* No. 16).

229 Bacon (Francis) Sylva Sylvarum, published by William Rawley, London, 1626, *on title,* 1627 *on illustrated title by Thomas Cecill, portrait by Cecill,* FIRST (? second) EDITION, *stained ;* also contains The New Atlantis, and Magnalia Naturæ, *s. a.*

230 Bacon (Francis) Francisci Baconi, Baronis de Verulamio, Vice-Comitis Sancti Albani, Operum Moralium et Civilium Tomus. Qui continet Historiam Regni Henrici Septimi. . . . Sermones Fideles. . . . Tractatum de Sapientiæ Veterum, Dialogum de Bello Sacro. Et Novum Atlantidem. ab ipso honoritissimo auctore, practer quam in paucis, Latinitate donatus. Curâ & Fide, Guilielmi Rawley. . . . In hoc volumine, iterum excusi, includuntur Tractatus de Augmentis Scientiarum. Historia Ventorum ; Historia Vitae & Mortis, *brilliant impression of the portrait by Pass, original calf*   *Londini,* 1638

   ⁎ A wonderful copy of the EDITIO PRINCEPS of Bacon, being in its original binding, and beautifully fresh and crisp. Refer to Mr. Hazlitt's *Shakespeare,* p. 236.

231 Bacon (Lord) Of the Advancement and Proficience of Learning ; interpreted by Gilbert Wats, *portrait, calf* 1674

 ₊ Originally in the possession of William Lilly, the astrologer, and bears his autograph in two places on fly-leaf, dated 1679 ; also on title is the autograph of his son, Robert Lilly.

232 Biblia. Liber Prophetiarum, *a finely executed* MANUSCRIPT ON VELLUM, *written in large* 𝔤𝔬𝔱𝔥𝔦𝔠 𝔠𝔥𝔞𝔯𝔞𝔠𝔱𝔢𝔯𝔰, *double columns, decorated with a great number of large and fine initial letters in red and blue, calf gilt, in fine preservation* *thick folio.* SÆC. XV

233 Biblia Sacra Latina cum Glossa Ordinaria, Nic. de Lyra Postilla, etc. Prima Pars (Pentateuchus solus), *title within woodcut border, woodcuts and ornamental initials, old English binding, oaken boards, leather, stamped with frame and diagonal figures and ornaments, and the device of* JOHN REYNES *as binder (Weale 181), (repaired), in new cloth lined case*

        Lugd. Jac. Mareschal, 1528

234 Bible (The) Genevan Version, revised by L. Tonson, with Booke of Common Prayer, and Psalmes in Meeter, *ruled throughout, old calf, R. Barker, etc.* 1611-12 ; etc. (3)

235 Binding. AN ANCIENT ITALIAN BOOK COVER of Oak Boards, with stamped compartments lacquered in gold, the outer borders having gilt floreate ornaments on blue grounds ; the centre panel of the upper cover containing a very finely painted full-length figure of a Warrior Saint with a long sword ; in the centre of the under cover 7 emblazoned shields of arms, with the following inscription : " *questo e Libō de la Generale Cabella del Magnifico Comuno di Siena fatto al Tempo del Venerabile Huomo Misser Balduccio Bandini Camari engho di Biccherna, Anno Domini* 1465 "

236 Biographia Britannica ; or, the Lives of the most eminent Persons who have flourished in Great Britain and Ireland, from the earliest Ages down to the present Times ; collected from the best Authorities, both printed and manuscript, and digested in the manner of Mr. Bayle's Historical and Critical Dictionary, 7 vol. *original calf* 1747

 ₊ Contains a biography of Shakespeare. The present copy belonged to Isaac Reed, and is annotated throughout by him.

237 BLAGDON (F. W.) History of Ancient and Modern India, from the Earliest Periods, *with 68 large and beautifully coloured plates, from the original drawings of Mr. Daniell, Col. Ward and Lieut. Hunter, in the original half binding* *E. Orme*, 1805

238 BLAKE. Young (Edward) Night Thoughts, FIRST EDITION, *with the large and beautiful designs by William Blake, contains the rare leaf at end* " Explanation of the Engravings," *fine uncut copy in half morocco, t. e. g.* *imp. 4to.* 1797

239 BLAKE. Illustrations of the Book of Job, in 21 plates (proofs), invented and engraved by William Blake, *original wrapper, with the paper label on side* *published by the author*, 1826

240 BLAKE. ILLUSTRATIONS OF THE BOOK OF JOB, in 21 plates, invented and engraved by William Blake, LARGE PAPER, ORIGINAL ISSUE, PROOFS, *original wrapper, with label*, RARE

     published by the Author, 3, Fountain Court, Strand, 1826

241 Boetius. De Philosophico Consolatu, sive de Consolatione Philo-
      sophiae cum figuris ornamentissimis noviter expolitus, lit.
      gotḥ. *and roman, numerous spirited woodcuts, Argent. Jo. Grü-
      ninger*, 1501—Virgilius, Opera, *lit. rom. title in* **gotḥic** (*some
      ll. at end water-stained*), *Mediol. A. Minutianus*, 1504 ; *in 1 vol.
      oaken boards, leather*   *sm. folio*

242 Boccaccio (Giov.) Genealogia Deorum Gentilium, *a large and
      sound copy, in vellum, with the book-plate of Joseph Smith, British
      Consul at Venice*   *Vincentiae*, 1487

243 Boccaccio (Giov.) The Decameron, translated into English, in two
      parts, *woodcut titles, and woodcuts* (First English Translation),
      two leaves at end soiled, morocco extra, g. e. by Riviere
                                          Isaac Jaggard, 1625, -20

244 Boisserée Gallery. Die Sammlung Alt-Nieder und Ober
      Deutscher Gemälde, den Brüder Boisserée und Bertram, 2 vol.
      in 1, *numerous large and beautifully executed plates, under the
      direction of J. N. Strixner, engraved in lithography, heightened
      by tints, and mounted on drab coloured drawing paper, half green
      morocco gilt*   *Stuttgart und München*, 1821-36

245 Boydell (J. and J.) History of the Thames, 2 vol.
      enlarged to 4 vol. 76 *coloured plates by Farington, and
      upwards of* 900 *extra illustrations,* 764 *being views, buildings,
      mansions, palaces, &c. on the banks of the Thames, from
      its source to the Nore, by Buck, Sandby, Westall, &c. and* (147
      being coloured impressions) *including the rare set of* 9 *plates of the
      Arches of Triumph erected in honour of the entry of James I into
      London,* 1603, *and the complete set of Ireland's Picturesque Views
      of the Thames ; the remaining* 150 *are portraits of celebrities, by
      Houbraken, Vertue, Van Dyck, &c.* (*many proofs and india proofs*) ;
      also 4 *original drawings in water-colour and sepia, an official
      document, signed by the Duke of Marlborough,* 1718 ; *Anthem
      with music for the funeral of the Duke, Vauxhall Songs with music,
      and specially printed titles, green morocco extra, tooled with a design
      of fish, &c. g. e. by the Guild of Women-Binders*   1794-96

246 Bridges (John) History and Antiquities of Northamptonshire,
      compiled by the Rev. Peter Whalley, 2 vol. *portrait and plates,
      half calf, scarce*   *Oxford*, 1791

247 Braithwait (R.) The English Gentleman and English Gentle-
      woman, third edition, *engraved title by Marshall, and leaf of
      explanation facing, calf gilt, by W. Pratt*   1641

248 Brooke (Lord) Certaine Learned and Elegante Workes of the
      Right Honorable Fulke Lord Brooke, written in his Youth,
      and familiar Exercise with Sir Philip Sidney (Plays, Letters
      and Poems), first edition, *original old calf, lettered up the
      back, with autograph of J. Holland on title*
                                          E. P. for H. Seyle, 1633

249 Brown (Sir Thos.) Works : containing Vulgar Errors ; Religio
      Medici ; Hydriotaphia, or Urn-Burial, and Miscellaneous
      Tracts, first edition, *fine copy, portrait by White, old calf,
      rebacked*   1686

250 Burton. The Anatomy of Melancholy, what it is, with all the kinds, causes, symptomes, prognostickes & severall cures of it. In three Partitions, Philosophically, Medicinally, Historically opened & cut up by Democritus Junior, with a Satyricall Preface conducing to the following Discourse, *very brilliant impression of the engraved title by C. Le Blon, calf extra, g. e.*

Oxford, 1628

*** "This third edition is the *first with the engraved title-page and portrait of the author.* The title occupies the centre of the page, having over it a representation of the ancient Democritus, and underneath a portrait of Burton. On either side are likenesses of the Jealous, the Lover, the Superstitious, Solitude, the Hypochondriac, and the Madman ; while in the corners are Borage and Hellebore,—

 'Soveraign plants to purge the veins
 Of melancholy, and chear the heart
 Of those black fumes which make it smart.'

Burton constantly made additions to the different editions of the 'Anatomy' up to that of 1651, which represents its final form."—*Grolier Club Catalogue of Early English Literature.*

SECOND DAY'S SALE.

OCTAVO ET INFRA.

LOT 251.

ATALOGUE (A.) of Choice and Valuable Books in most Faculties and Languages, being part of the Collection made by Thomas Rawlinson, Esq. which will begin to be sold by Auction at Paul's Coffee-House the West-End of S. Paul's, on Monday the 4th of December, 1721, by Thomas Ballard, Bookseller, &c. *in 2 parts,* 2 vol. *calf extra, with the original wrapper bound up,* UNCUT 1721

*** Amongst the 1438 lots in the above catalogue is a copy of the third Shakespeare Folio, 1664.

252 Catalogue (A) of the Library of Thomas Sclater Bacon, Esq. (deceas'd), which will be sold by Auction at Mr. Cock's in the Great Piazza, Covent Garden, on Monday, March 14th, 1736-7, and the following Days (Saturdays excepted), till all are sold, beginning each evening at Five o'clock, *half calf, uncut* 1736-7

*** Among the interesting volumes offered were, *Venus and Adonis,* 1602, *The Rape of Lucrece,* 1632, a collection of plays including *Timon of Athens ;* a copy of the Third Folio, 1664, which sold for 19s. 6d., and Shakespeare's *Poems,* 1640.

253 Catalogus Bibliotheca Harleianæ, in Locus Communes distributus cum indice Auctorum, 5 vol. *original binding,* UNCUT 1743-4

*** Dr. Samuel Johnson, who later in life was to be famous as an editor of Shakespeare, partly edited this catalogue of Lord Oxford's library. It contained *none* of the Shakespeare 4tos, but the folios of 1664 and 1685 are found, also the excessively rare *Venus and Adonis* of 1602, and the *Sonnets* of 1609.

254 Catalogue (A) of the Libraries of the late Dr. Cromwell Mortimer, Secretary to the Royal Society, Edmund Pargiter, Esq., and many others, too tedious to mention ; ..... Likewise a numerous Collection of curious Manuscripts, Prints and Drawings, the Whole together being a much larger Collection than any ever yet sold by any Bookseller in England, which will begin to be sold...(for Ready Money only), at T. Osborne's in Grays-Inn, on the 26th day of November, 1753, vol. I, *half calf* 1753

*** Two copies of the Fourth Folio Shakespeare 1685, are priced £1 5s., and £1 11s. 6d. respectively, a collection of 10 plays includes *King Lear,* and is offered for 10s. 6d., another collection of 14, includes *Othello,* and is priced the same, another

Lot 254—*continued.*

collection containing 11 plays and including *Troilus and Cressida*, 1679, and *Antony and Cleopatra*, 1677, is also offered for 10s. 6d., *The Tempest*, 1676, is priced 1s., *Venus and Adonis*, 1675, 1s. 6d. ; a collection of 10 plays including *Much Ado about Nothing*, 3s. 6d. ; another collection of 12 plays, all by Shakespeare, viz. *Much Ado about Nothing, The Winter's Tale, The Taming of the Shrew, The Puritan, All's Well that Ends Well, Two Gentlemen of Verona, Twelfth Night, a Yorkshire Tragedy, Midsummer Night's Dream, The Comedy of Errors, As you Like It, The London Prodigal,* is offered for 2s. 6d. *King John, King Richard II, King Richard III, and Henry VIII* are offered for 2s. ; *Henry IV 2 parts and Henry V,* 1s 6d, *Thomas Ld. Cromwell, Locrine and Titus Andronicus,* the three 1s. 6d., *Timon of Athens, The Tempest, and Troilus and Cressida,* the three 1s. 6d., *Measure for Measure, Cymbeline, and Pericles,* the three 1s. 6d., *Hamlet,* with another play, 1s. 6d.

255   Catalogue (A) of the Libraries of the Right Honourable Heneage Finch, Earl of Winchelsea, and the Reverend John Creyke, to which is added the large and curious library of Mr. Booth, late of Barnard's Inn, containing an uncommon Collection of scarce and curious Authors in all Languages, Arts and Sciences ...Which will begin to be sold on Wednesday the 26th of April, till the 31st of December, 1758, At T. Osborne's in Gray's Inn, *wrappers*   1758

*** A Fourth Folio 1685, with one leaf damaged, is offered at 15s. ; a Second Folio, 1632, neatly bound, at £1 5s. ; a collection of Plays (8) including *Much Ado about Nothing,* 3s. 6d. ; another collection of 9 offered at 2s., includes *Coriolanus and Julius Cæsar* ; another collection in 7 volumes offered at 15s. includes *King Lear, Timon of Athens,* with three other plays, 2s., *Thomas Ld. Cromwell, Titus Andronicus, and Locrine,* also offered for 1s. 6d. ; *Henry VI, 3 parts* 1s. 6d. ; *Timon of Athens, Tempest, Troilus and Cressida,* the three 1s. 6d. ; *Double Falsehood,* by Shakespeare, 1s.

256   Catalogue. The Second Volume of a Catalogue of a Further Part of the Stock of T. Osborne, which will begin to be sold ......this and every day till the 1st of January, 1766, *wrappers*   1766

*** Shakespeare's Fourth Folio is offered at 12s. ; seven Old Plays, including *Hamlet,* 5s. ; sixteen Old Plays, also including *Hamlet,* 7s.

257   Catalogue (A) Of a further Part of the Stock of T. Osborne...... vol. III, for the year 1766 ......Which will be selling every day (Sundays excepted) to the 1st of January, 1767. Containing the largest, most curious, and valuable Collection of Books, in all Languages, Manuscripts, Prints, &c., that have been exposed to Sale for many years, *half calf*   1766

*** Osborne prices a Fourth Folio, 1685, at 12s., and offers a Collection of Old Plays, twelve in number, and including *King Lear,* for 7s. 6d. ; in contrast with the sum required for the Fourth Folio we see Rowe's edition, dated 1765, valued at £2 8s., &c.

258 Catalogue. Wagstaff's Catalogue for 1769, containing A Choice
Collection of Books lately purchased, In all Languages, Arts,
and Sciences. Consisting of the best Pieces of the best
Authors, both Ancient and Modern, &c. *half calf* 1769

*** A good copy of the Second Folio, 1632, is advertised at
£1 10s. ; and under the heading of " Curious Quarto Tracts "
Troilus and Cressida is offered for 6d.

259 Catalogue. Wagstaff's Catalogue of Choice Books for 1771 ;
containing many Thousands of the most scarce and curious
Articles in all Arts and Sciences, and in Every Branch of
Polite Literature both in Print and in Manuscript, *half calf*
1771

*** A copy of the 1679 edition of *Troilus and Cressida* is marked
1s. ; *Poems written by William Shakespeare,* 1s. 6d. ; and *King
Henry the Fifth,* 6d.

260 Catalogue. Wagstaff's Second Catalogue for 1771 ; containing
a large and valuable Collection of Choice Books, in all
Languages, and in every Branch of Ancient and Modern
Literature, &c. *half calf* 1771

*** The Shakespearian items occuring in this Catalogue are :
King Heury V, 1723, priced at 6d. ; *Winter's Tale,* 1756, 6d. ;
Hamlet, 1709, 6d. ; *Tempest,* 1756, 6d. ; *King Richard II,* 1720,
6d. ; *Comedy of Errors,* 1709, 6d. ; *Timon of Athens,* 1709, 6d.

261 Catalogue. Wagstaff's New Catalogue of Rare Old Books, collected and imported since December, 1771. Consisting of a
Matchless Collection of such Articles as are seldom seen,
unless in the Libraries of the Greatest Connoisseurs. Which
will begin to be sold on Monday next, Nov. 2, 1772, &c. *half
calf* 1772

*** Shakespeare's *Hist. of Henry IV,* 1632, is offered for 3s. ;
The Tragedy of Richard III, 1629, also offered for 3s. ; *King
Henry V,* for 6d. ; *Midsummer's Night Dream, with alterations,*
6d. ; *Othello,* 6d. ; and *Comedy of Errors,* 1709, 6d.

262 Catalogues. Five Catalogues, including J. Edwards' of " A Very
Select Collection of Books in all Languages and Every Branch
of Literature," for 1794, *half calf*—A Catalogue of Books in
all Languages and Classes of Learning, for the year 1806......
selling by Lackington, Allen & Co. Temple of the Muses,
Finsbury Square, *half calf*—Merly Library—A Catalogue of
well-known and celebrated Library of the late Ralph Willett,
Esq.......Comprising a most rare Assemblage of the Early
Printers, Fine Specimens of Block Printing......Likewise, a
most Splendid Missal ; and a very Choice Selection of
Botanical Drawings, by Van Huysen, Taylor, Brown, Lee, &c.
which will be sold by Auction by Leigh & Sotheby, Book-
sellers, on Monday, December, 1813, and sixteen following
days, *half calf, uncut, with the names of purchasers and prices in
MS.*—Part V or Appendix of a General Catalogue of Books
......From the Libraries of the late Venerable Archdeacon
Wrangham and the late John Delafield Phelps......Particularly
rich in Privately Printed Works, &c. offered.........by Thomas
Thorp, No. 178, Piccadilly, 1843—Another Catalogue
1794-1843

263 Catalogue (A) of Books in all Languages and in every Branch of Literature, containing "La Guirlande de Julie," *printed on vellum with paintings of flowers, &c.* Now on Sale at J. Edwards', No. 77, Pall Mall   1796

    *** The Catalogue contains 7,743 items, among which a Second Folio Shakespeare, 1632, is priced three guineas, and another, wanting the title, £1 5s. A copy of Rowe's edition on LARGE PAPER, 6 vol. is offered for £2 12s. 6d.

264 Catalogues of an Useful, Curious, and Valuable Collection of Books, for the years 1800 and 1802, which are now selling... By R. H. Evans, No. 26, Pall Mall, 2 vol. *half calf*   1800-2

    *** Shakespeare Second Folio, 1632, "fine copy, in blue morocco," is priced five guineas.

265 Catalogue. Bibliotheca Brandiana ; a Catalogue of the Unique, Scarce, Rare, Curious, and numerous Collection of Works .. ..being the entire Library of the late Rev. John Brand...... which will be sold by Auction......By Mr. Stewart, at his room, No. 194, Piccadilly, on Wednesday, May 6, 1807, and thirty-six following days (Sundays, the King's birth-day, and from May 21st to 26th, both days inclusive excepted), *boards, uncut*   1807

    *** On the 25th day Shakespeare's *Poems*, 1640, sold for £1 11s. 6d., the 1714 edition for 6d., the "Sonnets never before Imprinted " (MS. title) "and are to be sold by Wm. Aspley, 1609," for 10s. 6d., and another copy of the *Poems*, 1640, for 6s. 6d., "*perfect.*" The 26th day's sale includes *The Tragedy of the Moore of Venice*, 1630, which realised 4s. 6d. ; *The Tempest*, 1676, with *Hamlet* (wanting title) and *Julius Cæsar*, which sold for 1s. and *Hamlet*, 1637, for 2s. 6d. A copy of Shakespeare's *Sonnets*, 1609, occurs in the 29th day's sale, and sold for £6 6s.

266 CATALOGUES OF PRINT SALES, 20 VOL. LARGE PAPER AND UNCUT, MOSTLY PRICED, WITH PURCHASER'S NAMES AND NOTES, ranging from 1786-1864, chief of which are as follows : — Gulston Catalogue, 38 days' sale ; among the purchasers were Walpole, Barnard, Bartolozzi, &c. 1786—Barnard, 26 days' sale, priced ; Rembrandt portrait inserted, 1798—Musgrave, 31 days' sale, priced ; among the purchasers were Sykes, Bindley, Tyson, &c. ; this copy belonged to Kirgate, Horace Walpole's printer, with his notes, 1808—Lake, 20 days' sale, priced ; in this Catalogue, on p. 65, lot 1152, is the original and copy of the Saracen's Head, the first mezzotint done in this country by Prince Rupert —Dowdeswell (2 vol.) 29 days' sale ; with History of Engravers, 1809 and 1810—Vernon, 24 days' sale, priced, Towneley, 5 days' sale, 1 vol. 1813—Bindley, 19 days' sale, priced, 3 parts complete ; with portrait and purchasers' names, 1819—Sykes, 42 days' sale, priced, 5 parts complete ; with portrait and purchasers' names, 1824—Baker, 13 days' sale, priced, with portrait ; a very large collection of Hogarth's works, 1825—Otley, 14 days' sale, priced, 1837

267 Cervantes (Miguel de) Two Humorous Novels : Scipio and Ber-
       ganson, Rinconete and Cortedello, now first translated
                                                        London, 1741

268 Cecire (F. Antonio Maria) La Dottrina della Chiesa sulle Indul-
       genze, *printed entirely on blue paper, in the old Italian morocco
       binding, tooled back and sides, with cardinal's arms as centre orna-
       ment, g. e.*   *in Napoli*, 1791

269 Chap Books. History of Jack and the Giants, in 2 parts,
       Nottingham, n. d.—Garland of New Songs, *n. d.*—Merry
       Frolics of Swalpo, *n. d.*—History of Tom Thumb, in 2 parts,
       n. d.—Guy Earl of Warwick, *n. d.* and 5 other scarce pieces,
       all with woodcuts, in 1 vol. *half bound*—Rider's British Merlin
       for 1738, *old red morocco gilt*   (2)

270 Chardin (Jean) Voyages en Perse, et autres lieux de l'Orient, 10
       vol. in 5, *portrait and folding maps, &c. vellum*
                                                Paris (Rouen), 1723

271 Charles I. Eikon Basiliké : the Pourtraicture of His Sacred
       Majestie, in his Solitudes and Sufferings, *portrait of the king
       and emblematic engraving, a large and fine copy in old morocco,
       richly tooled, g. e.*   1649

272 Charles I. Eikon Basiliké : the Pourtraicture of His Sacred
       Maiestie in his Solitudes and Sufferings, *portraits of Charles I
       and the Prince of Wales, folding plate by Marshall (small hole in
       one leaf), original calf rebacked, fine clean copy*
                                                no name or place, 1649

273 Chauncy (Sir Henry) Historical Antiquities of Hertfordshire,
       2 vol. *with 46 plates and a folding map, original boards, uncut*
                                                Bishop's Stortford, 1826

274 Chess. Stamma (Philip) The Noble Game of Chess, *folding
       diagram, &c. old calf,* THE AUTHOR'S AUTOGRAPH AT THE END
                                                                1745

275 CHILDREN'S BOOKS [Roscoe] The Butterfly's Ball and the Grass-
       hopper's Feast, *engravings (uncoloured),* 1807—The Elephant's
       Ball, by W. B. *engravings (uncoloured),* 1807—The Lion's Mas-
       querade, *engravings (uncoloured),* 1807—The Peacock at Home,
       engravings (uncoloured), 1807—Old Dame Trot and her Comical
       Cat, *engravings (coloured),* 1812—The Old Man, his Son and his
       Ass, *coloured engravings,* 1810—Little Nancy, *engravings (un-
       coloured),* 1813—The Thought : an interesting Game, *coloured
       engravings,* 1809—Think before you Speak, *coloured engravings,*
       1809—The Butterfly's Birthday, *engravings (uncoloured),* 1808
       —The Lobster's Voyage to the Brazils, *coloured engravings,*
       1808—Adventures of Capt. Lemuel Gulliver, *coloured engrav-
       ings,* 1808—Mounseer Nongton Paw, *coloured plates,* 1811
       —The Loves of Mr. Jenkins and Polly Pattens, *coloured plates,*
       1809—The Mice and their Picnic, *coloured engravings,* 1809 ;
       and others, *some imperfect, in the original half binding*   (5)

276 Children's Books. The Cries of London, drawn from Life, *coloured,*
       1823—Bishop (J.) The New Cries of London, *coloured,* 1824
       —The Little Tradesman, *coloured, n. d.*—Juvenile Sports,
       coloured, n. d. ; and others   (8)

D 2

277 Children's Books.   Johnny Gilpin's Journey, *coloured frontispiece
and woodcuts, n. d.*—Jack and his Rocking Horse, *coloured, n. d.*
—Jack the Giant Killer, *coloured frontispiece, n. d.*—Little
Peter Pry, *engravings, n. d.* ; and others   (6)

278 Children's Books.   History of Little Jack, *with cuts*, 1820—Jack
and the Bean-Stalk, *coloured engravings, n. d.*—Meeke (Mrs.)
The Parent's Offering, *coloured, n. d.* ; and others   (5)

279 Children's Books.   The Gaping Wide Mouth'd Waddling Frog,
a Game, *coloured, n. d.*—Adventures of a Dandy, *with* 15
coloured engravings, n. d.—Goody Two Shoes, *coloured, n. d.*—
Tom Thumb, *coloured, n. d.* ; and others, *scarce*   (6)

280 Children's Books.   Tommy Trip's Museum : The Feathered
Creation, in two parts, *coloured, n. d.*—The Quadruped Race,
in three parts, *n. d.* ; and others   (7)

281 Children's Books.   The Apple Pie Alphabet, *coloured, Bushnell,
n. d.*—The Yellow Dwarf, *coloured, n. d.*—The White Mouse,
with cuts, n. d.—Robinson Crusoe, *with cuts, n. d.* ; and others,
miniature size   (26)

282 Children's Books.   Franklin (Dr.) The Art of Making Money
Plenty, *with curious engravings*, 1817—History of Mary and
her Doll, *coloured, n. d.*—History of Little Jack, *coloured frontispiece, n. d.*—The Infant's Alphabet, *coloured, n. d.* ; and others
                                                                                        (7)

283 Children's Books.   Dame Wiggins of Lee and her Seven Wonderful Cats, written principally by a Lady of Ninety, *with* 16
*coloured engravings (this was reprinted by John Ruskin, with
additions), n. d.*—The History of Sixteen Wonderful Old
Women, *with* 16 *engravings (coloured)*, exhibiting their principal eccentricities and amusements, *n. d. fresh as when origin-
ally issued*   (2)

284 Children's Books.   Cock Robin and Jenny Wren, *with* 30 *coloured
engravings*, 1823—A Present for Youth, *frontispiece, &c. half
bound, n. d.*—Mr. Mathews "At Home," *coloured frontispiece,
n. d.* ; and others   *a parcel*

285 Cibber (Colley) An Apology for the Life of Mr. Tho' Cibber
Comedian, being a Proper Sequel to the Apology for the
Life of Mr. Colley Cibber, Comedian ; with an Historical
View of the Stage to the Present Year, supposed to be written
by himself, *old calf, Dublin*, 1741

₊ An interesting volume, containing numerous references to
Shakespeare and his plays. A Latin quotation of two lines
from the character of Pistol in Henry IV occurs on page 27,

LOT 285—*continued.*

    and a cast for Othello on page 45. The excellence of Betterton in the characters of Hotspur, Brutus, Cassius and Othello is commented upon on pages 48 and 49. A small portion of the text is missing on page 135.

286 Cibber (Colley) Papal Tyranny in the Reign of King John, a Tragedy as it is acted at the Theatre-Royal in Covent-Garden. By his Majesty's Servants, FIRST EDITION, *fine copy, contemporary red morocco, gold tooled on the sides, with a border containing eagle, acorn, rose and thistle ornaments, g. e.* RARE   *J. Watts,* 1745

    *** Dedicated to the Earl of Chesterfield, with an interesting " *Comparison between this Play and the King John of Shakespear.*" At the end is a catalogue of Watts' publications.

287 Cibber (Colley) The Lives of the Poets of Great Britain and Ireland, to the time of Dean Swift, FIRST EDITION, 5 vol. VERY FINE COPY, *original boards, uncut*   1753

    *** " The compiler of 'Lives of the Poets' was the *first* to relate the story that SHAKESPEARE'S original connection with the play-house was as holder of horses of visitors outside the doors."—SIDNEY LEE. Halliwell in his " Illustrations of the Life of Shakespeare," 1874, reprints Cibber's account.

288 Clavasio (A. de) De observantia cum quibusdam novis et opportunis additionibus ejusdem, lít. 𝔤𝔬𝔱𝔥. *double columns, title in red, with outline woodcut of St. Peter, in the original interesting binding of blind tooled leather, one side damaged,* VERY RARE
                        Venetiis, P. de Paganinis, 1499

289 Cleveland (John) The Idol of the Clowns, FIRST EDITION (*some leaves cut into*), *calf gilt*   1654

    *** The Woodhouse copy sold for £5 7s. 6d.

290 Cockton (H.) Sylvester Sound, the Somnambulist, FIRST EDITION, *portrait, engraved title, and plates by Onwhyn, clean copy in original red cloth, uncut*   1844

291 Coleridge (S. T.) Aids to Reflection, FIRST EDITION, *clean copy, in the original boards, uncut, with label*   1825

292 Collyns (C. P.) Notes of the Chase of the Wild Red Deer in the Counties of Devon and Somerset, *with numerous illustrations, half morocco gilt, t. e. g.*   1862

293 Combe (William) The English Dance of Death, with Metrical Illustrations, 2 vol. in 1, ORIGINAL EDITION, *numerous coloured plates by T. Rowlandson, fine impressions, half bound, m. e.*
                        R. Ackermann, 1815-16

294 Combe (William) The Three Tours of Dr. Syntax, 3 vol. third edition, *cloth, somewhat damaged*   *ib. n. d.*

295 Common Prayer (Book of) with the Psalms of David, *vellum gilt, with a beautifully executed painting of King David playing the harp on the upper side, and on the other side an allegorical figure of Faith, on a blue ground,* A PAINTING ON THE FORE EDGE *of a Roman aqueduct, with houses in the background, in a case* 1781

296 Compleat History of the Intrigues of Priests and Nuns, *plates,* 1746—Manley (Mrs.) Memoirs of Europe towards the close of the Eighth Century, 2 vol. in 1, 1716—Timon of Athens, made into a Play, by T. Shadwell, 1732—Ravenscroft (E.) The London Cuckolds, 1729 ; and other Plays and Operas, *old calf* (3)

297 Cooper (A.) and J. Scott. Impressions of a Series of Animals and Birds illustrative of British Field Sports from a Set of Silver Buttons, *engraved title and* 15 *illustrations, calf gilt* 1821

298 Cooper (J. F.) Ravensnest, or the Redskins, 3 vol. FIRST EDITION, *half calf* 1846

299 Corneille (P.) La Mort de Pompée, Tragédie, *calf* *Paris,* 1644

 *** Refer to Halliwell's Catalogue of Shakespeare (1862), No. 170.

300 CORNEILLE (P.) LE THEATRE DE P. CORNEILLE revue et corrigé, et augmenté de diverses pièces nouvelles, suivant la copie imprimée à Paris, 1664, 5 vol. in 4, *frontispieces*—Les Tragédies et Comédies de th. Corneille, revues et corrigées, et augmentées de diverses pièces nouvelles, suivant la copie imprimée à Paris, 1665, 1676-1678, 5 vol. ; *together* 10 *vol. in* 9, *frontispieces, brown levant morocco extra, finely gilt backs, inside borders, gilt and marbled leaves, by Traut-Bauzonnet* 1664-78

 *** This is ONE OF THE FINEST COPIES KNOWN, measuring 131 millim. It contains the ex-libris of M. de Montesson, and was sold in the Potier sale in 1870 for 2,400 francs. A minute description of this edition is given by M. E. Picot (Bibl. Cornélienne, No. 138).

301 Costello (Louisa S.) Clara Fane ; or, The Contrast of a Life, 3 vol. FIRST EDITION, *original boards, uncut* 1848

302 Cotton (Charles) Scarronides, or Virgil Travestie, FIRST EDITION, *calf* 1665

303 Cotton (Charles) The Wonders of the Peake, FIRST EDITION, *original calf* 1681

304 Counsellor Manners, his Last Legacy to his Son ; enriched and embellished with Grave Advisos, Pat Histories, and Ingenious Proverbs, Apologues, and Apophthegms, FIRST EDITION, *original calf* 1673

 *** At page 89 is a reference to Shakespeare's friend, Nat Field the Actor, " And be not of Nat Feeld the Players humour,

LOT 304—*continued.*

who vowed, that if the old Woman that crawled upon her tail at Holborn-Bridge, had a thousand pound for her Portion, he would marry her and adorn her Breech with a French Velvet Hood." (Refer to Halliwell's "Hand-List of Shakespeareana," 1862, No. 621.) Halliwell only possessed the late edition of 1699.

305   Cowley (A.) Works in Prose and Verse, *portrait*, LARGE PAPER COPY, 3 vol. *morocco extra, t. e. g. by Riviere, London*
John Sharpe, 1809

306   Cowper (William) and the Rev. John Newton. Olney Hymns, in Three Books. Book I, on Select Texts of Scripture; Book II, on Occasional Subjects; Book III, on the Progress and Changes of the Spiritual Life, FIRST EDITION, *black morocco, g. e.*   *W. Oliver, &c.* 1779

307   Cox (N.) The Gentleman's Recreation, in four parts, viz. Hunting, Hawking, Fowling, Fishing, &c. (*some leaves wormed and plates inlaid by the binder*), FIRST EDITION, *quaintly bound in carved oak boards, covered with green morocco super extra, joints, silk ends, rich symbolical tooling on sides and back by T. Gosden, with his bookplate*   1674

309   Crown Garland (The) of Golden Roses, gathered out of England's Royal Garden, set forth in many Pleasant New Songs and Sonnets, with New Additions never before Imprinted, Divided into Two Parts, *calf extra, g. e.*
Printed by J. M. for W. and T. Thackeray, at the sign of the Angel in Duck Lane, near West Smithfield, 1662

  *** An excessively rare little volume (B. A. P. copy in 1815, £10). Some leaves are mended, but the bottom edges are uncut. Contains the famous ballad of " King Cophetua and the Beggar Maid," which is quoted by Shakespeare in *Romeo and Juliet*, and *King Henry IV* (Second Part).

310   CRUIKSHANK (G.) THE SCOURGE, or Monthly Expositor of Imposture and Folly, vol. I-III, 3 vol. 18 *coloured folding caricatures, of which 13 are by G. Cruikshank (one of which requires mending, and 2 of the others), half russia*   1811-12

311   Cruikshank (G.) The Greeks, being the Jeremiad of an Exiled Greek, a Poem, " venu de France d'une manière inconnu," and dedicated to all the Legs ! . . . . by Mr. B— not B—np—te, FIRST EDITION, 6 *coloured plates by G. Cruikshank*, VERY SCARCE, 1817—The Pigeons, by the author of " The Greeks," 6 *coloured plates by G. Cruikshank*, 1817 ; in 1 vol. *new calf extra, g. e.*

312   Cruikshank (G.) Billets in the Low Countries, *coloured plates by G. Cruikshank, clean copy in the original boards, uncut, very scarce*
Stockdale, 1818

313   Cruikshank (G.) The Ton : Anecdotes, Chit-Chat, Hints and On Dits, *coloured plates by G. Cruikshank (one wanting), uncut*
ib. 1819

314   Cruikshank (G.) The Englishman's Mentor, the Picture of the
       Palais Royal, describing its Spectacles, Gaming-rooms, ...
       Gamesters, Sharpers, Mouchards, Artistes, Épicures, &c.
       *coloured folding frontispiece by G. Cruikshank, extra illustrated by
       the insertion of 5 coloured plates from Carey's Life in Paris, by
       G. Cruikshank, half vellum, t. e. g. uncut*   1819

315   CRUIKSHANK (G.) THE HUMORISTS, a Collection of Entertaining
       Tales, Anecdotes, Repartees, Witty Sayings, Epigrams, Bon-
       Mots, Jeu d'esprits, &c. carefully selected, 4 vol. *40 humorous
       coloured plates by G. Cruikshank, red morocco extra, gilt backs and
       sides, inside dentelles, g. e. by Riviere, scarce,* FINE COPY
                                                       1822, 1819, 1820

316   Cruikshank (G.) Points of Humour, both parts, *original impressions
       of the etchings and woodcuts, slightly stained, half bound (the
       etchings and woodcuts in part II are on india paper)*   1823-4

317   Cruikshank (G.) [Apel (T. A.)] Der Freischütz, Travestie by
       Septimus Globus, FIRST EDITION, *12 etchings after Crowquill,
       by G. Cruikshank, coloured, calf extra gilt, g. e.*   1824

318   Cruikshank (G.) Peter Schlemihl, from the German of Lamotte
       Fouqué (Chamisso), FIRST EDITION, *plates by G. Cruikshank,
       russia extra, t. e. g. uncut, by Zaehnsdorf*   1824
   *** Special copy, having a duplicate set of plates on india proofs.
       First issue with the mis-spelt title-page, rare.

319   Cruikshank (G.) Grimm's German Popular Stories, *plates by
       G. Cruikshank, clean tall copy, half calf*   J. Robins, 1825

320   Cruikshank (G.) Paris (J. A.) Philosophy in Sport made Science
       in Earnest, 3 vol. FIRST EDITION, *22 illustrations by G. Cruik-
       shank, clean copy with half titles, in the original boards, uncut,
       with the paper labels*   1827

321   Cruikshank (G. and R.) The Universal Songster, 3 vol. *engraved
       frontispieces, and numerous illustrations by G. and R. Cruikshank,
       original illustrated boards (rebacked), uncut*   1828-9
   *** Inserted in the first volume is the very rare original cancelled
       plate, coloured, of which only a very few were issued.

322   Cruikshank (G.). [Defoe (Daniel)] Robinson Crusoe, 2 vol. LARGE
       PAPER, FIRST EDITION, *with the india proof frontispieces and
       numerous illustrations by G. Cruikshank, panelled calf extra, gilt
       back, tooled sides, t. e. g. uncut, by Riviere,* FINE COPY   1831

323   Cruikshank (G.) The Cat's Tail, *plates by G. Cruikshank, in the
       original paper covers,* 1831—Comic Alphabet, *26 illustrations by
       R. Cruikshank, in the original pictorial cover, Martin, n. d. 2 vol.*

324   Cruikshank (G.). Fielding (H.) Adventures of Joseph Andrews,
       plates by G. Cruikshank, original cloth, uncut
                                         Roscoe's Novelist's Library, 1832

325   Cruikshank (G.). Le Sage. Adventures of Gil Blas, translated by
       Smollett, with Memoir by Roscoe, 2 vol. *illustrations by G.
       Cruikshank, green cloth, uncut*   *ib.* 1833

326   Cruikshank's Comic Almanacks, 19 vol. a complete set, FIRST
       EDITION, *coloured folding plates and several hundred etchings by
       G. Cruikshank, original wrappers, uncut, scarce*   1835-53

327 Cruikshank (G.). Inglis (H. D.) Rambles in the Footsteps of Don
       Quixote, FIRST EDITION, *illustrations by G. Cruikshank, half
       bound*   1837

328 Cruikshank (G.) George Cruikshank's Table Book, edited by Gilbert
       Abbott à Beckett, FIRST EDITION, *plates and other illustrations
       by G. Cruikshank, crushed levant morocco, extra gilt, g. e. by
       Zaehnsdorf*   imp. 8vo.   *Punch Office,* 1845

329 Cruikshank (G.) Table Book, edited by G. A. à Beckett, FIRST
       EDITION, *plates and numerous illustrations by G. Cruikshank, calf*
                                                                 1845

330 Cruikshank (G.) Omnibus, edited by L. Blanchard, *engravings on
       s'eel and wood, title and frontispiece soiled*   1869

331 Cruikshank (G.) Mayhew (Bros.) The Greatest Plague of Life,
       or Adventures of a Lady in Search of a Good Servant, *illus-
       trations by G. Cruikshank, original cloth*   *Bogue, n. d.*

332 Cruikshank (G.) Fairy Library. Jack and the Bean-stalk, Hop
       o' My Thumb, and the Seven League Boots, 2 vol. FIRST
       EDITIONS, *illustrations by G. Cruikshank, in the original pictorial
       covers*   *ib. n. d.*

333 Cruikshank (G.) Authentic Account of the Assassination of the
       Hon. Spencer Perceval who was shot by J. Bellingham, *folding
       frontispiece by G. Cruikshank, uncut*   *Lee, n. d.*

334 Cruikshank. The Political Dr. Syntax, a Poem, with Satyrical
       Designs by I. R. Cruikshank, 2 *full-page coloured plates, Grove
       & Co.* 1820, *very scarce*—Political House that Jack Built; The
       Queen and the Magna Charta; The Queen's Matrimonial
       Ladder, *with the ladder;* The Acts of Adonis the Great; Lost
       Mutton Found; Non Mi Ricordo; Man in the Moon; The
       Spirit of Despotism; The Sinecurist's Creed; Political Litany;
       Trial between Mr. J. Rogers and Parr Popkin, 1818; and
       others, *many with illustrations by G. Cruikshank*; and a number
       of single printed leaves at the end, *half calf*   *in 1 vol.*

335 Cumberland (Richard) First Love, 1799—The Sailor's Daughter,
       1804; and a number of Eighteenth Century Plays, &c.
                                                            a bundle

336 Cunningham (J.) Poems, chiefly Pastoral, FIRST EDITION, *frontis-
       piece, dedicated to David Garrick, original calf* *Newcastle,* 1766

337 DANCING MASTER (THE), or, Directions for Dancing Country
       Dances, with the tune to each Dance, for the Treble-Violin,
       *with view of "The Dancing Schoole" on title, original calf, very
       scarce*   oblong 8vo.   *W. Pearson,* 1716

338 Daniel (Samuel) A Panegyrike Congratvlatorie delivered to the
       Kings Most Excellent Maiestie at Bvrleigh Harrington in
       Rvtlandshire, by Samvel Daniel; also Certaine Epistles, with
       a Defence of Ryme heretofore written, and now published by
       the Avthor. Carmen amat, quisquis carmine digna gerit,
       large and beautiful copy, olive morocco, by Charles Lewis
                                    Imprinted for Edward Blount, 1603

     ₊ See the Grolier Club's Catalogue of Early English Literature
          (no. 58).

339   Dante col Situ et Forma dell' Inferno, dedicated to Vittoria
        Colonna, *with three woodcut diagrams at end, a large and clean
        copy of a scarce edition, vellum gilt, g. e.*   *Vinegia, Aldo,* 1515

340   Dasent (G. W.) Story of the Burnt Njal: or Life in Iceland at
        the end of the Tenth Century, with an Introduction, *maps
        and plans,* 2 vol. *original cloth*   1861

341   Dasent (G. W.) The Vikings of the Baltic, 3 vol. *original cloth*
                                                                         1875

342   Davidson (John) Plays, FIRST COLLECTED EDITION, *frontispiece by
        Aubrey Beardsley, original cloth, uncut, limited issue*   1894

343   Defoe (Daniel) Collection of the Writings of the Author of the
        True-born-Englishman, collected by himself, *portrait engraved
        by Vandergucht, after Taverner*   1703

344   Defoe (D.) Vox Populi, Vox Dei; being True Maxims of
        Governments, *printed for the author,* 1709; An Argument
        proving that the Design of employing and enobling foreigners
        is a treasonable conspiracy against the Constitution, &c.
        printed for the Booksellers, 1717; Secret History of the October
        Club, 1711; Secret History of the White Staff, Purse and
        Mitre, *S. Keimer,* 1715; *all unbound*   (4)

345   Defoe (D.) The Life and Adventures of the famous Moll Flanders,
        calf gilt   1765

346   Defoe (D.) The Life and Surprising Adventures of Robinson
        Crusoe, *numerous engravings from drawings by George Cruik-
        shank,* 2 vol. LARGE PAPER, *marble calf extra, m. e. Mayor,* 1831

347   DE L'OEIL des Rois et de la Justice, Remonstrance faite en la ville
        de Bourdeaux à l'ouverture de la Cour de Justice envoyée par
        le Roy en ses pais & Duché de Guienne, FINE LARGE COPY,
        red morocco extra, g. e. [*fleuron*] *à Paris, chez Robert le Mangnier,
        rüe neufue nostre Dame, à l'image sainct Jean Baptiste,* 1584

    *** During the last sixty years a succession of enthusiastic workers
          has done its utmost to elucidate the public and private career
          of one of the brightest literary ornaments of France, if not of
          Western Europe, during the sixteenth century, MICHAEL DE
          MONTAIGNE. The broad result of modern researches has
          been to place the author of the Essays in the ranks of those
          select few, who at different periods and in different countries
          have acquired high distinction in more than a single field of
          activity. Of course Montaigne is for us all at the present
          time essentially and primarily the man of letters, the thinker,
          the painter of men on paper; but if we more rarely regard
          him as the *homme d'affaires,* the relations of such a man to the
          public concerns of his age and of the part of France where
          most of his not very prolonged life was spent, inevitably ac-
          quire in our sight a peculiar and artificial value. Of the pre-
          sent small tract a long account was recently communicated
          (with facsimiles) to "*The Connoisseur,*" and there the writer of
          the paper proved that the composition, owing to certain in-
          disputable circumstances, was due to the pen of the famous
          essayist. The text of the volume purports in fact to be a
          printed transcript from the municipal registry of Bordeaux,

and it found its way into that record during the mayoralty of Montaigne. Never, before or since, most probably, has a similar composition found its way into local archives ; its structure and language are Montaignesque as such a thoroughly official paper could be by possibility, and in fact it is in places rather a supplement to the Essays than anything else. It is a tissue of quotations from Greek and Latin authors intermingled with expressions and sentiments, which seem unmistakably to betray its parentage. Take, for example, a paragraph which is, by the way, not quite accurately given in the periodical above cited : " Un hōme est bien malade quand il ne sent point son mal ; mais quand nō sentemēt il le sent & la cognoit, mais aussi scait & entend les causes et les remedes d' icelui, il est ja à demy guery." One of the facsimile pages in *The Connoisseur* illustrates a second very conclusive point, the citation of Chrysippus whom Montaigne almost stood alone in knowing and quoting ; and a third argument in favour of our view is the circumstance that such an address to the Bordeaux assembly could not have been drawn up by any third party without the ex-officio cognizance and sanction of the chief magistrate. The Essayist in his quality of Mayor presided over the meeting, and M. Bonnefon tells us that the allocution was orally delivered by Antonie Loisel, and that the Essayist in the chair highly approved of the terms of the inauguratory oration. He might have done so, as he laid down his pen at the conclusion of his unaccustomed task ; but a conversance with his style and method should go a very long way indeed to persuade us that Loisel was simply a mouthpiece for M. Le Maire. It is very much as if Shakespeare had been Mayor of Stratford, and had chosen to delegate to someone else a public speech, in which were passages reminding a hearer or reader of something which he had seen in *Hamlet* or *Lear*. NO OTHER COPY OF THIS EXTRAORDINARILY RARE LITTLE TRACT APPEARS TO HAVE OCCURRED FOR SALE IN ENGLAND.

QUARTO.

348   Costume. Picturesque Representations of the Dress and Manners of the Turks, *illustrated in* 60 *finely coloured engravings,* with Descriptions, *original half binding, uncut*   *M'Lean, n. d.*

349   Cowley (Abraham) The Guardian, a Comedie, acted before Prince Charles His Highness at Trinity-Colledg in Cambridge, upon the twelfth of March, 1641, FIRST EDITION, *unbound*   1650
*** Very rare. Contains allusions to SHAKESPEARE and Ben Jonson.

350   Crabbe (Rev. G.) The Library, a Poem, FIRST EDITION, 1781—Peacock (Lucy) The Adventures of the Six Princesses of Babylon, FIRST EDITION, *dedicated to Princess Mary, with autograph of the authoress on the last leaf,* 1785 ; &c. ; *half calf*
in 1 *vol.*

351   Creighton (Bp.) The Story of some English Shires, *with a photogravure frontispiece and* 98 *engravings, uncut, t. e. g.*   1897

352 Creighton (Bp.) Story of some English Shires; another copy
(*as the preceding*) 1897

353 [Croce (G. C.)] Bertoldo con Bertoldino e Cacasenno in ottava
rima, *full-page copperplates by L. Mattiola, half vellum*
Bologna, 1736

354 Cromwell (Richard) The Happy Sinner or Penitent Malefactor,
being the Prayers and Last Words of one Richard Cromwell
(some time a Souldier and Chyrurgion in the late D. of Mon-
mouth's Army), who was executed at Lichfield for murder, 3 July, 1691; also his Legacy to his County of Choyce,
Physical and Chyrurgical Receipts; together with a strange
and wonderful Account of Three Ravens flying against the
walls of his Chamber, *morocco, very rare; from the Bliss and
Corser collections*
*printed by R. Clavell, and to be sold by Mich. Johnson, Book-
seller in Lichfield*, 1691
₊ A literary curiosity. It is one of the few tracts printed for
sale by Johnson's father, then a bookseller at Lichfield. The
curious advertisement at the end shows that he also sold
quack medicines.

355 Cruikshank. Tales of the Cordelier Metamorphosed, as nar-
rated in a manuscript from the Borromeo collection, and in
the Cordelier Cheval of M. Piron, with Translations (by Geo.
Hibbert), *etchings on india paper by George Cruikshank, half
bound, uncut* 1821
₊ Only 64 copies privately printed. This is a presentation copy
from the translator, *vide* fly-leaf, very scarce.

356 D'Annunzio (Gabriele) Francesca da Rimini : Tragedia, rappre-
sentata in Roma nell' Anno MCMI, A.D. IIX del mese di
Decembre, impressa in Milano, per i fratelli Treves, nell' Anno
MCMII A.D. IXX del mese di Marzo, *beautifully printed in the
Kelmscott style, vellum, uncut, with tyers* 1902

357 Davenant (Sir W.) Love and Honour, presented by his Majesties
Servants at the Black-Fryers, *unbound* 1649
₊ With the rare extra leaf of Dramatis Personæ.

358 DAVIES (John, *of Hereford*) Mirum in modum. A Glimpse of
God's Glorie and the Soules Shape, *calf extra, g. e. by Bedford,
a few headlines shaved* 1602
₊ Dedicated to the Earl of Pembroke, Sir Robert Sidney, and
Edward Herbert. VERY RARE. It was the FIRST publication
of John Davies, of Hereford. *There was no copy in the
Bibliotheca Anglo-Poetica.*

359 DAVIES (John, *of Hereford*) Wittes Pilgrimage (by Poeticall
Essaies) Through a World of Amorous Sonnets, Soule-
passions, and other Passages, Divine, Philosophicall, Morall,
Poeticall, and Politicall, by John Davies, Jucunda vicissitudo
rerum, FIRST EDITION, *morocco extra, g. e.*
*At London. Printed for John Browne, and are to be sold at his
shop in Saint Dunstones Church-yard in Fleet streete, n. d.*
₊ A fine copy of this rare Elizabethan volume of poetry. See
Grolier Club Catalogue of Early English Literature, no. 68.

360 Day (J.) A New Spring of Divine Poetrie, FIRST EDITION, *calf gilt, by Riviere* sm. 4to. *London*, 1637

361 Deacon (John) Tobacco tortured, or the filthie fume of Tobacco refined, *black and roman letter, a few headlines cut into, title soiled, half bound, very scarce* 1616

362 Decker (T.) The Gull's Hornbook, with Notes and Illustrations by Dr. Nott, *only a few copies printed, uncut*
Bristol, 1609, *reprinted for J. M. Gutch*, 1812

363 DESPAUTÈRE (Jean) Syntaxis, *Lugduni* (1528) ; Ars Versificatoria, *Lugduni* (1528); *in* 1 *vol. calf, a curious specimen of early binding, sides and back blind tooled, the edges gilt and gauffred with the following motto, " Tel garde le corps qui ne garde le cœur "* 1528

₊ Despautère or Despauterius was one of the most popular teachers and writers of educational works of the sixteenth century, and his publications were employed in England and Scotland as well as in France.

364 Diario per l'Anno MDCCLXXXVIII, di Enrico Benedetto, Cardinale Duca di Yorck, *one of* 75 *copies, privately printed, uncut*
1876

365 Dickens (C.) Memoirs of Joseph Grimaldi, 2 vol. FIRST EDITION, INLAID TO 4TO SIZE, *portrait and plates by G. Cruikshank, with* 184 *extra illustrations, including* 41 *original Grimaldi playbills, many coloured portraits and plates, and* 10 *autograph letters by Kemble, Fawcett, Keeley, Macready, Miss Kelly, G. Cruikshank, &c., also the additional notes from Whitehead's edition of* 1846, *red morocco, g. e. with* 4 *inlaid character-portraits of Grimaldi on the sides (reproduced from rare engravings), by the Guild of Women-Binders* 1838

366 DIGGES (L.) A PROGNOSTICATION everlasting of ryght good effecte, conteyning playne, brief, pleasant, chose rules to iudge the Weather by the Sunne, Moone, Sterres, Cometes, Raynbowe, Thunder, &c. profitable to al maner of men of Understanding, **black letter**, *woodcuts and diagrams, large copy, in original binding* *T. Gemini*, 1556

₊ VERY RARE. The leaf between pp. 27 and 29 is blank, but forms part of the sheet. Mr. Hazlitt says it ends on Dii ; this copy ends on Diii, with the colophon. The British Museum copy wants the last two leaves. As copies differ, this will be sold not subject to return ; but it is believed to be the most complete copy known.

367 [DIRNE (Thos.)] The Life of the Dutches of Suffolke, as it hath beene divers and sundry times acted, with good applause, *part of last leaf missing* 1631

₊ FIRST AND ONLY EDITION.

368 [Doddridge (Sir John)] The Lawes Resolutions of Womens Rights, or the Lawes Provision for Women, a Methodicall Collection of such Statutes and Customes, with the Cases, Opinions, Arguments and points of Learning in the Law, as doe properly concerne Women, together with a Compendious Table, whereby the chiefe matters in this Booke contained, may be the more readily found, **black letter**, *unbound* 1632

₊ A long account will be found in Mr. Hazlitt's " Shakespeare." A volume of considerable rarity.

369   Dolce (Lodovico) Le Trasformationi, in questa Quinta Impressione da lui in molti luoghi ricorrette, *woodcut title, fine cuts in the text and figured initials, vellum*

       sm. 4to. Vinegia, Giolito, 1558

370   DONNE (John) Letters to Several Persons of Honour, written by John Donne, Sometime Deane of St. Paul's, London, published by John Donne, Dr. of the Civill Law, FINE LARGE COPY, *original sheepskin*

       London, printed by J. Flesher for Richard Marriot, and are to be sold at his shop in St. Dunstan's Church-yard, under the Dyall, 1651

    *** The portrait of Donne at the age of fifty-nine, engraved by Lombart, is a very brilliant impression. See Grolier Catalogue of Early English Literature, no. 73.

371   DONNE (John) Poems, by J. D. with Elegies on the Author's Death, FIRST EDITION, *original sheepskin*   1633

    *** A fine large copy, *in its original binding*, with the rare blank leaves before the title. See Grolier Club's Catalogue of Early English Literature, no. 71.

372   Doré. Aventures du Baron de Munchausen, traduction nouvelle par Théoph. Gautier fils, *illustrées par G. Doré, half morocco*

       Paris, Furne, s. d.

373   Drama. The Whole Art of the Stage, written in French by the command of Cardinal Richelieu, by M. Hedelin, and now made English, *old calf, fine copy,* 1684 ; and another   (2)

    *** Richelieu intended to appoint the writer of this work " Overseer of the Theatres of France."

374   Dryden (John) An Evening's Love, or the Mock Astrologer, FIRST EDITION, *unbound*   *sm. 4to.* 1671

375   Dryden (J.) Aureng-Zebe, a Tragedy, FIRST EDITION, *half calf*

       sm. 4to. 1676

376   Dryden. Malone (Edmond) Dryden Correspondence, a Collection of upwards of 100 Original Autograph Letters sent to him while engaged upon his edition of Dryden's Works, comprising Letters from Blakeway, Dr. Vincent, John Gutch, Chetwood, Lady Dryden, Bishop of Killala, Jas. Bindley, Charles Burney, Bishop Percy, Sir N. W. Wraxall, and others, *nearly all of them endorsed in Malone's handwriting, and some having his notes, bound in a vol. half morocco*   *thick 4to*

377   Durfey (Thos.) Madame Fickle, a Comedy, FIRST EDITION, *unbound, with autograph of John Genest*   *sm. 4to.* 1677

378   Durfey (T.) Squire Oldsapp, or the Night Adventurers, a Comedy, FIRST EDITION, *title slightly cut, autograph of John Genest*   1679

379   Du Bec (Jean, *Abbot of Mortimer*) The Historie of the Great Emperor Tamerlan, drawen on from the auncient Monuments of the Arabians, newly translated out of French into English by H. M. (Humphry Mildmay), *limp vellum*

       sm. 4to. Wm. Ponsonby, 1597

380   Early Book Sale. Catalogue of the Library of Richard Davis, Bibliopole, sold by Auction at Oxford, by Cooper and Millington, April, 1686, 208 *pp.* ; Catalogue of a Medical Library, sold by Auction at Child's Coffee House, by W. Cooper, July, 1686, *very rare*   (2)

381 Edda. De Yfverborna Atlingans, Eller, Sviogötars ok Nord-
männers, Edda, edited from MS. in Upsala Library by
Johannes Göransson, *wants last blank* *Upsala* (1746)

382 Essex's Innocency and Honour Vindicated : or Murder, Perjury,
&c. justly charged on the Murtherers of the Earl of Essex,
by L. Broddon, *frontispiece*, 1690—True and Perfect Journal
of the Affairs in IRELAND, 1690—Remarks on the Affairs and
Trade of England and Ireland, 1691—On the Causes of the
Present Disasters in England and who they are that brought
the French Fleet into the English Channel, 1690—Brief and
True Account of the Sufferings of the CHURCH OF SCOTLAND,
1690—NEW-YEARS GIFT for the late Rapparees, a Satyr (IN
VERSE), *E. Smith*, 1691 ; and others, *old calf, shabby* *in 1 vol.*

383 EVANGELIA SANCTI LUCÆ CUM GLOSSIS, MANUSCRIPT ON VELLUM
(150 *ll.* 10 *by* 7 *in.*) *the text written in the centre in neat* 𝔤𝔬𝔱𝔥𝔦𝔠
*contracted letters, 15 lines to a page, within marginal glosses on
each side, in a smaller hand, and numerous interlinear glosses,
oaken boards, doeskin with clasp* SÆC. XII

*** A VERY WELL WRITTEN CODEX IN FINE AND PERFECT
PRESERVATION, probably the work of an English scribe of
the Augustinian Monastery of Canterbury. The first leaf
bears the inscription "*Liber Sancti Augustini Cantuariensis.*"

384 Everitt (Graham) English Caricaturists and Graphic Humourists
of the XIXth century, *numerous illustrations, also 102 extra
plates, &c. including caricatures by Woodward, Bunbury, Gillray,
Heath, Cruikshank, Doyle, Buss, Seymour, Phiz, &c. red morocco,
uncut, t. e. g. by the Guild of Women Binders* 1882

385 Ex-Libris. BOOK-PLATES. A COLLECTION OF 729 SPECIMENS,
arranged in alphabetical order and mounted on hinges in an
album, *half red morocco extra, g. e.*

*** This is a representative collection of early Plates, consisting
with very few exceptions of specimens before 1800, many of
them of extreme rarity. It would be impossible in the limited
space of an auction catalogue to give a full list of the plates
contained in this volume, but an idea may be gathered from
the following few selected at random and classified in groups.

Dated. Duke of Bedford 1703 and 1736, C. Bush 1734, Archi-
bald Campbell 1708 (2 *sizes*), Sir W. Dawes 1704, Sir W.
Forbes 1760, Geo. Farmor 1756, Lord Halifax 1702 (2 *sizes*),
E. Haistwell 1717, G. Montagu 1705, Francis North 1703,
T. Nicholson 1798, J. Percival 1715 and 1736, C. Palmer
1783, Earl of Roxburghe 1703, John Stearn Bishop of Clogher
1717 (*friend of Dean Swift*), S. Strode 1723, T. Thoroton
1703, J. A. Tronchin 1779, A. Udny 1726, S. Willis 1756, &c.

Chippendale. B. Annington, T. Arlington, J. Adcock, J. Ainslie,
Rev. R. H. Brandling and Chas. Brandling, James Bindley,
Dr. Blackett, S. Buckle, P. Blake (*by Forth*), J. Bunbury,
H. J. Brownrigg, G. Colebrooke, J. Cracroft, F. Cook, E.
Cooper, R. Congreve, R. Cox, S. Dayrolles, Bryan Edwards
(*of Jamaica*), W. Horton, J. Hallet, J. Hollinworth, T. Johnes,
P. Justice, H. James, S. Mills (*by Kirk*), T. Martin, Sir J.

Lot 385—Ex-libris, *continued.*

> Mawbey (2 *varieties*), S. Pemberton, W. Phillips, J. Pellat,
> R. Rogers, W. Richardson, E. Smith, C. Spooner, G. Scott,
> T. Viner, W. Vachell, Vaughan, Sir J. Wright, T. C. Wilkes,
> Sir John and Sir R. Wilmot, John Wilkes, &c.

> *Early English.* Rt. Hon. Robt. Arbuthnott, Richd. Banner (2
> *varieties*), Earl of Buchan, Gilbert Burnet (*author of History of
> the Reformation, &c.*), Lord Elphinstone, G. Hillborne, G. Lock-
> hart, Marquis of Cornwallis (2 *varieties*), W. Cowper, (*uncle of
> the Poet*), T. Callis, B. Cowell, J. Conduit, A. Clarke, Sir Paul
> Methuen (*fine plate*), &c.

> *Ladies.* P. Cotton, Charlotte Drummond, Anna Damer, Mar-
> chioness of Exeter, M. Verney Fermanagh, Henrietta Duchess
> of Gordon, Anne Countess of Galloway, Lady Mary Howe,
> Mary A. Jackson, Honble. Henrietta Knight, Helen F. Max-
> well, Catherine M. Mellish, Mary Martineau, Catherine
> Neville, Katherine G. Robinson, M. Richmond, &c.

> *Pictorial.* Earl of Aylesford, J. Symmons, John Bullock (2
> *varieties*), P. Beaumont (*Bookpile*), J. Brand, J. Burton (*by J.
> Pine*), T. Baskerfield, W. Edkins (*by Howitt*), E. F. Fischer,
> O. Grogan, B. Granger, C. Hawkins (*Bookpile*), F. B. Hawkins,
> P. Hussey, W. Kops, J. Lowes, B. Lyon, E. Place, T. Sher-
> wood, &c.

386   Ex-Libris. Book-Plates. A Collection of 766 Specimens,
> arranged in alphabetical order and mounted on hinges in an
> album, *half red morocco extra, g. e. uniform with the preceding vol.*

> *** This forms a companion to the previous volume and consists
> of Plates chiefly of the Sheraton, wreath and ribbon, floral
> wreath and other lighter decorative styles, with a few
> Chippendale, Dated and Pictorial Plates, amongst which
> may be enumerated :—R. Austin (*Pictorial*), J. Aylmer, T.
> Bell (1797), J. Freke (*in blue*), G. Birch and W. Birch, Duke
> of Bavaria 1618, R. H. Bennett (*Pictorial*), J. Blackburn
> (*Pictorial*), Rev. W. Barrow 1789, W. Bucknell, S. J. Collins,
> J. Cockshutt, Louisa Cornwallis, Geo. Chapman (2 *varieties*),
> W. Christmas (*Bookpile*), P. C. Crespigny, Margaret Camp-
> bell, A. Donkin, C. W. Dilke, B. Didier, H. Dawkins (2
> *varieties*), F. Dickens 1795, John Gore (*large early plate*), J.
> Gilpin (2 *varieties*), N. Green, T. Hudson, J. Harcourt, 17—,
> Joseph Hume, John Haldane 1707, Charles Keene, F. Lawson,
> T. Lister, J. Losh, T. Markham 1780, Countess of Mornington,
> Charles, Francis and Thomas Otway 1752, R. Pevison, J.
> Piggott, A. L. Pointer, Madame Ronde, R. Stewart, Z. Suger
> 17—, Shrewsbury 1788, Earl of Shannon, John and Charles
> Selwyn, T. Salwey (2 *varieties*), Sir Philip Sydenham 1735,
> A. Thompson, Lord Trevor 1788, John Towneley (3 *varieties*),
> A. Villettes, W. Wyndham, E. Wither, E. Woodcock, W.
> Wilberforce, Sir Thomas Cooks, Robert Walpole, Margaret
> Woodifield, &c.

387   Fane (Sir Francis) Love in the Dark, a Comedy, first edition
>   *sm. 4to. In the Savoy,* 1675

388 Fletcher (John) Rule a Wife and have a Wife, a Comedy, acted
by his Majesties Servants, FIRST EDITION, *red morocco extra,
gilt leaves* *Oxford*, 1640
**** A very fine large copy of this rare play.

389 Fletcher (John) The Faithfull Shepherdesse, acted at Somerset
House before the King and Queene on Twelfe night last 1633,
and divers times since with great applause at the Private
House in Blackefriers by his Majesties Servants 1634
**** Passages from this edition are reprinted in Capel's "School
of Shakespeare."

390 Flowers. Davidischer Lust ünd Blumen Garten das ist 150 der
furtrefflichsten Blumen, Krauter ünd Garten-Bewachse, nicht
nür nach ihrer naturalichen Beschaffenheit, Bürkel, &c.
engraved title and 74 *plates of flowers, half morocco*
Nurnberg (circa 1670)

391 Flowers. Print-Boeck door Salvator Rosa, J. B. Piazzetta, *com-
prising* 28 *engravings after Salvator Rosa,* 17 *engravings after
Joh. Bapt. Piazzetta, amongst which figure Christ and his Twelve
Apostles,* 2 *engravings after Callot, Andere,* 1767; 12 Cartouches
de Différentes Inventions Utiles à plusiers sortes de persones, à
Paris, n. d. ; *and* 12 HAND-PAINTED PLATES OF TULIPS AND
CARNATIONS, BEAUTIFULLY EXECUTED ; *in* 1 *vol. original calf*
1767

392 Foreign Field Sports, Fisheries, Sporting Anecdotes, &c. 50 *finely
coloured plates by Howitt, Atkinson, Clark and others, half
morocco* *n. d.*

393 F[ountain] (John) The Rewards of Vertue, a Comedie (*part of last
leaf missing*) 1661
**** THE ONLY EDITION. Revised by Shadwell after the author's
death, under the title of the Royal Shepherdess.

394 Gauden (Bishop) Hieraspistes : a defence by way of apology for
the Ministry and Ministers of the Church of England, *beautifully engraved title-page by Cross, contemporary citron morocco, gilt
leaves* *sm. 4to.* 1653
**** Bp. Gauden is the reputed author of the celebrated "Eikon
Basilike." The above is a presentation copy to the Earl of
Westmoreland, and has an inscription on fly-leaf in the
author's handwriting.

395 Gardening. Duhamel du Monceau (M.) Traité des Arbres Frui-
tiers, contenant leur figure, leur description, leur Culture, &c.
numerous fine plates, 2 vol. *old French red morocco extra, g. e. by
Derome* *Paris,* 1768
**** A very beautiful copy.

396 GARDENS. JARDIN ROYAL des Plantes de Nancy, A collection
of engravings of Flowers, Fruit, Plants dissected, by Desehrt,
Collin, Madame Pinard, Fontaine, Fessard, Cor, &c. with
plans of the gardens of Nancy, Lunéville, D'Arry, &c. and
portrait of F. Nic. Marquet 1er Doyen du College Royal des
Medecins de Nancy, by Nicole, *all coloured by hand,* 2 vol.
Nancy (1763)
**** The arms of the nobility to whom several of the plates are
inscribed are engraved beneath them and are also coloured by
hand.

E

397 Gauvres. Des Sires de Gauvres, Roman du XVe Siècle, publié
      par Van Dale, *facsimile production of the original MS. with
      coloured drawings, half green morocco gilt, t. e. g. Bruxelles, s. d.*

398 Garrick (David) Ode upon Dedicating a Building and Erecting a
      Statue to Shakespeare at Stratford upon Avon, by D. G. FIRST
      EDITION, *uncut*   1769

399 Ganzoni (Tomaso) L'Hospidale de Pazzi Incurabili Nuovamente
      Ristampato, con tre Capitoli in fine sopra la Pazzia, *original
      vellum*   *Venetia*, 1589

   ₊ Refer to Douce's " Illustrations of Shakespeare," pp. 151 and
      592.

The Property of a Gentleman.

OCTAVO ET INFRA.

400 GENEALOGIST (THE) edited by Geo. W. Marshall, FIRST SERIES,
      7 vol. 1877-83—NEW SERIES, edited by W. D. Selby and
      others, 11 vol. 1884, *&c. illustrations and facsimiles; together
      18 vol. half calf gilt*   1877-95

401 Guigard (Joannis) Armorial du Bibliophile, 2 vol. in 1, *numerous
      coats of arms, half calf gilt, y. e.*   1870-73

402 HARLEIAN SOCIETY'S PUBLICATIONS, edited by J. J. Howard, C. J.
      Armytage, &c. complete, 41 vol. *original cloth imp. 8vo.* 1869-97

403 Herald (The) and Genealogist, edited by J. G. Nichols, complete
      in 8 vol. *illustrations, half calf gilt*   1863-74

404 Miscellanea Genealogica et Heraldica, edited by J. J. Howard,
      FIRST SERIES, 2 vol. 1868-76—NEW SERIES, 4 vol. 1874-84—
      SECOND SERIES, 5 vol. 1886-94; *numerous facsimile and other
      illustrations, together 11 vol. half calf gilt*   1868-94

405 Patrician (The) edited by John Burke, 6 vol. *half calf gilt* 1846-48

405* Topographer (The) and Genealogist, edited by J. G. Nichols,
      3 vol. *illustrations, uncut*   1846

OTHER PROPERTIES.

A Valuable Collection of Roman Catholic Books,

Chiefly printed and often written abroad, including many of great rarity.

All Octavo et Infra unless otherwise expressed.

406 Anderton (J.) Protestant's Apology for the Roman Church, with
      a conclusion to the Reverend Judges, and other grave and
      learned Sages of the Law, *very fine copy, calf extra, g. e. by
      Bedford*   4to. (*Printed abroad*) *Permissu Superorium*, 1608

407 Anderton (T.) History of the Iconoclasts during the Reign of
      the Eastern Emperors, *original calf, g. e. printed abroad*, 1671

408   Augustin (St.) A Heavenly Treasure of comfortable Meditations
        and Prayers, written by S. Augustin, Bishop of Hyppon, in
        three severall treatises of his Meditations, Soliloquies, and
        Manual.   Faithfully translated into English by the R. F.
        Antony Batt, Monke, &c. *original sheep, with clasps*
                                                    at S. Omers 1624

409   Bossuet (J. B.) Treatise of Communion under both species, *old
        calf, unknown to Lowndes*   *Paris,* 1685

410   Bossuet (J. B.) Exposition of the Doctrine of the Catholic Church,
        FIRST EDITION, 1685—Exposition of the Doctrine of the
        Church of England, 1688 ; 2 vol. in 1, *original calf* 4*to.* 1685-8

411   Broughton (R.) True Memorial of the Religious State of Great
        Britain, Flourishing with Apostles, Apostolic Men, Monas-
        teries, Religious Rules and Orders, *russia*
                                                    printed abroad, 1650

412   Canes (J. V.) Stillingfleeton, or an Account of Dr. Stillingfleet's
        Book against the Roman Church, *calf extra, g. e. by Riviere*
                                                    Bruges, 1672
      ₊ This rare volume is written in a very able and popular
        manner, and contains an abundance of allusions to Fencing,
        Feasting, and other interesting topics, not often found in
        such treatises.

413   Cantilupe. Life and Gests of S. Thomas Cantilupe, Bishop of
        Hereford, *very fine copy, contemporary calf*   *Gant,* 1674

414   Catholic.   The Guide in Controversie, or a Rational Account of
        the Doctrine of Roman Catholics, concerning the Ecclesiastical
        Guide in Controversies of Religion by R. H. *original calf*
                                                    4*to.*   1667

415   Catholic.   The Nature and Practice of the celebrated Devotion
        of the Holy Rosary, *frontispiece and numerous blank leaves with
        woodcut borders, original rough calf*   1754

416   Catholic.   Short Account of the Life and Virtues of Mary of the
        Holy Cross, abbess of the English Poor Clares at Rouen,
        original boards, uncut   1767

417   Catholic.   To the Honourable The Knights, Citizens, and Bur-
        gesses of the Common House in Parliament now assembled,
        in Answere to the Humble Petition of the Lay-Catholikes of
        England, *calf extra, g. e. by Riviere*   4*to.*   1641

418   Causin (N.) Entertainments for Lent, translated into English by
        Sir B. B(rook), *original calf*   1687

419   Causin (N.) Entertainments for Lent, written in French by the
        R. F. N. Causin, S. J. Translated into English by Sir Basil
        Brook, *original sheep*   *Liverpool,* 1755

420   Champney (A.) Treatise of the Vocation of Bishops and other
        Ecclesiasticall Ministers, proving the Ministers of the Pre-
        tended Reformed Churches to have no calling, *fine copy, calf
        extra, g. e.*   4*to. Douday,* 1616

421   Constable (John) A Specimen of Amendments candidly proposed
         to the Compiler of a Work, which he calls The Church History
         of England from the year 1500 to the year 1688, by Cler-
         ophilus Alethes, *old calf*   1741
   *** A sharp attack on the Rev. Charles Dodd, with special refer-
         ence to the manner in which he speaks of the Jesuits and
         their policy.

422   Cousturier (John) Nichodemus, his Gospel, *calf*
                                             (*Rouen, circa* 1610)

423   Declaration of the Principal Pointes of Christian Doctrine set
         forth by the English Priests dwelling in Tournay, *old calf*
                                             Paris, 1647

424   Devotions in the Antient Way of Offices with Psalms, Hymns,
         and Prayers for every day in the Week and every Holiday in
         the Year, *morocco extra, g. e.*   *Roan*, 1672

425   Disputation of the Church, wherein the old Religion is main-
         tained, *fine copy, russia extra, g. e.*   *Doway*, 1632

426   Franciscans.   Life of St. Francis, compiled by S. Bonaventure,
         Douay, 1635—The Rule of the Religious of the Thirde Order
         of Saint Francis, by Francis Bel, *Bruxelles*, 1624 ; 2 vol. in 1,
         curiously bound in contemporary vellum, with russia back
                                             1624-1635
   *** From the Library of the Poor Clares at Gravelines, and
         possibly bound in the convent. The second piece is peculiarly
         rare.

427   Garden (The) of Our Lady.   Three Inseparable Companions of
         Devotion towards the Sacred Virgin Mary, the First is Dili-
         gence and Favour, &c. *manuscript of the 17th century, original
         calf*

428   Gonzaga.   Life of B. Aloysius Gonzaga of the Society of Jesus,
         written in Latin by Virgilius Ceparius, and translated into
         English by R. S. *engraved title containing portrait, calf*
                                             Paris, 1627

429   Life of the Most Learned Father Paul, translated out of Latin by
         a Person of Quality, *fine portrait by Lombart, original calf* 1651

430   Mercy and Truth, or Charity Maintayned by Catholiques, *calf
         extra, g. e. by Riviere*   4to.   *printed abroad*, 1634

431   Miracles lately wrought by the Intercession of the Glorious Virgin
         Marie at Montaign, nere unto Siché in Brabant, *calf extra, g. e.
         attributed to Robert Chambers*
                                 printed at Antwerp by A. Conings, 1606
   *** Rare.   The translator, a priest, dedicates his book in a long
         epistle of 44 pages to his Sovereign Lord James I, "a
         Christian, and the sonne of a most glorious Christian martyr."
         This epistle, and the long epistle to the reader which follows,
         are well worthy of attentive reading.

432   Mumford (James) Question of Questions which Rightly Resolved
         resolves all our Questions in Religion, *very fine copy, calf extra,
         g. e. by Riviere, unknown to Lowndes*   1686-7

433 Oates (Titus) Vindication of the English Catholiks from the pre-
     tended Conspiracy against the Life and Government of His
     Sacred Majesty discovering the Chiefe Falsities and Contra-
     dictions in the narrative of Titus Oates, *calf extra, g. e. by
     Riviere*   4to.   *Antwerp,* 1680

434 Our Lady of Loreto. History of our Blessed Lady of Loreto,
     translated out of Latyn into English, *engraved frontispiece and
     plate, beautiful copy, blue morocco extra, g. e.*
                              imprinted with licence, 1608

435 Phillips (Thomas) To the Right Reverend and Religious Dame
     Elizabeth Phillips on her Entering the Religious Order of St.
     Benet (a Poem)   4to.   *(Gant) n. d.*

436 Richome (L.) Holy Pictures of the Mystical Figures of the most
     Holy Sacrifice and Sacrament of the Eucharist, *calf extra, by
     Riviere*   4to.   *printed abroad,* 1619

437 Richworth or Rushworth (Wm.) Dialogue, or the Judgment of
     Common Sense in the choice of Religion, *in the original vellum*
                              Paris, John Mestais, 1640
       **** In the Preface "To the Reader" is found the following
       account of the author of this volume :—" Mr. William Rich-
       worth, born in Lincolnshire, studied in the English College at
       Doway, there was made priest, and afterwards discharged the
       place and office of Prefect with much commendation, all
       which time he was knowne by the name of Charles Rosse.
       Comming into England, he lived in divers places with good
       esteeme untill the yeare 1637, in which he died. He was a
       man curious in Divinitie, Controversies, Mathematikes, and
       Physicke, but cheefly delighted in Mathematickes, and by the
       name of Robinson entertained correspondence with the learned
       Oughtred."

438 Right (The) and Jurisdiction of the Prelate, and the Prince, or
     A Treatise of Ecclesiasticall and Regall Authority, compyled
     by J. L. &c. *calf extra, g. e.*   1617

439 Roderiguez (A.) The Stoope Gallant, or a Treatise of Humility,
     calf extra, g. e. by Riviere   *Rouen,* 1631
       **** At the end is a contemporary manuscript poem : " An Anti-
       dote against pride." *Stoop Gallant* was probably, if rather
       unusually, chosen as the title of this religious treatise from
       the popularity of the term, under which a ballad, no longer
       known, is found registered at Stationers' Hall, July 9, 1580.

440 Roman Martyrologie (The) set forth by the command of Pope
     Gregory XIII, and reviewed by the authority of Urban VIII,
     original calf   *St. Omers,* 1667

441 Rushworth's Dialogues, or the Judgment of Common Sense in
     the Choyce of Religion, *calf extra, g. e. by Bedford   Paris,* 1654

442 Safegarde from Ship-wracke, or Heaven's Haven, *calf extra, g. e.
     by Riviere*   *Douay,* 1618

443 Sales (Francis) Introduction to a Devoute Life, translated into
     English by I. Y. *blue morocco extra, g. e.   printed abroad,* 1622

444 Sancta Sophia, or Directions for the Prayer of Contemplation,
     extracted out of more than XL Treatises, by Father Augustin
     Baker, *portrait,* 2 vol. *calf extra, g. e. by Bedford   Douay,* 1657

445   Schism Despach't, or a Rejoynder to the Replies of Dr. Hammond
and the Ld. of Derby, *calf*   *printed abroad,* 1657

446   Stillingfleet (Dr.) Just Discharge to Dr. Stillingfleet's Unjust
Charge of Idolatry against the Church of Rome, *calf extra,
g. e. by Riviere*   *Paris,* 1677

447   The Christian Sodality, or Catholik Hive of Bees Sucking the
Honey of the Churches Prayers from the Blossomes of the
Word of God, &c. *original calf*   *printed abroad,* 1652

448   The Office for the Dead, according to the Roman Breviary Missal
and Ritual, *contemporary morocco extra, g. e.*   1762

449   Treatise of the Grounds of the Old and Newe Religion, *calf extra,
g. e. by Riviere*   *4to. printed abroad,* 1608

450   Treatise of the Difference betwixt the Temporal and External,
composed in Spanish by Eusebius Nieremberg, translated by
Sir Vivian Mullineaux, *calf extra, g. e. by Riviere*
                               printed abroad, 1672

451   Villegas (Alfonsus) The Lives of Saints gathered out of the R.
Father Alfonsus Villegas, of the Order of S. Dominicke, Fa.
Peter Ribadineyra, and other most authenticall Authors, &c.
engraved title, original calf   *Paris,* 1634

452   Wenefrede (St.) Life and Miracles of St. Wenefrede, together
with Her Litanies, *half calf*   1713

453   White (T.) Apology for Rushworth's Dialogues, by T. White,
wherein the exceptions of the Lords Falkland and Digby are
answered, *calf extra, g. e. by Bedford*   *Paris,* 1654

454   White (T.) Religion and Reason mutually corresponding and
assisting each other, *calf extra, g. e. by Bedford*   *ib.* 1660

Another Property.

455   DUCIS (JEAN FRANÇOIS, *the first French editor of Shakespeare*) The
COMPLETE SERIES OF 26 AUTOGRAPH LETTERS, addressed by
Ducis to the Prince of Wurtemberg, these letters date from
1763-1773, and cover 81 pages folio or 4to   (26)

   **** A most important literary and dramatic correspondence,
containing several references to Ducis' acting editions of
Macbeth, Romeo and Juliet, and Hamlet. These letters were
only brought to light in 1882, and in 1899 Monsieur E. de
Refuge issued a (*privately printed*) pamphlet descriptive of them,
together with biographies of Ducis and the Prince of Wurtemberg, *a copy of this pamphlet accompanies the letters.*

Other Properties.

FOLIO.

456   Butler (Capt. H.) South African Sketches, illustrative of the
Wild Life of a Hunter on the Frontier of the Cape Colony,
frontispiece and 15 plates, mostly coloured, original cloth
                                 Ackermann, 1841

456* Calvin (John) Commentaria in Acta Apostolorum, *in a most
elaborate binding by Hagué, calf super extra, the sides covered with
interlaced designs in the Grolier style, enamelled in various colours,
with clasps and bosses*   *apud Jo. Crispin,* 1554

457   CARDS. Playing Cards of the Revolution, 1688, 2 vol. *bound in whole calf, wanting 2 cards*

457* Playing Cards. Reign of Queen Anne and Marlborough's Victories, *bound in whole calf*

458   Playing Cards. Reign of Queen Anne, 2 vol. (*wanting 4 cards*), *bound in whole calf*

459   Playing Cards. Bubble Schemes, 1720, 2 vol. *bound in whole calf*

460   Another set in one volume (*incomplete*)

461   Another set in one volume (*incomplete*)

462   CARICATURES. A Collection of 178 coloured and other Caricature Engravings, Political Cartoons, Humorous Subjects and Satirical Prints, by Gillray, Rowlandson, Pether, Bunbury, Saulcy and others, including : Westminster School, the Privy Council, Which is the Dirtiest, Trying on the Breeches, the Duchess Canvassing, Old Snuffy, Beauty in a Coal Skuttle Bonnet, the Bishopric, the Renversement, Mr. Mathews in the character of cypher, the Presentation, the R—l Libertine reclaimed, Sales by Auction, the Head of the Family in Good Humour, &c. *neatly mounted, half bound*   *in 1 vol.*

463   Catalogue. The General Catalogue of Books printed in England Since the Dreadful Fire of London, 1666, to the end of Trinity Term, 1680, *calf*   1680

∗ The works of Shakespeare mentioned are *Venus and Adonis* (1675), *Antony and Cleopatra* (1677), *Hamlet* (1676), *Macbeth* (1674), *The Tempest* (1670), *Troilus and Cressida* (1679)

464   Catalogus Impressorum Librorum Bibliothecæ Bodleiana in Academia Oxoniensi, *fleuron on title, frontispiece containing portraits of Thos. Bodley, Archbishop Laud, John Selden, Kenelm Digby, and William Count of Pembroke, numerous vignettes,* 2 vol. *old calf*   *Oxonii*, 1738

∗ LARGE PAPER. This catalogue is remarkable on account of the exceedingly small collection of Shakespeariana contained therein, covering as it does 1325 folio pages, there are yet only half a dozen items under the heading " Shakespeare."

465   CHAUCER (GEOFFREY) THE WOORKES of Geffrey Chaucer, newly printed, with divers Additions, which were never in printe before, with the Siege and Destruccion of the Worthy Citee of Thebes, compiled by John Lydgate (edited by John Stowe), FIRST EDITION, black letter, *arms on title, new calf gilt*
      Jhon Kyngston for Jhon Wight, 1561

∗ This copy belonged originally to MARGARET RADCLIFF (*Radcliffes of Ordsdale*), a favourite Maid of Honour to Queen Elizabeth, who died in 1599, and was buried at S. Margaret's Westminster. There is an Epitaph upon her :—
      " Here lies, Lord have mercy upon her
        One of Elizabeth's Maids of Honour
        Margaret Radcliffe, fayre and wittie
        She died a mayde, the more's the pittie."
On the title is the following inscription, "*Donum Honoratissimæ Virginis reginæ Margaretæ Radcliff, Co. Buc.* 1597."

466   Chaucer (Geffrey) Workes, newly printed, with divers addicions, whiche werc never in printe before, with the siege and destruccion of the worthy citee of Thebes, compiled by John Lidgate, **black letter**, *woodcut titles and numerous woodcut initials, including those to the Prologues, a few headlines slightly shaved, otherwise a sound copy, mottled calf extra, gilt back and edges*
John Kyngston, 1561

467   CHAUCER (Geoffrey) The Workes of our Ancient and Learned English Poet, Geffrey Chaucer, newly printed, to that which was done in the former Impression, thus much is now added. 1. In the life of Chaucer many things inserted. 2. The whole worke by old Copies reformed. 3. Sentences and Proverbes noted. 4. The Signification of the old and obscure words prooved ; also Caracters shewing from what Tongue or Dialect they be de-rived. 5. The Latine and French, not Englished by Chaucer, translated. 6. The Treatise called Jacke Upland, against Fri-ers, and Chaucer's A. B. C. called La Priere de nostre Dame, at this Impression added, A MOST BEAUTIFUL COPY IN THE ORIGINAL VELLUM
London, printed by Adam Islip, An. Dom. 1602

    *** Measures 14⅛ by 8¾ in., See Grolier Club's Catalogue of Early English Literature (no. 44).

468   CHAUNCY (SIR HENRY) Historical Antiquities of Hertfordshire, *portrait, map and plates (7 additional engravings inserted), wants 3 plates, which are frequently missing, and directions for placing the cuts,* there is a duplicate of the engraving of " Knebworth Place," *old russia, sold not subject to return*   1700

469   Cicero. Tusculanarum Questionum libri V, ejusdem Verrinarum Invectivarum liber, *fine* MANUSCRIPT *of the* XVTH CENTURY ON VELLUM, *calf*   *folio*

470   Cicero. Epistolæ ad Familiares, *s. l.* 1471, *wants first page. Though attributed to the Venetian press of Adam of Ammergau (4143), this seems to be an amalgam of two editions described by Serna of Santander, no. 459, of 40 lines a page, and dated 1471, ascribed by him to Vindelin of Spira, and no. 465 (ascribed by him on account of the similarity of type to that of the 1476 Virulus, to Veldener of Louvain, ? 1476), for this contains the metrical colophon, " Tullius ingenua," &c., found in that issue*

471   Clouet. Three Hundred French Portraits, representing Personages of the Courts of Francis I, Henry II and Francis II, auto-lithographed from the Originals, by Lord Ronald Gower, 2 vol. *gilt cloth*   1875

472   Collection of Copperplates. Woodcuts and Tracings arranged in a Scrap Book, including Dance of Death series, Dutch Drinking Scenes, and Copperplates illustrative of the Alva Campaign in the Netherlands, *half bound*   SÆC. XVI-XVIII

    *** Compiled by Stacy Marks, with his bookplate.

473   Collection of Engravings of the 17th and early 18th Centuries,
        including a number by Hugo Goltzius and Hollar, *and 50
        engraved titles and frontispieces, several of which are in colours, all
        neatly arranged in scrap-book*

474   Costume. Libro di Moda, 37 *full-length figures, chiefly of ladies,
        contemporary red morocco*
                              G. G. de Rossi le Stampa in Roma, 1688-9

475   Costume. A collection of 60 engravings, chiefly full-length figures
        of Old English and French Costume, by Collet, Paul Sandby,
        Fruchy, St. Aubin, and others, *mounted or inserted loosely, in a
        volume, half bound*   1773, *&c.*

476   Cotgrave (Randle) Dictionarie of the French and English Tongues,
        calf gilt, g. e.   *A. Islip*, 1611

477   CROMWELL. A collection of 80 Portraits, Views, and Printed
        Matter, Memoirs, &c. relating to Oliver Cromwell, inclu-
        ding portraits after Walker, Cooper, Wale, &c. there are
        also scarce Portraits of Thomas Lord Fairfax, Major-Gen.
        Mitton, Henry Cromwell, Col. John Okey, John Bradshaw,
        Col. John Hewson (*mezzotint*), Lieut.-Gen. Fleetwood, and
        others, *the whole neatly mounted on loose sheets*

478   Cruikshank. Scenes in Montrose, or, The Children of the Mist,
        and Side Wings in Montrose, 22 *plates by G. Cruikshank*,
        ORIGINAL IMPRESSIONS, *half calf*, VERY SCARCE
                              oblong. Hodgson & Co. 1822

479   Decker (Paul) Repraesentatio belli ob successionem in Regno
        Hispanico gesti, 57 *large and finely coloured plates of Battles,
        with elaborate borders, heightened with gold, original half binding*
                              Aug. Vind. n. d.

480   DE COMMINES. THE HISTORIE OF PHILIP DE COMMINES, KNIGHT
        LORD OF ARGENTON (translated by Thomas Danett), *in the
        original calf*   *Imprinted by Ar. Hatfield for J. Norton*, 1596
        ₊ QUEEN ELIZABETH'S COPY, with her arms, the Tudor rose
        surmounted by the royal crown, stamped in gold on the sides
        of the binding. This is the earliest known English version
        of De Commines. The impression of 1596 (which is far rarer
        than that of 1601, and is not quite correctly described by
        bibliographers), has the powerful interest, that it appeared
        just at the point of time when Shakespeare had in hand his
        "Tragedy of King Richard II," printed in the following year,
        and was naturally led to look about for information about
        Italy, between which and England the relations had then
        grown regular and intimate. In the drama the author intro-
        duces the banishment of Mowbray, Duke of Norfolk, his
        settlement at Venice, and death there, and he elsewhere refers
        to the "fashions of proud Italy."
                "————whose manners still our tardy
                    apish nation
                Limps after in base imitation."
        De Commines who was well acquainted with Italy and with
        Venice itself, describes the country and the place in his book
        in flattering colours, and it was just that sort of personal,
        picturesque way of narrating scenes and experiences, which

Lot 480—*continued*.

would impress Shakespeare. Capel reprinted a portion of this edition of De Commines in his "School of Shakespeare" (pages 201-3).

481 DRAKE (NATHAN) " A JOURNAL OF THE FIRST SIEGE OF PONTE-FRACT (1644), kept by Nathan Drake, a Gentleman Volunteer in it. " I desire that this MS. in my Great-Grandfathers writing may never go out of the Family, Francis Drake." (*Historian of York*), ORIGINAL MANUSCRIPT, *mostly in cipher* (32 pp.), *some damaged, used by Francis Drake for his History of York* ; and printed in the " Sieges of Pontefract Castle, 1644-48," edited by R. Holmes, published in 1887 ; with a neat Transcript *on* 33 *ll.* mostly in Francis Drake's hand ; Contemporary Copies of King James' and others Speeches in Parliament—Autograph Letter of Sir William Knolleys, 1626—Abstracts of Acts of Parliament made in the Reign of Philip and Mary, &c. interesting MSS. by Descendants of Sir Francis Drake the Circum-navigator, *loose in a vol. vellum*

482 DRESDEN GALLERY. Recueil d'Estampes d'après les plus célèbres Tableaux de la Galerie Royale de Dresde, 3 vol. *portraits, and numerous fine engravings, recent impressions, half green morocco gilt*   *Dresde et Leipsic* (1753, '67, 1850)

483 DUGDALE (SIR WILLIAM) Monasticon Anglicanum, or The History of the Ancient Abbies and other Monasteries, Hospitals, Cathedral and Collegiate Churches in England and Wales, with divers French, Irish and Scotch Monasteries, formerly related to England, *numerous plates representing the habits worn by the various Monastic Orders, original calf*   1693

  *** This particular edition contains a curious reference to Shake-peare. The preface alludes to two of the most famous writers in England, Dugdale and Shakespeare, " *both Williams*," and the editor places the poet *second* in order !

484 Dumont (Jean) et J. Rousset. Histoire Militaire du Prince Eugène de Savoye, du Prince et Duc de Marlborough, et du Prince de Nassau-Frise, vol. II, and Supplement (vol. I), *numerous large plans and plates, half bound*   *La Haye*, 1729

485 EDMONDSON (JOSEPH, *Mowbray Herald Extraordinary*) Scrap-Book originally his property, containing several hundred carefully emblazoned coats of arms, pen and ink trickings, tracings, reverses for copper engraving, book-plates, orders for Heraldic work, and other miscellaneous scraps, drawn and engraved, &c. *this interesting and unique collection was formed about the year* 1780, *neatly mounted, old vellum*

486 Engravings (Early Wood) A Collection of 500 specimens, from 1484 to 1631, but chiefly from the beginning to the middle of the XVIth Century, *neatly mounted*   *in 1 vol.*

487 Engravings. The Complete Set of 30 Illustrations to the Charac-ters of Theophrastus, by R. Austin, S. Williams, H. White, T. Branston, &c.   (30)

488 Engravings. Figures de La Fontaine, a Collection of 49 beautiful plates after Moreau, Simonnet, Desenne, Colin, &c. *mostly proofs before letters, neatly mounted in a vol. morocco extra, g.e.*

489 Essex and Southampton (Earls of) The Arraignment of the Earles
of Essex and Southampton at Westminster Hall on Thursday,
the 19 of februarii, 1600, Manuscript 23½ pages
XVIIth Century

   **** A contemporary manuscript giving an account of the trial,
probably by an eye-witness (*Sir Francis Bacon wrote a tract
relative to this trial*). Together with the above are three other
MSS. one referring to a projected voyage by Sir Walter
Raleigh to the South Seas "of America or els where in
America inhabited by the heathen and savage people to
thende to finde out some m chandizes (merchandize) and
comodities in those countryes," &c.

490 Eugene of Savoy. The Military History of Prince Eugene of
Savoy, and John Duke of Marlborough, with a Supplement,
2 vol. *numerous plates of battles, sieges, plans, &c. engraved by
Claude du Bosc, original calf gilt* 1736

491 Flowers. Ehret (Georgius Dionysius) Plantæ Selectæ Quarum
imagines ad exemplaria naturalia Londini in hortis curiosorum
nutrita manu artificiosa doctaque pinxit, *mezzotint portraits of
the author, D. Christophorus, Jacobus Trevv, and Joannes Jacobus
Huid, and 100 beautifully coloured plates of flowers*, VERY FINE
COPY, *old French green morocco* 1750-73

492 Flowers. Firens (Petrus) Theatrum Floræ, In quo ex toto Orbe
Selecti Miribiles Venustiores ac præcipui Flores tanquam ab
ipsus Deæ sinu proferuntcr, *engraved titles and 69 plates of
flowers, original vellum* Paris, 1634

493 Flowers. Robert (N.) Variæ ac Multiformes Florum species
appressæ ad Vivum et aeneis tabulis incisæ. Diverses Fleurs
dessinées et gravées d'après le Naturel par N. Robert, 31
plates of flowers, engraved by N. Robert *ib.* 1760

494 FRANKAU (JULIA) EIGHTEENTH CENTURY COLOUR PRINTS: an
Essay on certain Stipple Engravers and Their Work in Colour,
*illustrated with 52 beautiful characteristic pictures printed in colours
from copper-plates, original cloth, uncut, edition limited to 200
copies* 1900

495 FRANKAU (JULIA) EIGHTEENTH CENTURY COLOUR PRINTS: an
Essay on certain Stipple Engravers and Their Work in Colour,
*with 52 characteristic pictures printed in monochrome, and one in
colours, one of 60 copies*, with a Portfolio containing 50 Proof
Impressions of the Plates, *printed in colours on India paper* 1900

496 Fraser (J. B.) Views in the Himala Mountains, 20 *large and
beautifully coloured plates, original half binding (broken)* 1820

497 Fuller (Dr. Thos.) The Church History of Britain, FIRST EDITION,
(*slight defect in p. 219*) with Index, *plan, plates, &c. old calf
rebacked* 1655

498 Fuller (Dr. Thos.) A Pisgah-sight of Palestine and the Confines
thereof, *folding map of Canaan and other maps (appears to want
that of the Jewish Habits)*, FIRST EDITION, *fine copy in the original calf* 1650

499 Fuller (Dr. Thos.) The History of the Worthies of England,
FIRST EDITION, with the Index, *portrait by Loggan, original
calf* 1662

500   Geiler (J.) Sermones Præstantissimi Sacrarum litterarum Doctoris
Joannis Geilerii Keiserbergii, *gothic letter*, *printed in double
columns, woodcut border to title, large woodcut " Figura Mortis "
and other woodcuts of the Dance of Death, &c. by Hans Wächtlin,
and woodcut initial letters*, FINE LARGE COPY, *oak boards covered
with stamped pigskin, from the Monastery of S. Udalrici*
Argentorati per J. Grüninger, 1515

501   Gerard (John) Herball, or General History of Plants, FIRST
EDITION, *numerous woodcuts, wants the title, old calf, covered with
vellum*   (1597)

502   Gilray. A Collection of 179 Rare Coloured Caricature Engrav-
ings by James Gilray, including : Begging no Robbery,
Fashionable Jockeyship, Zenith of French Glory, Pizarro, a
Bravura Air, a Cognocenti, Lady Godiva's Rout, ci-devant
Occupations, Posting in Ireland, Hounds in Full Cry, &c. 8
plates, a Phantasmagoria,, a Vestal of 93, Tales of Wonder,
Dido in Despair, La Promenade en Famille, King of Brob-
dingnag and Gulliver, Contemplations upon a Coronet, Sand-
wich-Carrots, le Baiser, Progress of the Toilet, 3 plates, the
Nuptial Bower, Marriage of Cupid and Psyche, &c. *the whole
in fine condition and neatly mounted, half morocco*   *in 3 vol.*

503   Glanville (Bartholomei) Liber de Proprietatibus rerum Bartholomei Anglice, *gothic letter*, *printed in double columns in a
large clear type, 47 lines to a full page, capitals rubricated, fine
large clean copy with many uncut leaves, oak boards covered with
stamped pigskin, clasps, from the " Monasterii S. Emmerani
Ratisbona."*   *Argentine*, 1485

504   Glanville (Bartholomæus) De Proprietatibus Rerum (translated
by John of Trevisa), newly printed with many places therein
amended by the Latyne exemplare, &c. *black letter, wants
title, plain margins damaged by damp injuring several letters in
the table and last two ll. (?) the body of the book in good
condition, has leaf with Berthelet's device at end (sold with
all faults), oak boards, leather (1 cover missing)*
*printed by me Thos. Berthelet the XXVII Yere of
Kynge Henry the VIII.*   (1535)

THIRD DAY'S SALE.

OCTAVO ET INFRA.

Lot 505.

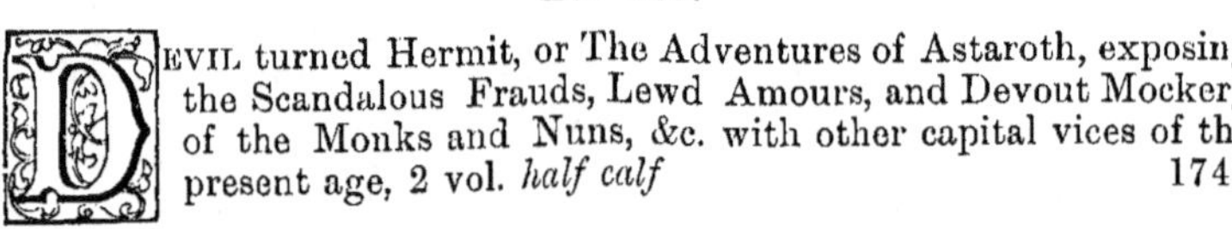

EVIL turned Hermit, or The Adventures of Astaroth, exposing the Scandalous Frauds, Lewd Amours, and Devout Mockery of the Monks and Nuns, &c. with other capital vices of the present age, 2 vol. *half calf*   1742

506 Dibdin (T. F.) Bibliotheca Spenceriana: a Descriptive Catalogue of the Books printed in the Fifteenth Century, &c. in the Library of Earl Spencer, 4 vol. *with original impressions of the beautiful portraits, views, and facsimiles, morocco gilt, g. e.*
imp. 8vo.   1814-15

507 Dibdin (T. F.) Bibliographical Decameron, 3 vol. *numerous beautiful engravings, some of which are on india paper, half morocco gilt, uncut, t. e. g.*   *imp. 8vo.*   1817

508 Dickens (Charles) Sketches by "Boz," FIRST SERIES, 2 vol. FIRST EDITION, *illustrations by George Cruikshank, original cloth (damaged)*   *J. Macrone,* 1836

509 Dickens (C.) Pickwick Papers, FIRST EDITION, 43 *plates by Seymour and Phiz, and extra illustrated by the insertion of the set of 24 humorous etchings, india proofs, by F. W. Pailthorpe, fine copy in crushed levant red morocco, extra gilt back and sides, inside dentelles, g. e. by Rivière*   1837

510 Dickens (C.) Oliver Twist, or The Parish Boy's Progress by "Boz," 3 vol. FIRST EDITION, *plates by G. Cruikshank, including the suppressed plate of the Parlour Scene "Rose Maylie and Oliver," half morocco*   1838

511 Dickens (C) Pickwick Papers, 43 *plates by Seymour and Phiz (spotted), half calf*   1838

512 Dickens (C.) A Curious Dance round a Curious Tree, FIRST EDITION, *very fine copy, in original wrapper*   (1860)
**** A most interesting lot. The pamphlet is accompanied by the original stamped wrapper used for posting, and has the stamped envelope for sending contributions to St. Luke's Hospital. With it is also a long letter of 8 pp. from T. C. Walker, who was Steward of the Hospital from 1849 till 1882, giving an account of Charles Dickens' visit to the Hospital and definitely ascribing the authorship of the pamphlet to him and not to W. H. Wills, who is sometimes accredited as its writer.

513 Dickens (C.) The List of Sibson's Illustrations to Master Humphrey's Clock, 8 *pp. uncut, very rare*

514 Dickens (C.) Sketches by Boz, *unique proof of a design by Cruikshank for the cover of the proposed re-issue by Macrone, and an impression showing variations of the same design as published by Chapman & Hall*

515 Dickens (C.) Works, "Edition de Luxe," 30 vol. *illustrations by Geo. Cruikshank, "Phiz," Seymour, &c. original boards, uncut, limited issue*   *imp. 8vo.* 1881

516 Dictionnaire Historique et Biographique de la Révolution et de l'Empire (1789-1815) par Robinet, Robert et Chaplain, 2 vol. *half red morocco, t. e. g.*   *n. d.*

517 Dillingham (W.) Vita Laurentii Chodertoni cum Vita Jacobi Usserii Archp. Armachani, *with Autograph of* "SAM RICHARDSON, *ex dono Editoris," and errata in MS. old calf with ex-libris of W. Richardson (defective) on back of title, and ex-libris of Richard Langley inside cover*   *Cantab.* 1700

518 Diurnale Monasticum secundum Rubricam romanam et secundum Ritum et Consuetudinem Monasterii Beatæ Mariæ Virginis al's Scotorum Viëne Ordinis Sci. benedicti, 2 *full-page woodcuts with opposite borders in compartments of figures and numerous ornamental and figured initials, in the original oaken boards covered with stamped ornamental pigskin, with the arms of a German Abbot, the initials* I. A. L. *and date* 1606, *impressed on the upper cover, with clasps*
      Venet. impressus L. A. de Giunta impensis
       L. et L. Alantsee Viennium, 1515

   *** An extremely rare Diurnale, for Scottish use. This pocket Breviary, in a small clear type, with numerous well-executed *woodcuts,* commences with a Calendar in which are some very curious verses descriptive of the twelve months. It was published for the use of the Scotish Benedictine Monastery at Vienna called the "Schottenhof," and still existing, but it is not local or peculiar in its scope, and includes in the hagiology German and Hungarian Saints. The little volume is in *immaculate condition, in the original stamped vellum binding.* Some bibliographers, owing to the intimate relations between Venice and Vienne in Dauphiny, and to the absence of the usual distinctive addition of *Pannoniæ* or *Austriæ,* have questioned whether the volume was not intended for the service of a French community.

519 Dobson. Eighteenth Century Essays, selected and annotated by Austin Dobson, LARGE PAPER, *one of 50 copies, uncut* 1882

520 Downman. A pair of Portraits of Ladies, executed in pastel (probably by Downman)   (2)

521 Dowton (W.) Job Thornberry in John Bull, MS. partly in Dowton's handwriting—The School for Scandal—Sir Peter Teazle, Downton's part, in manuscript—Fielding, The Mock Doctor, with Dowton's alterations—Otway's Venice Preserved, 1682; and four others   (9)

522 Downes (John) Roscius Anglicanus, or An Historical Review of
the Stage, after it had been suppress'd by means of the late
Unhappy Civil War, begun in 1641, till the time of King
Charles the II.'s Restoration in May, 1660, giving an account
of its Rise again, of the Time and Places the Governours of
both the Companies first erected their Theatres, the Names
of the Principal Actors and Actresses who perform'd in the
Chiefest Plays in each house, with the names of the most
taking Plays, &c. FIRST EDITION (*some leaves shaved*), *old calf*
1708

*** A most interesting copy. From the collections of Isaac
Reed, Henderson (the actor), and Charles Mathews, senior
(with ex-libris). A most important *Shakespearian* volume
(refer to Halliwell-Phillipps' Calendar of Shakespearean
Rarities, No. 61). Lowe, in his "Bibliographical Account
of English Theatrical Literature," says "*The first edition is
now practically of priceless value—not over half-a-dozen copies
can be located.*"

523 DRAMA. A pleasant and comical History of the Life of Scara-
mouche, translated by A. R. from the French, *frontispiece, old
green morocco, g. e.* 1696

*** Believed to be unique. The frontispiece is very curious as
showing *a five-stringed guitar of the period.* The hero is described as the player to the King of France, and one of the
Italian Company of Comedians.

524 Dryden. The Satyrs of Juvenal and Persius, translated into
English verse, *portraits, and many other copper-plates, old calf,*
SIR M. SYKES' *book-plate, and his autograph when at Cambridge,*
1730 1726

525 Dunton (John) Religio Bibliopolæ, in Imitation of Dr. Brown's
Religio Medici, with a Supplement to it by Benj. Ergwater
(*sic*), FIRST EDITION, *old calf, with ex-libris of A. Villettes, Esq.
H.M. Minister in Switzerland* P. Smart, 1691

526 Dunton (John, *the bookseller*) The Hanover Spy, or Secret History
of St. James's, *half calf,* 1718—Royal Gratitude : or King
George's Promise never to forget his obligations to those who
have distinguished themselves in his Service, *half roan,* 1716
(2)

527 Dürer (A.) Passion of Our Lord, edited by (Sir) Henry Cole,
*facsimile reproduction of the fine woodcuts, stamped ornamental
leather, g. e.* J. Cundall, &c. 1844

528 DYCE (Rev. Alexander) A Catalogue of the Printed Books and
Manuscripts bequeathed by the Reverend Alexander Dyce,
Manuscripts, Printed Books, A to K—Catalogue of Printed
Books (continued), including I to Z with Additions, *portrait,
thick half morocco extra, g. e.* 1875

*** J. O. Halliwell-Phillipps' copy with an autograph note, "This
is my London Copy," on the fly-leaf, and several annotations
of Shakespearian interest throughout the volume.

529 Edwards (J.) Companion from London to Brighthelmston in
Sussex, FINE COPY, *with all the plates, calf, back restored,* 1801
—Two imperfect copies of the same (3)

530   EGAN (PIERCE) LIFE IN LONDON ; or, The Day and Night Scenes of Jerry Hawthorn, Esq. and his elegant friend Corinthian Tom, accompanied by Bob Logic, the Oxonian, in their Rambles and Sprees through the Metropolis, FIRST EDITION, 3 *folding plates of music and* 36 *coloured plates by I. R. and G. Cruikshank, red levant morocco extra, g. e.* FINE TALL COPY
1821

531   Egan (Pierce) Life in London, or The Day and Night Scenes of Jerry Hawthorn, and Corinthian Tom, FIRST EDITION, *with* 36 *finely coloured plates, and numerous woodcuts, by I. R. and G. Cruikshank, title defective and mended, sold not subject to return*
1821

532   EGAN (PIERCE) LIFE IN LONDON : or The Day and Night Scenes of Jerry Hawthorn, and Corinthian Tom, accompanied by Bob Logic, in their Rambles and Sprees through the Metropolis, *with* 36 *coloured plates and numerous woodcuts by I. R. and G. Cruikshank, some leaves a little soiled, but an uncut copy in the original boards*   *Sherwood, Neely & Jones,* 1822

533   Egan (Pierce) Life in London, *numerous coloured plates by G. Cruikshank, original calf gilt*   *roy. 8vo.*   1823

534   Elder (W.) Pearls of Eloquence : or, The School of Complements (*partly in verse*), wherein Ladies, Gentlewomen, and Schollars may accomadate their Courtly practise with Gentile Ceremonies, Complemental, Amorous, and high Expressions of speaking or writing of Letters, *frontispiece, calf*   1656

535   Enchanted Plants (The) Fables in Verse, LARGE PAPER, *beautiful frontispiece engraved by Bartolozzi, in the original boards, uncut*
Bensley, 1800

536   Eutropius. Breviarium Historiæ Romanæ, *fine frontispiece by Eisen, and vignettes by La Fosse, old French red morocco extra, g. e.*
Paris, J. Barbou, 1754

537   Evelyn (John) Acetaria, a Discourse of Sallets, FIRST EDITION, *dedicated to Lord Somers, with the folding leaf sometimes wanting, hand-dyed calf extra, g. e. fine copy*   *B. Tooke,* 1699

538   Fanshawe (Sir R.) Il Pastor Fido, The Faithful Shepherd, with an Addition of divers other POEMS, with a Discourse of the Civil Wars of Rome, *with plate* (*usually wanting*), *forming A. VIII, which is not mentioned by Mr. Hazlitt, and containing commendatory verses by Sir J. Denham, with autograph on title of Thos. Herring, Archbishop of Canterbury, old calf*
H. Herringman, 1676

539   Fielding (Henry) A Charge delivered to the Grand Jury, at the Sessions of the Peace held for the City and Liberty of Westminster, &c. on Thursday, the 29th of June, 1749, FIRST EDITION, VERY FINE COPY, *calf extra, t. e. g.* UNCUT   1749

540   Fielding (Henry) Proposal for making an Effectual Provision for the Poor for Amending their Morals and rendering them useful members of Society, FIRST EDITION, VERY FINE COPY, *calf extra, t. e. g.* UNCUT   1753

541   Fisherman's Magazine and Review, edited by H. C. Pennell, vol. I and II, *numerous coloured plates, vol. I wants title and index, half calf gilt*   1864-5

542   Fitzgerald (E.) Autograph Letter, addressed to the Rev. G. Crabbe, Beccles, filling a whole page in 4to, as follows : " My dear Crabbe, George will forward you an Athenæum w^h has little in it : only in an article about Ebenezer Elliott, you will see a side compliment to your Life of your Father : which I always told you, and Every one else thinks, is an excellent thing. You must not let your contempt, of some theology therein blind you to them, nor make you resent people's expressing to you the pleasure they take in it. I was for 2 days last week at N'ham. and am just going for 2 days more to Bramford. I suppose you and I shall meet at the end of the week. Harvest begins to-day in the golden fields hereabout : and yesterday George laid widow Fulcher's blind son in his grave—yrs. E. F. G."

     *_*_* Interesting and very scarce. As far as we can ascertain the letter remains unpublished.

543   Fitzgerald (E.). A Collection of Twelve Autograph Letters, by W. Aldis Wright, Sir F. Pollock, &c. the former dealing with the correspondence left by Fitzgerald, which he subsequently edited for publication by Macmillan, the latter quoting a letter he received from Lord Tennyson, dated 17*th June*, 1883, wherein he mourns over the loss sustained by the demise of Fitzgerald, exclaiming : " Dear old Fitz—I had no truer friend …There are now left to me only two or three of my old College companions and who goes next ? " the remainder of the letters all deal with the genius of the departed author, deeply deploring his loss   (12)

544   FITZGERALD (E.) EUPHRANOR, a Dialogue on Youth, FIRST EDITION, *in the original cloth, uncut*   *Pickering*, 1851

     *_*_* VERY RARE. The author's first publication, of which only a few copies were printed.

545   Fitzherbert (Anthoine) La Nouvelle Natura brevium avecques un Table compose par Guilliaume Rastell, **black letter**, *title within woodcut border*, FINE COPY *in old calf*
      Imprinted at London by Richarde Tottell dwelling in Fleet Street, at the signe of the hand and Starr within Temple barre, 1567

     *_*_* With autograph on title of Sir William Cornwallis, author of " The Praise of King Richard the Third, 1617," and a few MS. notes.

546   Flatman (Thomas) Poems and Songs, FIRST EDITION, *fine copy, full dark blue morocco extra, g. e.*   1674

547   Forbes (John) Cantus, Songs and Fancies, to Three, Four or Five Parts, both apt for Voices and Viol. with a brief Introduction to Musick, as is taught in the Musick-School of Aberdeen, the Third Edition, much enlarged and corrected, with the second part, severall of the choicest Italian Songs, together with some of the best New English Ayres, *curious woodcut title, a tall and perfect copy, blue morocco*
                                        oblong 8vo. Aberdeen, 1682

     *_*_* A rare book, of which few perfect copies exist. Laing's copy sold for £18 18s.

                              F

548   Fowling, a Poem (in five books), descriptive of Grouse, Partridge,
      Pheasant, Woodcock, Duck, and Snipe Shooting, FIRST EDITION,
      *portraits of T. Gosden and of his favourite Pointer "Doll," green
      morocco extra, rich symbolical tooling on sides and back, by T.
      Gosden, with his book-plate*   1808

549   Freemasonry.   The Antient Constitutions and Charges of the
      Freemasons, with a True Representation of their Noble Art,
      and a Complete Collection of SONGS AND ODES by the most
      celebrated masters, *frontispiece by Cole, old calf, rare*
                            Printed and Sold by Brother Benj. Cole, 1762

550   Freemasonry. Preston (W.) Illustrations of Masonry, with
      Collection of Songs, *calf,* 1796 ; another edition, *calf,* 1804
                                                                  2 vol.

551   Frere (Miss) History of the Reign of Henry IV, King of France
      and Navarre, 2 vol. *portraits,* FIRST EDITION, *clean copy, in
      original cloth*   1860

552   Froude (J. A.) Nemesis of Faith, FIRST EDITION, *original cloth* 1849

553   Fry and Steele.   Specimens of Printing Types, Metal Cast
      Ornaments, &c. 2 vol. in 1, *in the original boards, uncut, with
      ex-libris of the Duke of Sussex*   *roy. 8vo.*   1795-4

554   Galeries Historiques du Palais de Versailles, vol. I to IX, *half
      morocco gilt, g. e. Paris, Impr. Royale,* 1839-47 ; and Atlas,
      100 *plates, half morocco gilt, g. e. Garnier, n. d.*   *10 vol.*

555   Galt (John) Ringan Gilhaize, or The Covenanters, 3 vol. FIRST
      EDITION, *with half titles, clean copy in original boards,* UNCUT,
      with paper labels   *Edinb.* 1823

556   Gardens.   Le Prieur (M.) Description d'une partie de la Vallée
      de Montmorency et de ses plus agréables jardins, ornée de
      gravures, par M. (Le Prieur), BEAUTIFUL COPY, *old calf gilt*
                                                            Paris, 1784
        ₊ " 26 jolies figures gravées à l'eauforte d'après les dessins de
      Marie de Lussy et de la Comtesse d'Albon.   L'une d'elles
      représente le ballon de Franconville, parti le 16 janvier 1784.
      Curieux volume."   From the De Bure collection.   A unique
      copy, see note in volume.

557   Garrick (D.).   Pittard (J.) Observations on Mr. Garrick's Acting ;
      in a letter to the Earl of Chesterfield, *clean copy,* UNCUT, 1758
      —Last Will and Testament of David Garrick of Hampton,
      dated 1790, *signed with seal and witnessed,* MANUSCRIPT *on three
      folio sheets*   (2)

558   [Gaskell (Mrs.)] Cranford, by the author of "Mary Barton,"
      FIRST EDITION, *very clean, in original cloth*   *sm. 8vo.* 1853

559   Gay (John) Trivia ; or The Art of Walking the Streets of London,
      FIRST EDITION, *half calf gilt, B. Lintott (his engraved device of
      the cross-keys on title)*   *n. d.*

560   Gessner (S.) Œuvres, 4 vol. LARGE PAPER, *portrait and plates by
      Moreau,* PROOFS BEFORE THE LETTERS, *white calf extra, back
      and sides inlaid with green gilt, g. e. fine copy*
                                          Paris, A. A. Renouard, 1795

561 Gildon (Charles) A Comparison between the Two Stages, with an Examen of the Generous Conqueror, and some Critical Remarks on the Funeral, or Grief Alamode, The False Friend, Tamerlane, and others, in Dialogue, *old calf*   1702

   ₊ A reference to *Shakespeare* occurs in the preface, Gildon also refers to *Antony and Cleopatra*, and on page 42 Betterton's supposed invocation to Shakespeare occurs, &c.

562 GOLDSMITH (OLIVER) THE VICAR OF WAKEFIELD, A TALE, suppposed to have been written by himself, FIRST EDITION, 2 vol. in 1, *old calf gilt*, VERY RARE   *Salisbury*, 1766

563 GOLDSMITH (O.) The Vicar of Wakefield, a Tale, supposed to be written by himself, 2 vol. FIRST EDITION, 5 *leaves torn and defective, and a few stained, old calf; sold not subject to return*
ib. 1766

564 Gosden. A Treatise on Greyhounds, with Observations on the Treatment and Disorders of them, *plate, uncut*; a Catalogue of Engravings and Books on Angling and Field Sports on sale by T. Gosden, *is bound up with this vol. T. Gosden*, 1825

565 Gray. Odes written by Mr. Gray, author of an Elegy in a Country Church-Yard, *Dublin*, 1757—Mason (W.) Elegies, *ib.* 1763—Hammond, Love Elegies, *ib.* 1762 ; and another piece, *half bound*   *in* 1 *vol.*

566 Gray (T.) Poems : this Collection contains all the Author's Poetical Works, among which are Three, never before published in Ireland, *red morocco, g. e.*   *Cork*, 1768

567 Gray (T.) Poetical Works, *frontispiece*   1785

568 Gregorius (Pape) Secundus liber Dialogorum : Regale Sanct. patris nostri Benedicti abbatis et Speculi D. Bernardi abbatis (*sig. & 1 missing*), l𝔦t. 𝔤ot𝔥. *woodcut borders containing figures of saints surrounding opening pages of the 3 opuscula, and full-page cuts of SS. Benedict and Bernard, contemporary colouring, early Venetian stamped binding, lower cover gone, rare*
Venetiis, Lucan. de Giunta, 1505

569 Greville Memoirs. A Journal of the Reigns of King George IV and William IV, by C. C. F. Greville, edited by H. Reeve, 3 vol. *original cloth, uncut*   1874

570 GRIMOALD (NICHOLAS) CHRISTUS REDIVIVUS COMEDIA TRAGICA, SACRA ET NOVA. AUTHORE NICOLAO GRIMOALDO, *fine large copy, morocco extra, g. e.*   1543

   ₊ The *Christus Redivivus* of Nicholas Grimoald is an early English miracle play by a poet who subsequently attained considerable distinction, not only as a principal contributor to the earliest English Poetical Miscellany (published in 1557), but, as Professor Arber considers, the person to whom we are indebted for editing it. His share in the volume is just equal to that of his friend the Earl of Surrey, and comprises some very interesting productions, including an Elegy on his mother. There is a good account of Grimoald in Mr. Hazlitt's edition of Warton's Poetry, 1871, with extracts, and in Professor Arber's biographical notices prefixed to his re-impression of *Tottel's Miscellany*, 1870, in both of which places it is

Lot 570—*continued*.

shown that the writer of *Christus Redivivus* was of both universities, being admitted to Merton College, Oxford, in 1542. The present dramatic composition, which is not mentioned by Lowndes or in Hazlitt's *Manual of Old Plays*, 1892, and is not in the British Museum, was evidently a very early work of the author, and was probably committed to the press at Cologne through the offices of Bishop Bale. Its rarity is such that in the *Dictionary of National Biography* its very existence is questioned, for the writer remarks : " Grimald is also credited with a similar work, *Christus Redivivus*, said to have been published at Cologne in 1543, but no copy is now known."

571   H. (R.) The School of Recreation, or a Guide to the most Ingenious Exercises of Hunting, Riding, Racing, Hawking, Cock-Fighting, Angling, &c. *frontispiece, morocco extra, with rich symbolical tooling on back and sides, by Zaehnsdorf, g. e. scarce* 1720

572   Hafiz. The Poems of Shamseddin Mohammed Hafiz of Shiraz, now first completely done into English Verse, from the Persian, by John Payne, 3 vol. *parchment, uncut, t. e. g. printed for the Villon Society by private subscription* 1901

573   [Hall (Bp. Joseph)] Virgidemarium Sixe Bookes. First three Bookes of Tooth-lesse Satyrs, 1 Poeticall, 2 Academicall, 3 Morall, *John Harison, for Robert Dexter,* 1602 ; Virgidemarium, the three last Bookes of byting Satyrs, *for Robert Dexter,* 1599, both parts in 1 vol. FIRST EDITIONS, *printed within ornamental top and bottom borders, a few fore-edges slightly cropped, crushed blue morocco extra gilt, g. e. scarce* 1602, 1599

574   Hallam (Isaac) The Cocker, a Poem, &c. humbly inscribed to the Honourable Society of Sportsmen at Grantham, *frontispiece,* FIRST EDITION, *half morocco, with gamecock on back, by T. Gosden, m. e. rare*   *sm. 4to.   Stamford,* 1742

575   HALLIWELL-PHILLIPPS (J. O.) Memoranda on the Tragedy of Hamlet, *original cloth, uncut*   1879
   *** Presentation copy, with inscription in the author's autograph. Only 50 copies were privately printed.

576   HALLIWELL-PHILLIPPS (J. O.) Memoranda on the Midsummer Night's Dream, A.D. 1879 and A.D. 1855, *original cloth, uncut*
                                                                Brighton, 1879
   *** Presentation copy, with inscription in the author's autograph.

577   HALLIWELL-PHILLIPPS (J. O.) A Catalogue of the Shakespeare-study Books in the Immediate Library of J. O. Halliwell-Phillipps, at No. 11, Tregunter Road, London, *t. e. g. uncut*
                                                            privately printed, 1876
   *** Presentation copy, with inscription in the author's autograph.

578   HALLIWELL-PHILLIPPS (J. O.) Memoranda on All's Well that Ends Well, The Two Gentlemen of Verona, Much Ado About Nothing, and on Titus Andronicus, *original cloth, uncut ib.*1879
   *** Presentation copy, with inscription in the author's autograph.

579   HALLIWELL-PHILLIPPS (J. O.) A Hand-List of the Drawings and Engravings illustrative of the Life of Shakespeare, preserved at Hollingbury Copse, near Brighton, *original cloth, uncut*
                                                    Brighton, for private circulation only, 1884
   *** Presentation copy, with inscription in the author's autograph.

580 HALLIWELL-PHILLIPPS (J. O.) Outlines of the Life of Shakespeare, 2 vol. *uncut* 1886

  *** Presentation copy to Moy Thomas (editor of the *Daily News*),
with inscription in the author's autograph ; inscription dated
Hollingbury Copse, June, 1886.

581 Hamilton (Walter) French Book-plates, *numerous facsimile illustrations, tall Japanese vellum paper, one of 38 copies, uncut* 1896

582 [HARINGTON (SIR JOHN)] A New Discourse of a Stale Subject,
called the Metamorphosis of Ajax ; written by Misacmos to
his friend and "cosin" Philostilpnos, *most curious woodcuts,
original vellum (a few leaves slightly wormed)* 1596

  *** "We shall conclude these observations on the miscellaneous
literature of Shakespeare's time, by noticing one of the earliest
of our Facetiæ, the production of an author who may be termed,
in allusion to this *jeu d'esprit*, the Rabelais of England. Had
the subject of this satire been exceptionable in its nature, the
popularity which it acquired for a season might have been
permanent ; but its grossness is such as not to admit of ade-
quate atonement by any portion of wit, however poignant.
It is entitled 'A New Discourse of a Stale Subject, called the
Metamorphosis of Ajax. Written by Misacmos to his friend
and cosin Philostilpnos.' London, 1596 ; and is said to have
originated from the author's invention of a water-closet for
his house at Kelston. The conceit, or pun upon the word
Ajax, or a jakes, appears to have been a familiar joke at the
time, and had been previously introduced by Shakespeare in
his *Love's Labour Lost*, when Costard tells Sir Nathaniel, the
curate, on his failure in the character of Alexander, 'You will
be scraped out of the painted cloth for this ; your lion, that
holds his poll-ax sitting on a close-stool, will be given to
A-jax : he will be the ninth worthy."—*Drake's "Shakespeare
and his Times."*

  *** AN EXCEEDINGLY RARE BOOK, even as far back as 1814,
when it was reprinted in facsimile.

583 Harris (Edmond) A Sermon preached at Brocket Hall before the
Rt. Worshipfull Sir John Brocket, and other gentlemen THERE
ASSEMBLED FOR THE TRAYNING OF SOULDIERS, **black letter**, *a
few head-lines slightly cut, old calf*
                    T. Orwin for J. Daldern and W. Haw, 1588

  *** A copy of this volume is in the British Museum, but *no other,
except the present*, is recorded. It is of historical interest and
importance as showing how, at the critical juncture of the
Armada, the English were actively preparing, not only on the
coasts, but in the inland shires, to repel the Spaniard.

584 Hawker (Lt.-Col. P.) Instructions to Young Sportsmen, with
Directions for the choice, care and management of Guns ;
hints for the preservation of Game ; and Instructions for
Shooting Wildfowl, FIRST EDITION, *uncut, exceedingly scarce*
                                    1814

585 Hawker (Lt.-Col. P.) Instructions to Young Sportsmen in all that
relates to Guns and Shooting, *morocco extra, with rich symbolical tooling, g. e. by T. Gosden* 1830

586 Hawkins (Edward) The Silver Coins of England, arranged and
described, second edition, with alterations and additions, by
R. Ll. Kenyon, *plates, half bound, uncut, t. e. g.* 1876

587 Hebrew. Pentateuchus, Hebraicè, 6 vol. *old Dutch polished sheep,
gilt ornamental borders and arms and name (David Bon Hain) in
gold on sides* Amst. *anno* 5486 (A.D. 1726)

588 Helps (Sir A.) Thoughts in the Cloister and the Crowd, FIRST
EDITION *with half title, clean copy, in original boards, uncut, with
label* 1835

   ✱ Suppressed by the author; his earliest work, printed at Cambridge during his residence at Trinity College. Tennyson's
poem of Œnone is quoted in this little volume. Interesting
copy, having the following autograph inscription on fly-leaf:
"The O'Dowd" (Charles Lever?) from The McLean (James
Maclean?).

589 Herbert (George) The Temple, eighth edition, 1660—The Syna-
gogue, or the Shadow of the Temple, by Harding, fourth edition *in 1 vol.*

590 Heures Nouvelles ou Prières Choisies, *frontispiece,* EMBROIDERED
BINDING *of green silk, large conventional flower and curved stem
worked in raised filigree and various shades of silk on both covers,
portion of border defective, g. e.* Paris, 1760

591 Hewlett (Maurice) The Forest Lovers: a Romance, 1898—Pan
and the Young Shepherd: a Pastoral, 1898; FIRST EDITIONS,
original cloth, uncut (2)

592 Heywood (Thos.) Pleasant Dialogues and Drammas; as also certaine Elegies, Epitaphs and Epithalamions or Nuptiall Songs,
&c. FIRST EDITION, *calf (border of title cut)* 1637

593 Hindley (C.) Life and Times of Catnach, *one of 25 on cartridge
paper,* 230 *cuts,* 1878—Cockton, Silvester Sound, FIRST EDI-
TION, *plate torn, half calf,* 1844—Collins (Wilkie) Mr. Wray's
Cash Box, FIRST EDITION, *frontispiece by Millais, half calf, t. e. g.
uncut,* 1852; and another (4)

594 History of the Theatres of London from 1771-1795, 2 vol. *half
calf, uncut,* 1796—Richardson (W.) Essays on Shakespeare's
Dramatic Characters, FIRST EDITION, *uncut,* 1784—A Philosophical Analysis of some of Shakespeare's Remarkable
Characters, *uncut,* 1774 *4 vol.*

595 Holmes (Oliver Wendell) Astraca: the Balance of Illusions, a
Poem delivered before the Phi Beta Kappa Society of Yale
College, August 14, 1850, FIRST EDITION, *original boards*
Boston, 1850

596 Hood (Thos.) Whims and Oddities in Prose and Verse, *with* 40
original designs, 2 vol. *half red morocco extra, t. e. g. by F. Bedford* L. Relfe, Hirst, &c. 1829

597 Hone (Wm.) Ancient Mysteries described, FIRST EDITION, *copper-
plates and woodcuts (Gog and Magog coloured), half calf,* 1823—
Malden (Henry) Account of King's College Chapel, *portrait of
the author and view of the chapel, old calf, Cambridge,* 1769; and
2 others (4)

   ✱ The Hone is a specially picked copy. See letter inserted.

598 "HORÆ BEATÆ MARIÆ VIRGINIS SECUNDUM STYLUM ANGLIÆ," cum Calendario, ENGLISH MANUSCRIPT ON VELLUM (173 *ll.* 4¼ *by* 3 *in.*) *written in neat* 𝔤𝔬𝔱𝔥𝔦𝔠 𝔩𝔢𝔱𝔱𝔢𝔯𝔰 *in red and black, long lines,* 14 *to a page, with* 6 PAINTED AND ILLUMINATED MINIA- TURES *within floreate borders, the opposite page to each having a large illuminated ornamental initial within similar borders ; nume- rous small initials and decorative details, old calf* SÆC. XIV

 *** Although not in fine condition this little MS. is interest- ing for its ancient English origin. The calendar is in red and black and is full of English saints, as St. Wulfstan Epi. St. Vedast, St. Patrick, St. Edwardi Regis, St. Cuthbert, St. Alphege, St. Erkenwald, St. Dunstan, St. Aldchlm, St. Alban, St. Ethelreda, St. Kenelm Reg. St. Editha, St. Edmund Archiep. St. Thomas (à Becket) Archiep. &c. In the Litany of the Saints is an old MS. note in English.

599 HORÆ BEATÆ MARIÆ VIRGINIS AD USUM EBORACENSEM, *a remark- ably fine* ENGLISH MANUSCRIPT PRIMER *of York use, of the late XIIIth Century, written on vellum, in* 𝔤𝔬𝔱𝔥𝔦𝔠 𝔠𝔥𝔞𝔯𝔞𝔠𝔱𝔢𝔯𝔰, *in red and black,* 105 *leaves, long lines, richly decorated with* 13 *miniatures enclosed in large initials, with ornamental strap borders appended,* 91 *similar borders, many of them charged with curious and fanciful grotesque figures,* 15 *beautiful large initials of inter- laced work and numerous smaller initials containing grotesques, all illuminated in gold and colours by one of the best artists of the time ; ends of many of the borders slightly cut into and a number of plain margins written upon, else well preserved, old English red morocco, ornamental border and centre on sides in gold, g. e.*

           SÆC. XIII (*c.* 1280)

 *** An excessively rare English liturgical manuscript of York use. That the present manuscript is of York use can be proved, for, in addition to the special office given for the Archbishop St. William it agrees in every point with the variations noted by Mr. Hoskins between the respective uses of Sarum and York. Thus the Capitulum at Lauds is the " In Omnibus " of York, not the " Maria Virgo " of Sarum. The Antiphon at Prime is the York " Quando Natus," not the " O admirable " of Sarum. The Psalm at Prime is the " Beatus Vir " of York, not the " Deus in nomine " of Sarum, and so on throughout. It is also a most desirable example of the culminating period of the early English school of art, when the painting of this school was un- rivalled by that of any other country, the illuminated work throughout being of the finest quality. The miniatures repre- sent : 1, The Annunciation ; 2, Christ enthroned, in the accompanying border are eight saints climbing a flight of stairs towards him, beneath a devil and two angels with trumpets summoning the dead, seven of whom are emerging from their coffins, beneath is hell with burn- ing figures ; 3, The Visitation ; 4, The Nativity ; 5, The Magi ; 6, The Presentation ; 7, The Flight into Egypt ; 8, A Funeral Scene ; 9, Coronation of the Virgin ; 10, Minia- ture in two compartments, in the first a Dominican monk with

Lot 599—*continued.*

a penitent, beneath in an oval, a nun; in the second, five penitents and a monk with scourge; 11, The Crucifixion, with six figures; 12, The Crucifixion, with four figures; 13, Pentecost, seven figures, the Virgin in centre. Among the fanciful figures attached to the borders the following are noteworthy, namely : a rabbit riding a dog and holding a pennon in triumph, another playing a violin, another with a spear, a monkey with a bow, another playing on cymbals, man blowing a trumpet with pennon, and two grotesque figures playing on a harp. It was apparently executed for use in some Dominican monastery in the diocese of York. Unfortunately the calendar, which might have located the manuscript, is wanting, as are also several leaves of text. Some leaves have been misplaced by the binder. A leaf of Prayers in a 15th century hand has been added.

600 Horæ Beatæ Mariæ Virginis (sine Calendario), richly illuminated Manuscript on vellum (105 *ll.* 8½ *by* 7¼ *in.*) *written in bold* gothic letters, *within inner illuminated frame borders, with rubrics, by a French scribe and illuminator, some Prayers in French ; commencing with " Obsecio te Domina Sancta Maria," &c. every page surrounded by elaborate floreate and leafy branch scrolls, in gold, red, blue and green;* 11 pages wholly occupied with large and small miniatures, 4 *on each page, interspersed with rich branch scroll ornaments, each thus presenting a most brilliant* tout ensemble, *the large centre ones having backgrounds mostly of landscapes or interiors, the smaller ones in the margins having chequered backgrounds of blue, red and gold ; also numerous large and small illuminated ornamental initials and decorative details ; boarded purple velvet binding, enclosed in an old French red morocco gilt case (Derome, 18th cent.)*   sm. 4to. Sæc. xv

    *** The miniatures in this fine manuscript are very rich, the figures are very much elongated, especially the Christ; the costumes are very fine and the colouring good. The following are the subjects : 1, The Virgin and Child in glory, on a crescent supported by angels, Deity and cherubim above (three other subjects connected with the Virgin in margins) ; 2, Betrayal of Christ, *very fine group*, Christ touching the ear of Malpas (Cock and St. Peter, Warning of Pilate by his wife, and another in margins) ; 3, The Agony in the Garden (three miniatures of the Disciples sleeping, in the margin) ; 4, Christ before Pilate (the same blindfolded and beaten before Pilate and Herod, in margin) ; 5, Christ Scourged (Examinations in margins) ; 6, Christ bearing the Cross (incident of Simon of Cyrene, &c. in margins) ; 7, Christ, Crucifixion with the two Thieves, soldier piercing His side, two Maries, John and officials (Nailing to the Cross, soldiers and group on horseback in margins) ; 8, Descent from the Cross (the Maries mourning in margins) ; 9, The Entombment (Officials, soldiers and Mary mourning in margins) ; 10, The Resurrection (the dead rising from their graves) ; 11, Vigiliæ Mortuorum, Death-Chamber Scene (crucifix *tres vifs et tres morts* in margins). A few top margins slightly cut into.

601 HORÆ BEATÆ MARIÆ VIRGINIS, SECUNDUM CONSUETUDINEM
ROMANÆ ECCLESIÆ ; Horæ de Sancta Cruce ; Horæ de Sancto
Spiritu ; Officium B.V.M. Septem Psalmi Penitentiales ; et
Vigiliæ Mortuorum (*sine Calendario*), ILLUMINATED MANU-
SCRIPT ON VELLUM (236 *ll.* 4¾ by 3½ *in.*) *written in small neat*
𝔤𝔬𝔱𝔥𝔦𝔠 𝔩𝔢𝔱𝔱𝔢𝔯𝔰 (*semi-bâtardes*) *with rubrics, long lines, 15 to a full*
page, by a Flemish scribe and miniaturist; 7 VERY SUPERIOR
LARGE MINIATURES, *beautifully painted and richly illuminated,*
within exquisite borders of natural flowers, fruits, birds, including
the peacock, on washed gold grounds; opposite each miniature a
similar border, enclosing a small historiated miniature; 14 *other*
pages have 3 borders of a similar nature, each with a small illu-
minated figure of a Saint, &c. and throughout are numerous delicate
ornamental initials and decorative details; bound in old French red
morocco (18*th cent.*) *full gilt back, line sides with corner fleur-de-lis,*
enclosed in red morocco boarded case   *sq.* 12*mo.* SÆC. XV

  *** A very charming manuscript, for drawing, costume, grouping
and harmonious colouring. The subjects of the miniatures
following the order of the volume are (1) Crucifixion, (2)
Pentecost, (3) Virgin and Child with Instruments of the Passion, (4) The Annunciation, (5) Christ in Judgment, (6) Vigilia
Mortuorum (a Death-chamber Scene). The 7th miniature is
a full-page one of Christ as *Redemptor Mundi* inserted in front
and apparently not belonging to the original MS.

602 HORÆ BEATÆ MARIÆ VIRGINIS, cum Calendario, RICHLY ILLU-
MINATED MANUSCRIPT ON THICK VELLUM (112 *ll.* 4⅝ by 4⅜ *in.*)
written in bold 𝔤𝔬𝔱𝔥𝔦𝔠 𝔩𝔢𝔱𝔱𝔢𝔯𝔰, *long lines, 17 to a full page, by a*
French scribe and illuminator, calendar in red and black; each
page of the calendar has a lateral border in 3 compartments, the
top one depicting an occupation of the month, the bottom one a
Zodiac sign, the middle one a floreate ornament; in the text are 92
very fine lateral borders richly painted and illuminated, consisting
chiefly of floreate scrolls, in which are introduced birds of brilliant
plumage, grotesques, fruits (chiefly strawberries), &c.; there are
also 10 LARGE RICHLY-PAINTED AND ILLUMINATED MINIA-
TURES *within rich borders in small compartments of various shapes,*
in which are depicted ornamental and floreate scrolls, nude children,
birds of gorgeous plumage (the peacock, &c.) grotesque animals, &c.
and there are many large and small illuminated ornamental initials
and decorative details; bound in modern calf with blind stamped
ornaments   *sq.* 8*vo.* SÆC. XV

  *** Although the figures in this MS. are far from gracefully
drawn, and the architecture in the backgrounds is of a sil-
houette character, the miniatures are striking, being drawn
chiefly in lines and in wash colours, causing them to resemble
some of the designs used for the early Block Books, and the
costume is good. They represent (1) The Annunciation, (2)
The Visitation, (3) The Nativity, (4) The Shepherds, (5) The
Offerings of the Magi, (6) Presentation in the Temple, (7)
Flight into Egypt, (8) Death of the Virgin, (9) David and
Bathsheba, (10) Raising of Lazarus.

603　Horæ Beatæ Mariæ Virginis, cum Calendario, RICHLY ILLU-
MINATED MANUSCRIPT ON VELLUM (174 *ll.* 7¾ *by* 5¼ *in.*) *finely*
written in 𝔤𝔬𝔱𝔥𝔦𝔠 𝔩𝔢𝔱𝔱𝔢𝔯𝔰, *long lines,* 14 *to a full page, by a French*
scribe and illuminator, the calendar and some prayers and rubrics
in French in red, blue and gold, the calendar having a small initial
miniature to each month of its special occupation, and a circular
miniature of the Zodiac signs in each outside margin ; in the text
are 12 *very fine* LARGE PAINTED AND ILLUMINATED MINIA-
TURES, *within broad and richly decorated borders of flowers, fruits*
and birds, a figure of the peacock in the first miniature, many pages
have decorated borders, and there are numerous large and small
illuminated ornamental initials, inner borders and decorative details,
five of the fly-leaves are occupied with prayers in a hand of the
16*th century ; bound in French green morocco of the* 19*th century*

sm. 4to. SÆC. XV

*** A BRILLIANTLY ILLUMINATED MANUSCRIPT. The miniatures
comprise : (1) The Annunciation in an architectural semi-trip-
tych, (2) The Visitation, (3) The Crucifixion (Mary and John),
(4) Pentecost, (5) The Nativity (three angels under a shed
with written scrolls), (6) The Shepherds, (7) Offerings of the
Magi, (8) The Flight into Egypt, (9) Coronation of the Virgin,
(10) David praying, (11) Vigilia Mortuorum (a churchyard
scene), (12) SS. Sergius and Bacchus.

604　Horæ Beatæ Mariæ Virginis, cum Calendario, MANUSCRIPT ON
VELLUM (109 *ll.* 6½ *by* 4½ *in.*) *written in Dutch in* 𝔤𝔬𝔱𝔥𝔦𝔠 𝔩𝔢𝔱𝔱𝔢𝔯𝔰,
very full calendar in blue and gold, many outside borders of flowers
and fruits, fine large and small illuminated ornamental initials,
and decorative details (*several entries of births and deaths of a*
Dutch family dating from 1605 *occur in the calendar*), *calf*

SÆC. XV

605　Horæ Beatæ Mariæ ad usum Romanæ Curiæ, cum Calendario,
𝔩𝔦𝔱. 𝔤𝔬𝔱𝔥. PRINTED UPON VELLUM, *within woodcut borders of com-*
partments of Scriptural subjects, Zodiac signs, grotesques, nude
figures, &c. (*several slightly shaved by binder*), 19 *full-page and*
28 *small woodcuts, the whole richly painted and illuminated, sig-*
natures F 4 *and* 5 *wanting, rare*

s. n. (*Paris. G. de Marnef, c.* 1490, *almanac* 1489-1508)

*** An undescribed edition, remarkable for the interesting and
unusual character of its woodcuts.

606　Horæ. Ces presentes heures a lusaige de Romme toutes au long
sans riens requerir, ont este imprimées à Paris pour Germain
Hardouyn, PRINTED ON VELLUM, 15 *fine miniatures engraved on*
wood, illuminated in gold and colours, also 6 *smaller miniatures,*
old French red morocco gilt　　　　　　　　　　　　Paris (1520)

607　Horæ. HEURES A LUSAIGE DE PARIS, tout au lōg sans requerir,
avec Calendrier, PRINTED UPON VELLUM, *in red and black, in*
a large 𝔤𝔬𝔱𝔥𝔦𝔠 𝔩𝔢𝔱𝔱𝔢𝔯, *with* 16 *full-page engravings, the figure of*
the Anatomical Man and printer's mark, all beautifully painted
and illuminated, 22 *small historiated miniatures, also illuminated,*
and numerous initial letters and finials, dark purple morocco, blind
tooled sides and back, vellum fly-leaves, g. e. by Riviere
imprimées à Paris, pour Germain Hardouyn (*Almanack,* 1524-1527)

608 Horæ Beatæ Mariæ Virginis, ad usum Romanum, lit. goth. *fragment of 109 ll. between b* III *and v* VIII, *initials and headings in
red, every page enclosed by border of Gospel characters or incidents,
contemporary binding of oak boards covered with calf, much dilap-
idated (Paris, circa* 1520). — La Bible (Genesis to Job only),
*engraved title, old brown morocco, elaborately gold-tooled, g. e.
Charenton,* 1652   (2)

609 Horses. Liberati (Fran.) La Perfettione del Cavallo, *nearly* 200
*cuts of the marks used by kings, cardinals, noblemen and gentle-
men to brand their horses, old limp vellum* (2 *copies*), *Romæ,* 1639
—Solleysel (Le Sieur de) La Parfait Mareschal, 2 vol. in 1,
portrait, engraved title, plates of horses and woodcuts, old calf—
Seventeenth Century French Manuscript on Horses, *neatly
written on* 32 *pp. signed, wrappers*   (4)

609* Horsfield (Dr. Thos.) Zoological Researches in Java, and the
neighbouring Islands, 64 *highly coloured plates from drawings by
W. Daniell, russia gilt, fine copy*   1824

610 Hunter (Dr. John) Catalogue of an elegant Selection from his
Library, 3 *days' sale of very rare books, with prices*   1813

611 IRELAND (W. H.) THE LIFE OF NAPOLEON BONAPARTE, 4 vol.
*numerous folding plates by Geo. Cruikshank, coloured by hand, half
calf gilt, t. e. g.*   *John Cumberland,* 1828

612 Joe Miller's Jests, or the Wit's Vade Mecum, inscribed to David
Garrick, Theo. Cibber, &c. *frontispiece, uncut*   *W. Lane, n. d.*

613 [Johnson (Dr. Sam.)] The False Alarm, FIRST EDITION, *original
wrapper, uncut*   *T. Cadell,* 1770

614 Jones (Stephen) Masonic Miscellanies in Poetry and Prose,
frontispiece, half calf   1811

615 KEATS (JOHN) POEMS, FIRST EDITION, *calf gilt, m. e.*
printed for C. and J. Ollier, 1817
**** This most interesting PRESENTATION COPY, bears on the title-
page the inscription in the POET'S AUTOGRAPH, "From J. K.
to his friend C. C. C." *i.e.* Charles Cowden Clarke.   It contains numerous marked passages and notes on pages 75, 92,
111 and 118, in Mary Cowden Clarke's handwriting, and
Charles Cowden Clarke's pictorial book-plate. A copy of
Joseph Severn's portrait-sketch of John Keats inserted.

616 KEATS (JOHN) ENDYMION : a Poetic Romance, "The Stretched
Metre of an Antique Song," FIRST EDITION, *a large and very
clean copy, in the original calf, rare*   1818

617 Keats (John) Endymion : a Poetic Romance, FIRST EDITION, complete with the half-title and the " errata," *morocco extra, g. e.*
1818

618 KEATS (JOHN) LAMIA, ISABELLA, The Eve of St. Agnes, and
other Poems, FIRST EDITION, *morocco super extra, g. e.*
by Riviere, 1820

619 Kidgell (John) The Card, 2 vol. *coloured frontispiece and plate, uncut*   *London, printed for the maker,* 1755
**** The existence of this book remained entirely unknown to
bibliographers, as no trace is to be found in any of their
works ; very scarce, particularly in the uncut state.

620 Killigrew (Sir Wm.) Mid-night and Daily Thoughts, in Prose
       and Verse, FIRST EDITION, *limp morocco*   1694
621 King (K.) New London Spy ; or a Twenty-four Hours' Ramble
       Through the Bills of Mortality, *frontispiece of a Duelling
       Scene at a celebrated Night House, uncut*   *A. Hogg, n. d.*
622 KIPLING (RUDYARD) ECHOES, by Two Writers, *in the original
       wrapper   Lahore, the Civil and Military Gazette Press* (1884)
       ₊ One of the scarcest of Kipling's writings, privately cir-
       culated while he was a young man on the staff of the "Civil
       and Military Gazette."
623 Kipling (Rudyard) Writings in Prose and Verse, vol. XVIII,
       XIX and XX, Early Verses, Stalky and Co. Kim, *silk bind-
       ing, uncut*   1900
624 LA FONTAINE (J. de) Contes et Nouvelles, en vers, 2 vol.
       *numerous beautiful plates after Eisen and Choffard, wants the
       portrait of La Fontaine, calf gilt, m. e.*   *Amst.* 1764

The Property of a Gentleman.

625 Coleridge. Matthiae (A) Copious Greek Grammar, translated
       by Blomfield, *with numerous marginal notes and comments by*
       S. T. COLERIDGE, *some of them initialled S. T. C.* 2 vol. *half
       russia (binding broken)*   1824
       ₊ On the fly-leaf is the autograph of " Edward Coleridge,
       Eton College, 1825."
626 Cunningham (Peter) Poems upon several occasions, FIRST EDITION,
       *in the original paper wrapper, 75 copies printed for private circu-
       lation*   1841
       ₊ Inserted is an autograph letter from the author to John
       Scott, Esq. asking him to review the volume.
627 Freshfield (Douglas W.) From Thuon to Trent, *a presentation
       copy from the author*   1865
                         ₊ RARE.
628 Freshfield (D. W.) The Italian Alps, 1875—King (S. W.)
       Italian Valleys of the Pennine Alps, *plates,* 1858   (2)
629 Gaskell (Mrs.) Ruth, a Novel, by the author of " Mary Barton,"
       3 vol.   1853
       ₊ Presentation copy from the author, with the inscription,
       " For dear Miss Nell from ' Mrs. Gaskell ' and Annie, Xmas
       Day, /65."
630 Hinchliff (T. W.) Summer Months among the Alps   1857
631 Longfellow (H. W.) Hyperion, *illustrations by Birket Foster,
       morocco, g. e.*   1853
       ₊ Inserted is a long autograph letter (8 pp.) from Longfellow
       to Robert Brigsby, containing references to Hyperion and to
       Longfellow's work at Cambridge, but principally concerned
       with a Poem by Brigsby entitled " Ombo," an enthusiastic
       appreciation of it, and excuses for not having read it and
       written sooner.

632 Hunt (Leigh) : Horne (R. H.) A New Spirit of the Age, *portraits
and numerous marginal notes in pencil by* LEIGH HUNT, 2 vol.
1844

⁎ The editor's own copy, with his autograph on each title-
page and the following note in his handwriting: "The
annotations in pencil are all by my friend Leigh Hunt, to
whom I lent the vols., R. H. H." At the end of vol. I (which
contains other marginal notes) is written "A million of un-
utterable thanks, L. H." At the end of the work is a short
criticism (11 lines) in which Leigh Hunt says "that with the
exception of Carlyle's books, I have not read anything containing so much thought and feeling for many a day," although
he considers the book very unequally written.

633 Prout (Father) Reliques, *illustrations by Alfred Croquis,* FRANCIS
MAHONEY'S COPY, *with his corrections, additions, and alterations
for a fresh edition, with an autograph letter from him to H. G.
Bohn, referring to the republication of this book,* 2 vol.   1836

634 Ruskin (John) Ethics of the Dust, FIRST EDITION, *with two autograph letters from the author (both signed J. Ruskin) inserted*
1866

⁎ The two letters are both interesting and characteristic, the
first, dated 1860, to Gerald Massey, thanking him for an
appreciative review in the "Witness," continuing—"At present I am in a bad humour with myself and all my work—as
far as art is concerned—it falls so wretchedly short of what I
hoped and believed myself once able to do ; so that I have little
comfort in praise, and take the sting of coarse blame more
home than I used to do." The second, also to Mr. Massey,
dated 1867, is regretting having to decline an invitation
owing to ill-health.

635 Smith (Albert) Story of Mont Blanc, 1853—Talfourd (T. N.)
Recollections of a First Visit to the Alps, 1841, *Presentation
copy with the author's inscription, printed for private circulation*
(1842)   (2)

636 Thackeray. The National Shakspeare Committee and the late
Mr. Thackeray, 24 pp.   (1864)

⁎ Refers to the National Shakspeare Committee refusing to
elect Thackeray as one of the Vice-Presidents of the Society.

637 Tyndall (J.) The Glaciers of the Alps, 1840—Tyndall's Moun-
taineering in 1861-62   (2)

638 Whymper (E.) Scrambles among the Alps, 1860-69, *many illustrations,* FIRST EDITION   1871

639 [Wild (R.)] Iter Boreale, together with some other select Poems,
not heretofore printed, *half calf*   1661

640 Wilson (Andrew) The Abode of Snow, *illustrated, half calf gilt,
t. e. g.* 1875—[Dempsey's] The Maritime Alps, *illustrated, half
calf gilt, t. e. g.* 1885   (2)

641 Wordsworth (W.) Lyrical Ballads, with other Poems, 2 vol. in 1,
vol. I second edition, vol. II FIRST EDITION, *morocco, edges
gilt*   1800

QUARTO.

642   Solemne League and Covenant, for the Reformation and Defence
of Religion, the honour and happinesse of the King, and the
peace and safety of the three Kingdomes of Scotland, England, and Ireland, *the* ORIGINAL BROADSHEET, *mounted on linen,
and folded to roy. 8vo*   1643

643   Tasso. Series of 41 finely engraved Plates from designs by
Cochin, to illustrate "Tasso's Jerusalem Delivered"

644   Thomson (James) The Castle of Indolence ; an allegorical Poem,
half bound, FIRST EDITION   1748

FOLIO.

645   Addison. A Poem to His Majesty, presented to the Lord
Keeper, 10 pp. FIRST EDITION, 1695—Prior (Matt.) To a
Young Gentleman in Love, *a single sheet*, FIRST EDITION, 1702
—Trappe, Aedes Badmintonianæ, a Poem presented to the
Duke of Beaufort, 1701 ; and many other pieces, 1 thick
vol. *calf*   *v. d.*

646   Chaucer. The Workes of Geffray Chaucer newlye printed,
wythe dyvers workes whych were never in print before,
BLACK LETTER, *with woodcut titles, folio, brown morocco extra,
edges gilt, by* RIVIERE, *Prynted by John Reynes dwellynge at the
sygne of saynte George in Pauls Churchyarde*   1542

647   Dryden (John) Comedies, Tragedies and Operas, FIRST EDITION,
2 vol. *calf*   1701

648   Dulwich Gallery. A series of thirty beautiful Plates coloured
like water-colour drawings, copied from pictures in the Dulwich Gallery, *mounted on stout card, morocco gilt*

649   [Hammond (James)] Love Elegies written in the year 1732,
20 pp. FIRST EDITION   1743

650   Pope (A.) Of Taste, an Epistle to the Earl of Burlington,
occasion'd by his publishing Palladio's Designs of the Baths,
Arches, etc. of Ancient Rome, 16 pp. FIRST EDITION   1731

651   Pope (A.) Of the Use of Riches, an Epistle to Lord Bathurst,
20 pp. FIRST EDITION   1732

652   Pope. An Epistle from Mr. Pope to Dr. Arbuthnot, 30 pp. FIRST
EDITION   1734

653   Pope (A.) Of the Characters of Women, an Epistle to a Lady,
16 pp. FIRST EDITION   1735

654   Pope (A.) Horace, his Ode to Venus, imitated by Mr. Pope,
8 pp. FIRST EDITION   1737

655   Pope (A.) Second Epistle of the Second Book of Horace,
imitated by Mr. Pope, 20 pp. FIRST EDITION   1737

656   [Pope (A.)] Art of Poetry, 14 pp. FIRST EDITION   1741

657   Popeiana. One Thousand Seven Hundred Thirty Nine, a
Rhapsody, by way of sequel to Seventeen Hundred Thirty
Eight, by Mr. Pope, 1740—Elegy to a Young Lady in the
manner of Ovid, with an answer by the Author of Verses to
the Imitator of Horace, 1733—The Man of Taste, occasioned by an Epistle of Mr. Pope's, 1733—Sober Advice from

Lot 657—*continued.*

Horace to the Young Gentleman about Town, imitated in the manner of Mr. Pope—First Satire of the Second Book of Horace, imitated in a Dialogue between Alexander Pope and his Learned Council, 1733—Verses addressed to the Imitator of the First Satire of the Second Book of Horace—Characters, an Epistle to Mr. Pope and Mr. Whitehead, 1739—Life and Genuine Character of Dr. Swift, dedicated to Mr. Pope, 1733—Tryal of Skill between a Court Lord and a Twickenham Squire (Mr. Pope), 1734—Bounce to Fop, an Heroick Epistle from a Dog at Twickenham to a Dog at Court, by Dr. S——t, 1736, *all sewed, v. d.*   (10)

658   Stepney (George) Epistle to Charles Montague, on His Majesty's Voyage to Holland, 10 pp.   1691

659   Wilkinson (H.) Sketches of Scenery in the Basque Provinces of Spain, 12 *beautifully coloured plates*   1838

*** Presentation copy from the late Queen Victoria, with the following inscription in her handwriting : " To (name erased) From his very sincere friend, Victoria ; 44th December, 1838."

660   [Young (E.)] The Complaint : or Night-Thoughts on Life, Death, and Immortality, 20 pp. FIRST EDITION   1742

Other Properties.

QUARTO.

661   General Catalogue of all the Stich'd Books and Single Sheets, &c. commencing from the first Discovery of the Popish Plot, very useful for Gent. that make collections, 3 parts, *unbound, very rare*   1680

662   George (H. B.) The Oberland and its Glaciers, explored and illustrated with Ice-Axe and Camera, 28 *photographs and a map,* 1866—Saint Juirs.   La Seine à travers Paris, *coloured plates and numerous illustrations, by G. Fraipont,* " Edition de Luxe," 1890   (2)

663   Gerard of Cremona's Theora Planetorium, and another kindred Opusculum by George Pierbach *in the same vol.*

664   GESTA ROMANORUM.   Le Violier des Hystoires rommaines : Moralisez sur les Nobles Gestes faictz vertueulx et anciēnes Croniques de toutes natiōs de gēs fort reccatif et moral. Nouvellement translate de latin en francois ; *woodcut title, printed in red and black, numerous woodcuts, with device of Ph. le Noir at end,* 𝔤𝔬𝔱𝔥𝔦𝔠 𝔩𝔢𝔱𝔱𝔢𝔯, *red morocco extra, gilt leaves, by Chambolle-Duru,* A BEAUTIFUL COPY   *Paris,* 1525

*** Shakespeare's indebtedness to the Gesta Romanorum is well known.   The various commentators only mention Latin editions.   *This French translation seems to have eluded their researches.*

665 Gesta Romanorum. A Record of Ancient Histories intitled in
       Latin Gesta Romanorum translated (auctore ut suppossitor
       Johane Leylando Antiquario) by mee (Richard Robinson)
       perused, corrected and bettered, *wants title and last leaf, vellum*
                                                 Thomas East, 1577
   *** One of the rarest and most important volumes in the whole
       range of *Shakespeareana.* For a full account refer to Douce's
       Illustrations of Shakespeare, pp. 517-575. Lowndes says
       that Shakespeare has manifestly borrowed many of his stories
       from this source.

666 GLAPTHORNE (Henry) Wit in a Constable.   A Comedy
       written 1639......And now Printed as it was lately acted at
       the Cock-pit in Drury Lane, by their Majesties Servants,
       with good allowance, FIRST EDITION, *boards*   1640
   *** A *fine large copy* of this rare play, with the blank leaf before
       the title.

667 [Googe (Barnabe)] A New Yeares Gifte, dedicated to the Pope's
       Holinesse and all Catholikes, in recompense of divers singular
       and inestimable Reliques, *folding-plate in facsimile, sm. 4to, red
       morocco gilt*   1579

668 Guerres Religieuses de France, les Calvinistes, &c. 120 *curious
       copperplate engravings, a few mended, calf (rebacked), r. e. sold
       not subject to return*   (1580)

669 Hall (Thos. B.D. and Pastor of King's Norton) Funebria Floræ,
       the Downfall of May-Games : wherein is set forth the rudeness,
       prophaneness, stealing, fighting, drinking, dancing, whoring,
       misrule, &c. in this their open profaneness and heathenish
       customs ; together with the addition of some Verses, FIRST
       EDITION, *panelled calf extra, g. e. by Zaehnsdorf, fine copy,*
       EXTREMELY RARE   *sm. 4to.   Printed for H. Mortlock,* 1660

670 HALLIWELL (James O.) Observations on the Shaksperian For-
       geries at Bridgewater House ; illustrative of a Facsimile of
       the Spurious Letter of H.S., *folding plate (facsimile of a forged
       letter from Lord Southampton), original cloth, t. e.* UNCUT
                                For private circulation only, 1853
   *** Inserted is an (signed) autograph letter of W. H. Ireland
       concerning his "first confession of the Shakespeare fabri-
       cations."

671 Hamilton (A.) Memoires de Comte de Grammont, 72 *fine portraits,
       by Harding, old calf, m. e.*   *Londres, Edwards,* 1793

672 Henry VIII.   Assertio Sacramentum, *wants sheet* A, *four leaves*
                                     Antwerp. Hillenius, 1522

673 HERCULES OF GREECE. The famous and renowned History of the
       Life and Actions of Hercules of Greece, *woodcut on title, half
       russia*   *London, for S. Bates, in Pye Corner, circa* 1680
   *** A very rare volume, of which we can trace no other copy as
       having occurred for sale. The present copy was described in
       Halliwell's *Catalogue of Chap Books.* Hazlitt, in his *Hand Book,*
       1867, describes it as "one of the scarcest of that series to
       which it belongs" ; but gives the title somewhat differently.
       He only cites the Bodleian copy, formerly Malone's.

674 Heylin (Peter) The Rebel's Catechisme   *s. l.* 1643

675 HORÆ BEATÆ MARIÆ VIRGINIS, cum Calendario, MANUSCRIPT UPON VELLUM, 152 *leaves, written in bold* gothic characters, *the outside border of each page composed of flowers, fruit, leaves, and other ornamentation, richly painted and illuminated, numerous large and small initials and finials, also illuminated, and a beautiful miniature of the Sacrament of the Mass on the first leaf, a fine copy, with exceptionally large margins, contemporary oak boards, covered with stamped leather, g. e.* SÆC. XV

676 Howgill (F.) Oaths no Gospel Ordinance but Prohibited by Christ, *in the year* 1666—The True Rule, Judge, and Guide of the true Church of God, *in the year* 1665—The Great Case of Tythes and forced Maintenance with Poems (4 pp.) The Poor Husband-man's Complaint, &c. *ib.* 1665, *original calf in* 1 *vol.*

*** From the library of the Poet John Scott of Amwell, with his autograph on the flyleaf and some earlier MS. memoranda relating to the Quakers.

677 Ibbetson (Julius) An Accidence, or Gamut, of Painting in Oil and Water Colours, part I (*all published*), *several original etchings, &c. original boards, lettered* "*Ibbetson's Oil Painting,*" VERY RARE *Darton & Harvey*, 1805

678 Illuminated Initial Miniatures of the XIVth Century, a Selection of forty-nine initials cut from an Italian Antiphonary, representing chiefly heads of monks, grotesques, &c. (*three are large and good*), *mounted on blank paper and bound in vellum*

679 Jonson. Ben Jonson's Execration against Vulcan, with divers epigrams by the same author, FIRST EDITION, *unbound* (*wants portrait*) 1640

*** Contains references to Shakespeare's Globe Theatre and Paris Garden. The Halliwell-Phillipps' copy also lacked the portrait.

680 La Fontaine. Fables Choisies, mises en vers, par M. de la Fontaine, *numerous vignettes by Chauveau, red morocco extra, gilt leaves*, EXTREMELY RARE
A Paris, chez Claude Barbin au Palais sur le Perron de la Sainte Chapelle, MDCLXVIII (1668) *avec privilege du Roy*

681 Langlande (Rob.) The Vision of Pierce Plowman, newlye imprynted after the Authour's olde copy......whereunto is also annexed the Crede of Pierce Plowman (*this latter wanting as usual*), black letter, *slightly wormed, but sound copy, old calf*
sm. 4to. Owen Rogers, neare Great Saint Bartholomews, 1561

682 Lansdowne (Lord) The Sho Gallants : a Comedy, FIRST EDITION, *unbound* *sm. 4to.* 1696
*** From John Genest's collection, with his autograph.

683 Le Maire de Belges (Jean) Les Illustrations de Gaule, et singularitez de Troyes, contenant troys parties, avec plusieurs additions faicte par le dict Autheur, nouvellement reveu et corrigé, *numerous ornamental woodcut initials, crushed red morocco extra, g. e.* (*Toovey*) *sm. 4to. Paris, Vivant Gualterot,* 1548
G

684 Lewes (G.) A Series of Groups Illustrating the Physiognomy, Manners and Character of the People of France and Germany, 60 *plates, india proofs, tree-calf gilt*   1823

685 L'Histoire de Huon de Bordeaux, *cut on title and at end, Troyes,* 1683—Livre Second, *cut on title and at end, Troyes,* 1701
in 1 *vol.*

686 L'Histoire de Huon de Bordeaux, *cut on title,* the first part only
Troyes, 1679

687 Limming. A very proper Treatise wherein is briefly sett forthe the Arte of Limming, which teacheth the order in drawing and tracing of letters, vinets, flowers, armes, and imagery, & the maner how to make sundry sizes or grounds to laye silver or golde uppon ... and diverse kyndes of colours to write or to limme withal vpon velym, parchement or paper, FIRST EDITION, black letter, *Richard Tottill,* 1573—Alphabetum Pauperis monachi fris. Thome Kempis ordis. regularium, Manuscript *on seven leaves of* Vellum, *written in* gothic letter, *large and handsome scrolled initials, curious drawings, and over* 200 *outline and* COLOURED *copies of beautiful illuminated capitals, &c. on* 57 *leaves of paper,* Sæc. XVI ; *together in* 1 *vol. dark blue morocco extra, g. e. by* Pratt, *ornamental letters pasted in covers*

688 Lloyd (Ludov.) The Marrow of History ; or the Pilgrimage of Kings and Princes, &c. corrected and revived by R. C. (Rob. Codrington), *original calf*   *E. Alsop,* 1653

FOLIO.

689 Godefroy de Bulloïgne. Histoire de la Conquest de Jerusalem, &c. [*begins on folio* 1*a*] " Ces anciens histoires dieut que Eracles fu ml't boens Crestiens et gouverna lempire de Roume ; mais a son tans Mahomes ot ia est ki fu messaiges au deable, et il fist en rendant ke il estoit Prophetes envoies de damelden," &c. [*the last four leaves are occupied by the letter of Prester John of Abyssinia*], MANUSCRIPT ON Vellum (359 *ll.* 13½ *by* 9¾ *in.*), *finely written in* gothic letters, *double columns,* 44 *lines, by a Northern French or Anglo-Norman scribe, with rubrics,* 15 FINE LARGE PAINTED AND ILLUMINATED FIGURED INITIALS, *the first in four compartments, all having docked marginal floreate and grotesque decorations, and many hundred very superior large and small ornamental pen letters, with marginal decorations ; numerous MS. explanatory notes (17th Century) in margins, new limp vellum, with ties, in new open cloth case* Sæc. XIV

    *** The large Illuminated Initials in this very well preserved MS. are very important for their Ecclesiastical, Civil, Domestic and Military Costumes.

690 Gower (John) Confessio Amantis: a most valuable and interesting Early English Manuscript of this celebrated poem, *written in double columns in red and black on vellum,* 348 *pp. with painted capitals (slightly imperfect)*   EARLY XV CENT.

    *** A fine and rare MS. of one of the earliest pieces of English Poetry. It was formerly in the Towneley Collection, and afterwards in that of Sir Thomas Phillipps, at whose sale it realised £132.

691   GOULD (JOHN) THE BIRDS OF EUROPE, 5 vol. *with numerous large
      and beautifully coloured plates, half morocco gilt, g. e.*
                                    Published by the Author, 1837

692   GRANGER (REV. JAMES) BIOGRAPHICAL HISTORY OF ENGLAND,
      EXTRA-ILLUSTRATED WITH OVER TWO THOUSAND FIVE HUN-
      DRED PORTRAITS, comprising mezzotints by J. Smith, J.
      Faber, J. McArdell, J. Beckett, E. Cooper, A. Blooteling, &c.
      including Mrs. Susanna Centlivre, by P. Pelham, after D.
      Fermin ; Countess of Roxburghe, by J. Smith, after Kneller,
      proof; Charles, Earl of Derby, by A. Blooteling ; Countess of
      Westmoreland, by J. Beckett ; Mrs. Marianne Herbert, by
      W. Faithorne, after Kerssaboom ; Mary Duchess of Rich-
      mond, by Bockman, after Sir A. Vandyck ; Frances Stuart,
      Countess of Portland, by A. Browne, after the same ; Louisa,
      Countess of Portsmouth, by G. Volck, after Sir P. Lely ;
      Eleanor Gwynn, by V. Green, after the same ; and others.
      Scarce early line portraits by W. Faithorne, W. Hollar, C.
      Pass, M. Delph, P. White, G. Vertue, and many other en-
      gravers ; *in ten volumes, half morocco*   1824

693   Harrington (James) The Commonwealth of Oceana, FIRST
      EDITION, with the sub-title dedicated to Oliver Cromwell
      (*reverse of 239 blank, then wrong pagination 255*), *&c. original
      calf*   *J. Streater, for L. Chapman*, 1656

694   Harrington (Jas.) The Commonwealth of Oceana, FIRST EDITION,
      title in red and black, old calf   *ib.* 1656

695   PAINTING IN OILS, by S. A. HART, *R.A.*, *signed and dated*—The
      three Inventors of Printing, Gutenberg, Faust, and Schoeffer,
      discussing the merit of moveable type   1852

696   Hearne and Byrne's Antiquities of Great Britain [vol. I], 60
      plates, tree-calf gilt, Earl of Fife bookplate, ORIGINAL SUBSCRI-
      BER'S COPY   1786

697   Hieronymus (S.) Epistolæ, a finely executed Manuscript of the XIIth
      Century, *written in double columns upon vellum, titles rubricated,
      in the original oak boards*   SÆC. XII
      **** This Manuscript at one time belonged to the Monastery of
      Royaumont in France. It subsequently formed part of the
      Chardin Collection.

698   Holland (H.) Bazilologia : a Booke of Kings, beeing the true and
      lively effigies of all our English Kings from the Conquest
      untill this present, with their severall Coates of Armes, Im-
      preses, and Devises, and a Briefe Chronologie of their Lives
      and Deaths, *elegantly graven in copper, original impressions of
      the engraved title by Elstracke (in 1st state), and 27 portraits by
      Elstracke, Francis Delaram, and Simon Pass, morocco extra*
              Printed by H. Holland and are to be sold by Comp. Holland, 1618
      **** A Portrait Collection of the greatest rarity. No copy appears
      to have been offered for public sale for many years. As copies
      all differ in collation, we give a list of the contents of this :—
      Engraved title by Elstracke, William I, William II, Henry I,
      Stephen, Henry II, Richard I, John, Henry III, Edward I, Edward II,
      Edward III, Edward the Black Prince, Richard II, Henry IV, Henry V,
      Henry VI, Edward V, Richard III, Henry VII, Henry VIII, Edward
      VI, Mary, Elizabeth, James I, Queen Anne of Denmark, Henry,
      Prince of Wales, Prince Charles.

699   Holbein (Hans) Œuvre, ou Recueil de Gravures par Chr. de
      Mechel, Partie I. Le Triomphe de la Mort. *47 subjects on* 12
      *plates, and the Triumph of Poverty and Riches on 2 separate plates
      at end, half calf*   *imp. 4to.   Basle,* 1780

700   JONSON (BEN) THE WORKES OF. Plays, Epigramms, Masques,
      &c. FIRST EDITION, *fine impression of the frontispiece by Hole,
      blank margins restored,* FINE SOUND COPY, *in old calf*
                                            Imprinted by W. Stansby, 1616
      *** Amongst the names of the actors appear those of Wm. Shake-
            speare, Burbage, Heming, &c. with Commendatory Poems by
            J. Selden, Geo. Chapman, Francis Beaumont, &c.

701   JOSEPHUS.   HISTOIRE DES JUIFS [*begins folio* 1*b*] "Ci Apres
      Commence le XV livre des anciennetes des Juifs selond le
      Sentence de Josephe" [*ends on folio* 286*b*]; "Ci fine le livre
      de Josephe contenant en tout XXVII livres historiaulx."
      MANUSCRIPT ON STOUT VELLUM (286 *ll.* 15 *by* 11 *in.*), *finely
      written in* 𝔤𝔬𝔱𝔥𝔦𝔠 𝔩𝔢𝔱𝔱𝔢𝔯𝔰, *double columns,* 36 *lines, with rubrics,
      the reverse of first leaf having a fine* LARGE PAINTED AND
      ILLUMINATED MINIATURE *of a portion of Solomon's Temple, the
      king on horseback, clad in gold armour, with armoured warriors
      and officials attending, people bathing in front, the twisted pillars
      and shrine in gold* (8 *by* 7 *in.*), *surrounded by a border of spiked
      ivy-leaves, numerous fine ornamental pen letters, old French red
      morocco with rich gilt borders; from the Towneley Library, with
      ex-libris,* A FINE MANUSCRIPT   SÆC. XIV

702   Juvenal.   Satires, translated into English Verse, by John Dryden
      and other Eminent Hands, together with the Satires of Persius,
      made English by Mr. Dryden, and Notes, *plates by W. Hollar,
      half bound*   1693

703   Killigrew (Thomas) Comedies and Tragedies, FIRST EDITION, *with
      a fine impression of the rare portrait by Faithorne, tall and very
      clean copy, full morocco extra, gilt leaves on the rough, by Riviere*
                                            Henry Herringman, 1664

704   La Motraye (A. de) Travels through Europe, Asia, and into
      parts of Africa, 2 vol. 50 *plates, many by* WM. HOGARTH, *old
      calf,* 1730—Icones Operum Misericordiæ, *engraved title and*
      17 *copperplates by C. Carr, Romæ,* 1585   (3)

705   Le Brun (M.) Expressions des Passions de l'Ame, *engraved title
      and* 19 *plates, with letterpress descriptions*
                                            Paris, Jean Audran, 1727

706   Leggi e Memorie Venete sulla Prostituzione, *plates, one of* 150
      *copies printed at the expense of the Earl of Orford, presentation
      copy, half morocco, uncut*   *Venezia,* 1870-72

707   Leggi e Memorie Venete; another copy (*as the preceding*)
                                                          ib. 1870-72

708   Leicester, both Countye and City described, the Honourable
      Famylies that have had the titles of Earls thereof, with other
      accidents therein observed, *a folding map of Leicestershire by
      John Speed, with numerous tricks of arms, boards*   1610
      *** Refer to the catalogue of Halliwell-Phillipps' Shakespearian
            rarities.

709 Lhuyd (E.) Archæologia Britannica, account of the additional to
what has hitherto been published of the Languages, Histories,
and Customs of the Original Inhabitants of Great Britain, *old
calf*   *Oxford*, 1707

710 Locke (John) An Essay concerning Humane Understanding,
FIRST EDITION, *original calf*   1690

  *** Contains illustrations of *Hamlet*. The Halliwell-Phillipps'
copy sold in 1889 for £6 6s.

711 Luther (Martin) Colloquie oder Tischreden doctor Martini
Luther so er in vielen jaren die zent alines, lebens gegen
Gelehrten Seuchen, &c. Durch herrn Johann Aurifaber,
*curious woodcut on title representing the Great Reformer at table
with some friends, original vellum, with numerous miniature portraits (including that of Martin Luther) impressed on the sides*
Franckfurt, 1567

  *** Excessively rare, every available copy having been destroyed
by order of Gregory XIII (*see* Retrospective Review, vol. V).
An account is given in Douce's "Illustrations of Shakespeare."

712 Lyndewode (Wilhelm) Constitutiones Provinciales anglie summa
diligentia et accuratione magri. Andree Bocard edidae, **gothic
letter**, *printed in red and black in double columns*, FIRST EDITION,
WITH NOTES, *slightly stained in top inner corner, old calf, rebacked*
Paris. May XXVIII, 1501

  *** Autograph Inscriptions on title : "Thomas Williams, 1566 ;
Johannis Westoni liber ex dono mei Thomas Williams
artium magi. Exon. 1578, 7th Jan.; Et emptus ab
eiusdem Magri. Weston mense Junii, 1587, per me Josperum
Bridgman, Archid. Exon. &c." and other interesting notes ;
also others on the margins.

713 Mabbes. The Spanish Bawd, represented in Celestina; or, the
Tragicke-Comedy of Calisto and Melibea, shewing the deceits
and subtilties housed in the bosomes of false servants and
Cunny-catching Bawds, FIRST EDITION   1631

  *** This play is the longest that was ever published, consisting
of twenty-one acts. It was written originally in Spanish by
Fernando de Roxas de Montalvan.

714 Maizeroy (R.) La Mer, *etchings and numerous other beautiful illustrations, half morocco, t. e. g.*   *Paris, n. d.*

715 Malone (Edmond) Catalogue of Early English Poetry and other
Miscellaneous Works illustrating the British Drama, collected
by Edmond (*sic*) Malone, Esq. and now presented to the
Bodleian Library, *uncut*   *Oxford*, 1836

  *** The entries under Shakespeare number no less than 124,
including the first two folios, several of the quartos, and
first editions of Venus and Adonis, Lucrece, &c.

FOURTH DAY'S SALE.

OCTAVO ET INFRA.

LOT 716.

AMB (Charles) Elia : Essays which have appeared under that signature in the London Magazine (First Series), FIRST EDITION, *uncut, in the original boards (damaged)* 1823

717 Lamb (C.). A Brief History of Christ's Hospital (contains a long article on "The Character of the Boys," by Charles Lamb, pp. 62-83), *coloured costume plate on title, and other plates, fine copy, in the original pictorial boards, uncut Effingham Wilson,*1830

   **** At the end is Wilson's 18 pp. catalogue of books, amongst which is Tennyson's Poems, chiefly Lyrical, 1830.

718 La Motte (Countess de Valois de) Memoirs of, a complete justification of her Conduct, Intrigues, &c. relating to the Diamond Necklace, &c. *uncut,* 1789—Adolphus (J. H.) The Royal Exile or Memoirs of Queen Caroline, 2 vol. *numerous portraits,* 1821—Death-Bed Confession of the Countess of Guernsey to Lady Anne H.(amilton), 1822, in 2 vol. *calf*   *3 vol.*

719 Landor. Idyllia Heroica decem librum Phaleuciorum unum, partim jam primo partim iterum atq. tertio edit Savagius Landor, FIRST EDITION, *presentation copy, with inscription* : "The Rev. W. Birch, with the Author's compliments," and a MS. note to Dr. Birch inside last cover, in the handwriting of Landor, *original boards, uncut*   *Pisis,* 1820

720 Lang (Andrew) XXII Ballades in Blue China, FIRST EDITION, *uncut*   1880

721 Lang (A.) The most pleasant and delectable Tale of the Marriage of Cupid and Psyche, done into English by Wm. Adlington, with a Discourse on the Fable by Andrew Lang, *the Editor's proof sheets, containing numerous corrections throughout, and having the dedicatory Poem to Lang, by R. L. Stevenson, which was suppressed, and never appeared in the published copies*
   David Nutt, 1887

722 Lang (A.) The Library, second edition, LARGE PAPER, *illustrations, buckram, uncut*   *imp. 8vo. Macmillan,* 1892

723 Leech. The Comic English Grammar, 1840—The Comic Latin Grammar, 1840 ; 2 vol. in 1, FIRST EDITIONS, *numerous illustrations by J. Leech, half calf*   *Bentley and Tilt,* 1840

724 Lathy (T. P.) The Angler, a Poem in ten cantos, with proper
Instructions in the Art, rules to choose fishing rods, lines,
hooks, floats, baits, &c. *portrait and engravings in text*, FIRST
EDITION, *one of 25 copies on large and thick paper, morocco extra,
the sides and back impressed with various Angling emblems in
blind and gold (viz. portraits of Walton and Cotton, scenes from
Walton's Angler, fish, angling implements, &c.) by T. Gosden,
g. e. scarce* 1819

725 Légende Celeste : nouvelle histoire de la Vie des Saints, par une
Société de Littérateurs et d'Ecclesiastiques, 2 vol. *illuminated
titles, initials, &c. coloured and illuminated portraits of Saints,
half calf* Paris, 1845

726 Légende Joyeuse (La) ou les cent une Leçons de Lampsaque,
*engraved throughout, frontispiece and vignette, old red morocco,
g. e.* Londres, chez Pynne, 1749

727 Leiningen-Westerburg (Karl Emich, Count zu) German book-
plates, an Illustrated Handbook of German and Austrian
Ex-libris, *tall Japanese vellum paper, one of 75 copies, uncut* 1901

728 Le Paysan Parvenu, or the Fortunate Peasant, *old calf*, 1735—
Des Ballets Anciens et Modernes selon les règles du Théâtre,
diagrams, old calf, Paris, 1682 ; and another (3)

729 Les Epistres de S. Paul : les Epistres canoniques, l'Apocalypse
["Mons" New Test. FIRST EDITION], *old French blue morocco,
gold-line borders, branches and fleurons forming diamond-shaped
compartments, morocco joints, g. e.*
Amst. Dan. Elzevir à Mons, 1667
*** Admirable example ; probably the work of Padeloup.

730 Lever (Charles) Charles O'Malley, edited by Harry Lorrequer,
FIRST EDITION, 2 vol. *illustrations by Phiz, half bound*
Dublin, 1841

731 Lever (C.) Charles O'Malley, The Irish Dragoon, Edited by Harry
Lorrequer, 2 vol. FIRST EDITION, *illustrations by Phiz, clean
copy, calf gilt, m. e.* ib. 1841

732 Lever (C.) Diary and Notes of Horace Templeton, Esq. 2 vol.
second edition, *clean copy, in the original cloth, uncut, very
scarce* 1849

733 Lever (C.) The Dodd Family Abroad, FIRST EDITION, *fine copy in
the original parts, illustrations by Phiz, in the original wrappers*
1854

734 Lever (C.) Tom Burke of "Ours," 2 vol. FIRST EDITION, *numerous
illustrations by Phiz, clean copy, in original cloth, uncut*
Dublin, W. Curry, n. d.

735 LILFORD (LORD) COLOURED FIGURES OF THE BIRDS OF THE
BRITISH ISLANDS, FIRST EDITION *throughout*, complete in 36
parts, *portrait of Lord Lilford, and numerous beautifully coloured
plates*, with Descriptive Text, *original wrappers* 1885-1897

736 [Linton (W. J.)] Famine, a Masque, design on the first page by
the author, *presentation copy to Wm. Morris, with inscription,
wrappers, privately printed* (1890)—MAGNÚSSON (E.) Dr.
Gudbrand Vigfusson's Idea of an Icelandic New Testament
Translation of the Gospel of St. Matthew (1540), *presentation
inscription from author to Wm. Morris, Cambridge*, 1879—
Scots Poems and Ballads, by J. WILSON MCLAREN, *half
vellum, also presentation copy to Morris, Edinb.* 1892 (3)

737   Little Hydrogen, or the Devil on Two Sticks in London, 12 *plates by Williams, clean copy, half calf gilt*   Stockdale, 1819

738   Lloyd (Charles, *friend of Charles Lamb*) The Duke d'Ormond, a Tragedy ; and Beritola, a Tale (in verse), FIRST EDITION, *original boards, uncut, very scarce*   1822

739   London and Paris (1798-1806), *with numerous satirical and humorous coloured plates, calf and boards*   (9)

740   Longfellow (Henry Wadsworth) The Seaside and the Fireside, FIRST EDITION, *four leaves stained, original cloth, uncut*
                                                                  Boston, 1850

741   Longus.   Les Amours Pastorales de Daphnis et de Chloe, 1718, *a complete set of the plates, with the title, after designs by Philip d'Orleans, by Audran, including the "Petits Pieds," uncut, sewed*
                                                                  (30)

742   LOVELACE (R.) and DAVIES (J.) Letters of Affaires, Love and Courtship, Written to several Persons of Honour and Quality, by the Exquisite Pen of Monsieur de Voiture, a Member of the Famous French Academy, established at Paris by Cardinall de Richelieu, *portrait, original sheep*   1657
      ₊ This is not only an exceedingly rare volume, but has a peculiar interest as presenting, beneath the fine portrait of Voiture, eight lines by Lovelace which are not found in his *Lucasta*, and are hitherto unknown, having been unseen by Mr. Hazlitt when he produced his new edition of Lovelace in 1864. These *inedited verses* show that Voiture was a favourite author of Lovelace, as he was of so many readers of those times. The translation is a perfectly distinct one from that mentioned by Lowndes, who evidently never saw a copy of the above volume.

743   Lover (Samuel) Handy Andy : a Tale of Irish Life, FIRST EDITION, 24 *plates by the author, clean copy in the original gilt cloth, uncut*   1845

744   Mackay (Charles) Legends of the Isles, and other Poems, FIRST EDITION, *clean copy in original cloth, uncut*   1845
      ₊ Presentation copy with autograph inscription on half-title : " To the Chevalier de Chatelain from the Author," with his ex-libris.

745   McLeod (J.) Voyage of H.M.S. " Alceste " along the Coast of Corea to the Island of Lewchew ; with account of her shipwreck, *portrait, and coloured plates, green morocco extra, gold borders on the sides, with elegant large fan-fare corners, deep gilt joints, watered silk linings, g. e.*   J. Murray, 1818

746   Manuscript.   La Pratique du Monde, ou le Miroir Universel, exactement recueilly et augmentée par Godens Bouck, MS. in French, on 86 leaves, 12mo, *in contemporary brown morocco, with the full title in large gold letters on side, interspersed with fleurs-de-lis*   *circa* 1680

747   Marguerite de Valois.   L'Heptameron des Nouvelles de tres illustre et tres excellente Princess Marguerite de Valois, Royne de Navarre, *beautiful copy, blue morocco super extra, g. e. by Lortic*   1560
      ₊ The excessively rare third edition. The first edition was published in 1559, and the second in 1560.

748 Marmontel (M.) Silvain, Comédie, en un acte, mêlée d'ariettes. La Musique est de M. Grétry, FIRST EDITION, *very scarce*
Paris, 1770

749 Marryat (Captain) Masterman Ready, FIRST EDITION, *illustrations, original cloth* 1841

750 Masks. A Collection of 39 very fine Line Engravings of Masks, *numbered 1-38 and 1 unnumbered, bound in a vol. old calf* 17—

751 Mason (J. Monck) Comments on the Plays of Beaumont and Fletcher, with an Appendix, 1798—Comments on the several Editions of Shakespeare's Plays, *Dublin*, 1807 ; *uncut* (2)

752 Matrimonial Preceptor (The) ; *engraved title and frontispiece, old calf,* 1759—An Essay on the Art of Ingeniously Tormenting ; with proper Rules for exercising of that pleasant art, *frontispiece, old calf* 2 *vol.*

753 Mayhew (A.) Paved with Gold, or, The Romance and Reality of the London Streets, FIRST EDITION, *illustrations by Phiz, clean copy in original gilt cloth, uncut* 1858

754 Melancthon (P.) Examen eorum qui audivntur ante ritum publicae ordinationis, qua commendatur eis ministerium Evangelii, *woodcut portrait on title, limp parchment cover*
Witebergae, L. Schwenck, 1558

755 Mellon (Harriet, Actress, afterwards Mrs. Coutts) Mr. Percy Wyndham's Strictures on an Impostor, and Old Actress, formerly Bet the Pt Girl, alias the Banker's Sham Widow, &c. *cuts of hatchments (pages 51 to 145 text perfect), unbound,* RARE, *having been suppressed*
Sold by W. B. Turner, 28 Litchfield Street, Newport Market, n. d.
(*about* 1822)

756 MEREDITH (GEORGE) POEMS, The extremely rare FIRST EDITION, with the slip of Errata, *autograph of George Meredith on title, original cloth* *J. W. Parker & Son, n. d.* (1851)

757 Meredith (George) Modern Love : and Poems of the English Roadside, with Poems and Ballads, FIRST EDITION, *original cloth, uncut* 1862

758 METASTASIO. Opere del Signor Abate Pietro Metastasio. Tomo Primo. In Parigi, Presso la Vedova Herissant, nella Via Nuova di Nostra - Donna, alla Croce d'oro M.DCC.LXXX (1780). Tomo Duodecimo, M.DCC.LXXXII (1782). *Portrait, by Steiner engraved by Gaucher, and 35 plates by Cipriani, Cochin, Martini & Moreau, engraved by Bartolozzi, Carmona, Delvaux, Duclos, Leveau, Martini, St. Aubin, &c.* 12 vol. A BEAUTIFUL COPY, *in old French red morocco, full gilt backs, gilt on marbled leaves* 1780-82

*** " Édition *la plus belle* et la plus complete qui eût paru jusqu' alors de ce poëte jadis fort célèbre."—*Cohen.*

759 Milnes (R. Monckton : Lord Houghton) Memorials of a Residence on the Continent, and Historical Poems ; *the Original Proof Sheets of the First Edition, with corrections in the autograph of the author on almost every page ; half morocco*
1838

760   Milnes (R. Monckton : Lord Houghton) Palm Leaves, FIRST
        EDITION, 2 vol. *calf gilt, Moxon*, 1844—Poems, Legendary
        and Historical, *Moxon*, 1844   (3)
      ₊ Both the above are presentation copies with autograph
        inscriptions.

761   MOLIÈRE (J. B. P.) LES FACHEUX, Comédie, représentée sur le
        Théâtre du Palais Royal, FIRST EDITION, *unbound*
                                          Paris, Gabriel Quinet, 1662

762   MOLIÈRE (J. B. P.) L'ESTOURDY : ou les Contre-Temps, Comedie,
        représentée sur le Théatre du Palais Royal, FIRST EDITION,
        unbound, rare   *ib.* 1663

763   Molière (J. B. P.) Dom Garcie de Navarre, ou le Prince Jaloux,
        Comédie (forms a portion of a collection of the works), *unbound*
                                                                 n. d.

764   Montaigne. Essays, done into English by John Florio, 1615,
        edited, with Introduction, by George Saintsbury (the Tudor
        Translations edited by W. E. Henley), *uncut*   1892

765   Montesquieu (C. S.) Le Temple de Gnide, *engraved throughout
        and illustrated with frontispiece, engraved title, and the series of
        9 beautifully engraved plates by Le Mire, after Eisen, in the
        earliest state, proofs before the letters, and before the numbers, 4 of
        the plates (all that were so issued) being in the excessively rare
        "découverte" state, full blue polished morocco, by Chambolle-Duru*
                                          roy. 8vo. Paris, 1772

766   Moore (Tom) Catalogue of his Books, Music and Engraved Por-
        traits, sold by Auction   1874

767   More (Henry) Philosophicall Poems, FIRST EDITION, *calf*
                                          Cambridge, 1647
            ₊ With the rare leaf of " Errata."

768   More (Sir Thos.) The Debellacyon of Salem and Bizance, the
        Second Part, 𝔟𝔩𝔞𝔠𝔨 𝔩𝔢𝔱𝔱𝔢𝔯, *fine large copy, unbound, quite com-
        plete, issued without separate title, and with the two leaves of
        errata*   *Printed by W. Rastell in Flete Strete*, 1533

769   Morris (Sir Lewis) The Epic of Hades, FIRST EDITION, *original
        cloth*   *H. S. King*, 1876

770   [Morris (W.)] The Oxford and Cambridge Magazine for 1856,
        conducted by Members of the Two Universities, *half bound,
        r. e. (some MS. notes)*   *Bell & Daldy*, 1856
      ₊ Contains the earliest writings of William Morris, also contri-
        butions by Burne-Jones, D. G. Rossetti, and others.

771   Morris (William) The Life and Death of Jason, FIRST EDITION,
        post 8vo, clean, in original cloth   1869
      ₊ Presentation copy, with inscription in Morris's autograph,
        " G. P. Boyce, from his friend the Author."

772   Morris. A King's Lesson, *original wrapper*, 1891—The Tables
        Turned, or Nupkins Awakened, *a few leaves ink-stained, original
        wrapper*, 1887   (2)

773   Morris. Alfred Linnell, killed in Trafalgar Square, Nov. 20,
        1887, a Death Song, *with a memorial design by Walter Crane,
        n. d.*—Monopoly, or How Labour is Robbed, 1890—Chants
        for Socialists, the Day is Coming, *n. d.*   (3)

774 Morris. Advertisements of the Kelmscott Press Publications,
June, August and December, 1894, July and November, 1895,
June and October, 1896, Feb. and November, 1897—Order
Forms (18)

775 Morris. Notice relating to "Laudes Beatæ Mariæ Virginis," *two
copies, Dec.* 1896—The Deaconess Institution for the Diocese
of Rochester, Associate's Card, *with woodcut border and initial,
printed at the Kelmscott Press for Wm. Morris's sister (Miss
Morris)*—Notice on "An American Memorial to Keats"—
L. C. C. Technical Education Board Certificate, *with woodcut
border, printed at the Kelmscott Press* (5)

776 Morris. Three Sheets of Original Ornamental Designs, Scroll-
Work, &c. by William Morris

777 Morris. First Annual Waysgoose of the Kelmscott Press, held
at the Royal Stag Hotel, Datchet, Sept. 5th, 1892, W. Morris,
Chairman, Menu and Programme, *printed at the Kelmscott Press*
—Hammersmith Branch, Socialist League, MS. Programme
of the Evening Entertainment (2)

778 Morris. Some Thoughts on the Ornamented MSS. of the Middle
Ages, Manuscript (7 *pp.*) in the handwriting of William
Morris *folio*

779 Morris. Five Sheets of Manuscript Matter (*some of which has
probably never been printed*) in the handwriting of William
Morris *folio*

780 Morris. The God of the Poor, originally published in the
Fortnightly Review, *in the original wrapper* *n. d.*

781 Moulin (P.) Theophilus, or Love Divine, translated by R. Goring
(*stained*), *calf, richly tooled back and sides, g. e. S. Macham,* 1612
—Rous (F.) The Mysticall Marriage (*wants pp.* 61-2), *calf,*
1631—Epicteti Enchiridion made English in a Poetical Paraphrase by E. Walker (*corner off p.* 91), *frontispiece, original calf,*
1701 ; &c. *4 vol.*

782 New Musical Charmer, being a Select Collection of the most
approved Modern Songs, *frontispiece, calf gilt,* 32mo, *Glasgow,*
1800—Defoe (D.) Life and Surprising Adventures of Robinson Crusoe, *woodcuts, old calf, n. d.* (17—)—Browne (Sir T.)
Tracts, *calf gilt,* 1822 (3)

783 Newton (Isaac) Sir Isaac Newton's Mathematick Philosophy, with
Dr. Halley's Account of Comets, edited by William Whiston,
diagrams *Senex & Taylor,* 1716

784 Northcote (J.) One Hundred Fables, Original and Selected, *portraits and numerous woodcuts (first series), original cloth,* 1829—
Vues des plus beaux Palais, Monuments et Eglises de Paris,
&c. 60 *plates by Couché fils, original boards, uncut, n. d.*—A
Booke of Christmas Carols, *illuminated from ancient manuscript
in the British Museum, original boards, g. e. Cundall,* 1846 ; and
others (5)

785 Oakley (Benjamin) Selections from Shakespeare, FIRST EDITION,
original boards, uncut 1828
  *** Presentation copy from the editor (Benjamin Oakley) to John
Bannister (the Shakespearean actor), with inscription in the
editor's autograph upon the title-page.

786   Officium Beatæ Mariæ Virginis, cum Calendario, an English
      Manuscript, *written in large* **gothic characters** *on 150 leaves of
      vellum, 17 lines to the full page, 10 finely illuminated borders,
      with capitals, composed of flowers, grylls, grotesques surrounding
      the entire page, and about 140 large illuminated capitals, with
      floral pendants, numerous initials and finials, calf, gilt sides
      (wants the first leaf of the Calendar)*   Sæc. XIV

   *** A valuable Early English Manuscript. It is of the use
      of Sarum. Among the names of the Saints in the Calendar
      are those of St. Cuthbert, St. Dunstan, St. Augustin, St.
      Kenelm, St. Thomas of Hereford, the latter a very unusual
      name in manuscripts. Towards the end of the volume will be
      found an Indulgence in English for 40 days.

787   Oriental Manuscript. A richly painted and illuminated
      decorated Manuscript, partly in Arabic and partly in
      Persian, *measuring 2 ft. 11 in. by 1 ft. 6½ in.* being the original
      Contract of Marriage between "The Nawab Ginat Mahil the
      Begum Sohelah the daughter of Rajah Nawab of exalted
      dignity" and "Sarazedin Mohammed Bahadur Shah the Ghazi
      King .. the Son of the late Mohammed Akbar Shah Padi-
      shah ; . in consideration of a dowry of the Sum of 15 Lakhs
      of Rupees ... The Knot of Marriage (has been) tied according
      to firm and lawful Wedlock, and it has taken place according
      to the best known custom and rule, and in the regular way of
      certainty and security ;" &c. with the Seals of the Bride and
      Bridegroom and Officials, *framed and glazed*

   *** The Marriage was celebrated " on the Night of the 23rd of
      Ranzan in the Year 1256 of the Prophet." The Empress to
      whom the MS. relates is said to have been one of the chief
      instigators of the Indian Mutiny. The MS. forms a portion
      of loot taken from the Palace of Delhi in the sack of the
      Palace in 1857, and was in the possession of Major Wreford the
      Prize Master. [See translation of the Document annexed].

788   Old Ballads, Historical and Narrative, collected from rare copies
      and MSS. by Thomas Evans, 4 vol. Best edition, *russia, gold
      line borders by Riviere, fine copy*   1810

789   Omar Kheyyam. The Quatrains of Omar Kheyyam of Nisha-
      pour, now first completely done into English verse, with an
      Introduction, &c. by John Payne, *printed for the Villon Society,
      for private circulation only, parchment, uncut, t. e. g.*   1898

790   Ovid. Metamorphoseon, *italic letter*, 187 *curious cuts, old calf gilt,
      covered with limp roan, Parisiis*, 1587 ; and another   (2)

791   Oxford (The) and Cambridge Magazine for 1856, conducted by
      Members of the Two Universities, *green morocco, by Miss
      Katherine Adams*
                                                                  1856
   *** This magazine was projected by William Morris, Sir E. Burne-
      Jones and R. W. Dixon, afterwards Canon Dixon, and the editor
      was W. Talfourd. It includes some of the earliest contribu-
      tions of W. Morris, D. G. Rossetti, W. Talfourd, W. Lushing-
      ton, &c.

792   Petrarch. Sonetti, Canzoni, e Triomphi con la Spositione di Bernardino D. da Lucca (*portion of the text on 3 ll. erased*), *woodcut title containing portraits, and cuts to the Triomphi, fine contemporary binding of claret morocco, both covers elaborately tooled in gold, an interlaced fillet painted light blue, sprigs of oak, pomegranates, flies and arabesques frequently introduced, central ovals painted in various shades, a remarkable Venetian binding* Vinegia, Pietro et Gionmaria Fratelli di Nicolini da Sabio, 1549

793   Phædri Fabularum, *curious copper-plates, none of which are mutilated, vellum,* 1667—Flores sev Formvlæ Loqvendi, ex P. Terentii Comœdiis excerpta, *Antv. Plantin.* 1597 ; and three others (5)

794   Phillips (Stephen) Poems, FIRST EDITION, *original cloth, uncut* 1898

795   Phillips (S.) Marpessa, FIRST EDITION, *illustrated by P. Connard, original cloth, uncut, t. e. g.*   1900

796   Phillips (S.) Herod, a Tragedy, FIRST EDITION, *in the original cloth, uncut*   1901

797   Phillips (S.) Ulysses : a Drama, in a Prologue and three Acts, FIRST EDITION, *in the original cloth, uncut, t. e. g.*   1902

798   Phillips (S.) Ulysses, another copy of the FIRST EDITION (*as preceding*)   1902

799   Phillips (S.) Ulysses, a Drama, in a Prologue and three Acts, FIRST EDITION, *original cloth, uncut, t. e. g.*   1902

800   Pike (Major Z. M.) Account of the Expeditions to the Sources of the Mississippi, and through the Western Parts of Louisiana, *portrait, maps and charts, original calf*   Philadelphia, 1810

801   Pinkerton (J.) Rimes (Melodies, Odes, Sonnets, &c.) FIRST EDITION, *fine clean copy, in the original paper covers, uncut,* 1781 (*Lowndes gives the date as* 1782)—The Works of the Caledonian Bards, translated from the Gaelic, vol. I (*all published ?*), *very clean in original wrapper, uncut, Edinb.* 1778   2 vol.

802   Playford (J. M.) A Brief Introduction to the Skill of Musick... To which is added the Art of Descant, by Dr. Thomas Campion, with Annotations thereon by Mr. Chr. Simpson (*wants pp. 49-50*), *portrait with verses beneath, original sheepskin*   1664

803   Playing Cards. A complete Pack of 52 engraved Geographical Playing Cards, with the extra card "Explanation of these cards," in all 53, *in beautiful condition*   circa 1670

    *** This pack consists of maps of the counties of England, with descriptions ; the court cards contain portraits, which, with the suits, are printed in colours. Complete sets are excessively rare.

804   Poetical Magazine, 4 vol. *original impressions of the beautifully coloured plates by Rowlandson, illustrating the* "Tour of Dr. Syntax in search of the Picturesque," *which appeared first in this serial under the title of the* "Schoolmaster," *fine copy in the original boards, uncut, with the paper labels, enclosed in 4 cases, book form*   R. Ackermann, 1809-11

805   Poggius, Asinus Luciani, &c. MANUSCRIPT *on 5 leaves of paper, in Italian characters,* SÆC. XV—Lincolnshire Document, *on vellum,* dated 1628   (2)

806   [Pope (Alexander)] An Essay on Man in Epistles to a Friend (4
      parts), *old calf, rare*   *Dublin, printed by S. Powell, 1733*
      *** Interleaved throughout, with Pope's later corrections in
      manuscript.

807   Pope (A.) Essay on Man addressed to a Friend, *Dublin, 1733*—
      The Man of Honour, to which is added The Curious Females,
      a Tale, 1737—Jones (Henry) Poems on Several Occasions,
      Dublin, 1735-6 (*unknown to Lowndes*)—Pope (A.) Of the
      Character of Women, an Epistle to a Lady, *ib. 1735*—The
      Weekly Amusement : or Universal Magazine, no. 1, *ib. 1735*
      —Are these Things so ? *ib. 1740*—Yes, they are, *ib. 1740*—
      The Impertinent, or a Visit to the Court, a Satyr, *ib. 1737*—
      Gardiner (Mat.) The Sharpers, a Ballad Opera, *ib. 1740*—A
      Modest Inquiry addressed to the Bishop of C——c, *no place
      or name, 1738*—The Preceptor, or the Loves of Abelard and
      Heloise, *ib. 1740*—A Supplement to 1738, not by Mr. Pope,
      Dublin, 1738 ; and others, *half bound, uncut*   *in 1 vol.*
         *** An extremely rare Collection.

808   Pope (A.) Letters to a Lady (Miss Martha Blount) never before
      published, FIRST EDITION, *original wrapper, uncut, t. e. g. rare*
      (*Col. Grant's copy produced £5 5s*)   *J. Dodsley, 1769*

809   [Porson (R.)] Eloisa en Déshabile, being a Parody on Mr. Pope's
      celebrated Epistle of that Young Lady to Abelard, by a late
      celebrated Greek Professor, *half bound, one of 12 copies
                                               privately printed, n. d.*

810   Pragmatica Sanctio sive decreta Basiliensia, Glosata per Cosman
      Guymier, 𝔤𝔬𝔱𝔥𝔦𝔠 𝔩𝔢𝔱𝔱𝔢𝔯, *commences on b* 1, FIRST EDITION, *printed
      by Pigouchet and undescribed by Brunet*
                              Paris. P. Pigouchet, 30 Apl. 1502

811   Prayers. A volume containing 100 leaves of writing paper, some
      of the leaves containing Prayers neatly written in an 18th
      century hand ; 3 copper-plates inserted, and Communion
      Service from Book of Common Prayer, *old red morocco, deli-
      cately gold-tooled dentelle borders, large centre ornament, metal
      clasp and fittings complete, Ludford book-plate*   Sæc. XVIII

812   Primavera : Poems by Four Authors [Stephen Phillips, L. Bin-
      yon, M. Ghose, and A. S. Cripps], *original wrapper, uncut*
                              Oxford, B. H. Blackwell, 1890

813   Primavera ; another copy, *as the preceding*   *ib. 1890*

814   Proceedings of the Society of Biblical Archæology, from the com-
      mencement in 1878 to Dec. 1901, with Indexes and the Ap-
      pendix, 23 vol. *in 122 parts, numerous plates and facsimiles, un-
      cut*
                                                      1879-1901

815   Procter (J. J.) Voices of the Night ; and other Poems, FIRST
      EDITION, *presentation copy with autograph inscription on fly-leaf :
      " Mary Snowball with best love, J. J. Procter," original cloth
      Montreal, printed and published by John Lovell, 1861*

816   PSALMS (The) of David, translated from the Vulgar, *original calf*
                                    (*St. Germains*), 1700

    **** FIRST EDITION. This prose version, now become very rare,
was executed by J. Caryl, of West Grinstead in Sussex, not
improbably a son of the Rev. Joseph Caryll, preacher at
Lincoln's Inn in the time of the Civil War. Caryl produced,
in 1667, a play called *The English Princess, or, the Death of
Richard the Third,* which Pepys describes as "a most sad
melancholy play, but pretty good." It was republished in
1674 ; but we hear nothing further of the author till we find
him an adherent of the Old Pretender, who created him Lord
Dartford. He seems to have been resident with his patron
at St. Germains, *where he probably devoted part of his time to
the execution of this work, and where he printed it.* The typography betrays on the part of the printer a deficiency of fonts,
and on that of the writer considerable negligence in reading
the proofs. Caryll explains that "In some places the Latin
text of the Psalms too rigorously translated would yeald a
scarce *untelligible* sense." He states that the faults were too
many to be all spy'd and amended ; but until a better version
is offered, "this Translater will thinк (*sic*) himself *very* happy,
and his pains well bestow'd." Such language appears almost to
intimate an ignorance of the barely numerable translations
already in existence.

817   Quarles (F.) Enchiridion, containing Institutions, Divine, Moral,
            portrait, old calf, g. e. 1681—Wesley (S.) History of the New
            Testament attempted in Verse, *plates by J. Sturt, old calf, r. e.*
            1701—Memoirs of the Life of the Rev. T. Halyburton, with
            an Epistle by I. Watts, *half calf,* 1718 ; and another   (4)

818   Quarles (F.) Boanerges and Barnabas, Judgment and Mercy, or
            Wine and Oil for Wounded and Afflicted Souls, *brilliant im-
            pression of the scarce portrait, fine copy in the original calf*   1690

819   Rabaut (M. J. P.) Almanach Historique de la Révolution Fran-
            çoise pour l'année 1792, *plates by Moreau, calf gilt, m. e.*
                                        Paris, Didot l'Ainé

820   Racine (R.) Œuvres, avec des Commentaires par J. L. Geoffroy,
            7 vol. *portraits, plates and vignettes, after Garnier, by Choffard,
            Halbon, Masquelier et Masquelier Jeune, half russia, contents
            lettered, with ex-libris in each vol*   *Paris, Le Normand,* 1808

    **** JOHN PHILIP KEMBLE'S COPY, with his arms surrounded by
            his name in gold, on leather impressed on both sides of each
            volume.

821   Radcliffe (F. P. Delmé) The Noble Science : a few general Ideas
            on Fox-Hunting, FIRST EDITION, *numerous illustrations, from
            original designs, fine copy in the original cloth, g. e.*
                                        R. Akermann, 1839

822   Railroadiana. A New History of England, Descriptive of the
            Railroads, "London and Birmingham Railway," *folding map
            in pocket, coloured folding frontispiece, and other plates, original
            pictorial cloth*   *Simpkin & Marshall,* 1838

823   Rainolds (Dr. J.) An Excellent Oration, very usefull for all such as affect the Study of Logick, and Philosophie, and admire profane Learning, translated out of the Latin by J. L(eycester), Schoolmaster, *title very slightly defective, original calf*
T. Harper for T. Slater and W. Aderton, 1638

    *** A very rare little volume, interspersed with couplets in verse, unknown to Lowndes, Hazlitt and other bibliographers. There is no copy in the British Museum.

824   Rawlinson (G.) The Sixth Great Oriental Monarchy, *maps and plans* 1873

825   Ray (J.) Complete Collection of English Proverbs, *calf gilt,* 1817 —Drayton (J. B.) Poems, *calf gilt,* 1813—Walford (Thomas) The Scientific Tourist through England, Wales and Scotland, *plates,* 3 vol. *calf gilt,* 1818 ; and others (7)

826   Recueil de Costumes Suisses, Allemands, Espagnols, &c. 135 *coloured plates, old tree-calf gilt*   *Paris, Martinet, n. d.*

827   Recueil (Nouveau) des plus belles Chansons et Airs de Cour de ce temps, *à Paris, chez* ANTOINE DE RAFFLÉ—Recueil Curieux des plus beaux Airs de Cour et Chansons Cachiques de le temps, *à Paris, chez A. R. rue de Petit Pont au Chaudron,* ORIGINAL MANUSCRIPT, *finely written (114 ll. 6 by 4 in.) with 2 private engravings in front of the vol. having blank spaces in centre, on one of which is written the above title ; and on the other, man and woman dancing round a tree with Death ; in the centre :* "Chantez mes Jens, dansez, joüez, faites l'amour, dit la Mort, mais pensez, que je viens à mon tour," *vellum*   *sm. 8vo.* 1672

828   Reid (Capt. Mayne) The Headless Horseman, a strange Tale of Texas, 2 vol. FIRST EDITION, *with the substituted titles, clean copy in original cloth*   *n. d.*

    *** Presentation copy, with the author's autograph inscription on fly-leaf : "Benjamin Moran, Esq. U.S. Secretary, from his Sincere Friend Mayne Reid, Dec. 1, 1866."

829   Restif de la Bretonne. Monument du Costume Physique et Moral du fin du dix-huitième Siècle, ou Tableau de la Vie, 2 vol. *plates, fine clean copy, original boards, uncut Londres, C. Dilly,* 1790

830   [Ritson (Joseph)] Remarks critical and illustrative of the text and Notes of the last edition of Shakespeare, *calf* 1783

    *** These remarks apply to Mr. Steevens' edition in 1778. A copy, with MS. notes by Tooke, sold for £7 2s. 6d.

831   Ritson (Joseph) The Quip Modest ; a few words by way of supplement to Remarks, critical and illustrative, on the Text and Notes of the Last Edition of Shakespeare ; occasioned by a republication of that edition, revised and augmented by the editor of "Dodsley's Old Plays," *half bound, uncut* 1788

    *** This copy of "Quip Modest" contains the remarkable note in the preface, p. vii, in which Ritson calls one of the editors (George Steevens) an infamous scoundrel, and predicts his coming to the gallows. This note was afterwards suppressed, and copies of the tract issued with a new preface, and the note altered in a milder form, but still in Ritson's sarcastic style.

832   Rochester. Works of the Earls of Rochester, Roscomon, and
        Dorset, &c. with Memoirs, 2 vol. in 1, including the "Cabinet
        of Love," *portraits and plates, original calf*   1752
833   Rochester. Works; another edition, including the "Cabinet of
        Love," 2 vol. in 1, *portraits and plates, original sheep*   *n. d.*
834   Rogers (S.) Italy: a Poem, FIRST EDITION, *with the beautiful
        vignettes by Turner and Stothard, many leaves stained, calf, g. e.*
                                                                   1830
835   Roscoe (Wm.) Lives of Leo X and Lorenzo de Medici, revised
        by his Son, *portraits,* 3 vol. *calf extra, g. e. by F. Bedford*
                                                          Bohn, 1846

*The following 21 Books were returned from the Sale of the Library of the
late Lieut-Col. E. G. Hibbert, and will be sold not subject to return.*

SIZES MIXED.

836   [Beckford (Wm.)] Vathek, THE EXTREMELY RARE ORIGINAL
        LAUSANNE EDITION, *title within border with a fleuron (pp.* 175-6
        *very slightly defective), crushed red morocco, plain, inside dentelles,
        g. e. (Janseniste) by F. Bedford*
                    sm. 8vo.   Lausanne chez Isaac Hignon and Co. 1787
837   BERTANDUS PETRAGORICUS (JOANNES) ENCOMIUM TRIUM MARI-
        ANUM cum earundem cultus defensione adversus Lutheranos;
        Solemnique Missa et Officio Canonico, &c.; HORARUM ET
        MISSALE EARUNDEM OFFICIUM, &c. **lit. goth.** *and roman, with
        fine woodcuts, " Prelum Ascensianum " on title and last leaf, wood-
        cut borders and large and small woodcuts, some with the Lorraine
        Cross, the mark of Geoffrey Tory, the three parts, in 1 vol., wants
        2 ll. in the Second Part without the woodcut borders, crushed red
        morocco gilt, antique style, by F. Bedford*
                           sm. 4to.   Paris. J. B. Ascensius, 1529
    *** A VERY FINE AND LARGE COPY (? LARGE PAPER) of this ex-
        ceedingly rare volume, remarkable for its woodcut borders
        and full-page woodcuts as used by Geoffrey Tory in his Books
        of Hours. EXTREMELY RARE.
838   Butler (Sam.) Hudibras, the First Part, the spurious first edition,
        rose and thistle vignette on title (pp. 53-4 *slightly defective), mottled
        calf extra, inside dentelles, g. e. by Riviere*
                           12mo.   Printed in the year 1663
839   [CAXTON (WILLIAM)] THE CRONYCLE OF ENGLANDE WITH THE
        FRUYTE OF TYMES; with the Descrypcion of Englonde, newly
        imprynted, **black letter,** *woodcut title and numerous cuts in the
        text (the title in facsimile), brown morocco extra, antique style, g. e.
        by F. Bedford,* AN EXCELLENT COPY OF A VERY RARE EDITION
                *sm. folio.   emprynted in Powlys Chyrche Yarde at the West
                dore of Powlys, besyde my larde of Londons Palays by me*
                    JULIAN NOTARY *in the yere* MCCCCCXV (1515)
840   Charles II. Boscobel; or the History of his Sacred Majesties
        most miraculous preservation after the Battle of Worcester,
        3 Sept. 1651, *Part I,* ORIGINAL EDITION, 2 *fine portraits, one
        by Hertochs, and plate of the Oaks (mended), crushed crimson
        morocco extra, ornamental back end frame sides, g. e. by F. Bedford,*
        FINE COPY   *12mo.   H. Seile,* 1660

841 [Collier (J.)] "*Tim Bobbin.*" A View of the Lancashire Dialect
    by way of Dialogue ; containing the Adventures and Misfor-
    tunes of a Lancashire Clown, *with the original portrait (a re-
    impression inserted) and 7 plates, calf, gilt and gauffred edges*
    sm. 8vo. *Printed for the Author and Mr. Haslingden,*
    Bookseller in Manchester, 1775

842 Costumes Français depuis Clovis jusqu'au nos Jours, avec un
    Texte historique et descriptif, publiés par A. Miflies, 640 *fine
    coloured plates of costume (No.* 109 *missing*), 4 vol. *green morocco
    extra, g. e.* 8vo. *Paris,* 1835-39

843 [Defoe (D.)] Life and Adventures of Mrs. Christian Davies, com-
    monly call'd Mother Ross, a Foot Soldier under King William,
    &c. FIRST EDITION (*wants frontispiece*), *sprinkled calf extra, g. e.*
    8vo. *R. Montague,* 1740

844 [Defoe (D.)] Memoirs of an English Officer who served in the
    Dutch War in 1672 to the Peace of Utrecht in 1713, by Capt.
    George Carleton, FIRST EDITION, LARGE PAPER (*few letters
    missing from the title*), *straight grained red morocco extra, inlaid
    back and borders, g. e. (B. M. Pickering*), FINE COPY, RARE
    8vo. *E. Symon,* 1728

845 DORAT (C. J.) FABLES NOUVELLES, PREMIÈRE ÉDITION (second
    issue), LARGE FRENCH PAPER *of a bluish tint (9 in.)* 2 *frontis-
    pieces,* 99 *vignettes and* 99 *tail-pieces after Marillier by various
    engravers, portrait of Dorat after Denon by St. Aubin, inserted,*
    VERY BRILLIANT EARLY IMPRESSIONS, 2 vol. in 1, *crushed yel-
    low morocco super extra, full gilt floreate back, broad and rich orna-
    mental scroll borders (Derome style), inside dentelles, cerise silk
    linings, edges gilt on the rough, by F. Bedford,* A VERY FINE
    COPY
    roy. 8vo. *La Haye et se trouve à Paris, chez Delalain,* 1773

846 Leicester (Robert Dudley Earl of). Leicester's Commonwealth,
    by Robert Parsons, Jesuite : whereunto is added Leicester's
    Ghost, *brilliant impression of the fine head by W Marshall (lower
    margin of pp.* 85-6 *torn away), original calf*
    12mo. *Printed Anno Dom.* 1641

847 Le Vayer de Boutigny. Tarsis et Zélie, nouvelle édition, beau-
    coup plus riche, plus correcte et mieux exécutée qu'autres,
    *brilliant impressions of the frontispieces, vignettes and fleurons after
    Eisen, Cochin, Moreau and others,* 3 vol. (*vol. III wants the
    frontispiece ; duplicate of the one to vol. II inserted in its place*)
    bright calf extra, inside dentelles, g. e. by F. Bedford, FINE
    LARGE COPY *with some uncut edges*
    roy. 8vo. *Paris, Musier Fils,* 1784

848 Lewis (M. G.) The Monk, a Romance, the spurious first edition,
    3 vol. *original half binding, uncut*
    sm. 8vo. *Waterford, J. Saunders,* 1796

849 Maxwell (W. H.) History of the Irish Rebellion in 1798, with
    Memoirs of the Union and Emmett's Insurrection in 1803,
    portraits and illustrations by G. Cruikshank (that at p. 154 *re-
    paired), crushed green morocco extra, inside dentelles, t. e. g. rough
    fore and lower edges, by Zaehnsdorf,* FINE COPY
    8vo. *Baily Bros.* 1845

850 Memoirs of Hariette Wilson, written by herself, twenty-fifth
edition, *plates (frontispiece to vol. I loose, and wants half titles to
vol. I and II and titles to III and IV),* 4 vol. *half bound*
12mo. *Stockdale,* 1825

851 MILTON (J.) PARADISE LOST, a Poem in Ten Books, the Author
J. M. FIRST EDITION, *fourth issue with a third title page, with
the argument and printers' advertisement (6 lines), (sig. Nn 2
defective in lower margin), old russia gilt, g. e.*
sm. 4to. *printed and are to be sold by Peter Parker, &c.* 1668

852 MORE (SIR THOS.) A FRUTEFUL AND PLEASAUNT WORKE OF THE
BESTE STATE OF A PUBLIC WEALE AND OF THE NEWE YLE CAL-
LED UTOPIA ; translated into Englyshe by Raphe Robinson at
the procurement of G. Tablowe, citizen and Haberdasher, FIRST
EDITION, black letter *(few letters on title restored in facsimile),
ornamental woodcut initials, brown morocco extra, antique style,
g. e. by F. Bedford*
12mo. *Abr. Vele,* 1551

853 Munchausen (Baron). Baron Munchausen's Narrative of his Mar-
vellous Travels and Campaigns in Russia, etc. FIRST EDITION
(published without plates, and wants catchword to p. 18), *sprinkled
calf extra, g. e. by F. Bedford,* RARE
sm. 8vo. *Oxford, for the Editor,* 1786

854 Pardoe (Julia) Life of Marie de Medicis Queen of France, *portraits,* 3 vol. *(wants pp. v and vi in vol. II), embossed blue cloth,
uncut*
8vo. *Bentley,* 1890

855 Rousseau (J. J.) Emile ou de l'Education, LARGE PAPER, 8 *(only)
of the fine plates after Moreau, by Delvaux,* 4 vol. *old red French
morocco, full gilt floreate backs, ornamental borders, blue watered
silk linings, g. e.* FINE COPY   8vo. *à Londres (Paris, Cazin)* 1781

856 Rowlandson (Thos.) Military Adventures of Johnny Newcombe,
with his Campaign on the Peninsula and in Pall Mall, by an
Officer, second edition, *coloured plates by T. Rowlandson, no.* 3
and 7 missing, half morocco gilt, t. e. g. uncut
8vo. *P. Martin,* 1816

Other Properties.

QUARTO.

857 LOMBARDUS (PETRUS) LIBRI SENTENTIARUM QUATTUOR, MANU-
SCRIPT ON VELLUM (359 *ll.* 10½ *by* 6¾ *in.) written in neat
gothic letters, in double columns,* 39 *lines, with rubrics ; the text
occupies the space of* 5¼ *by* 3 *in. only, surrounded by very wide
blank margins ; written probably by a French scribe, with numerous
contemporary notes in margins ; many small ornamental pen-
letters and marginal decorations, newly bound in oak boards, half
niger morocco, clasps, by D. Cockerell, ex-libris of a cardinal,
dated* 1605, *pasted in cover*
SÆC. XIV
  *_** The following MS. inscription occurs on the first leaf : "*Iste
liber est Beatæ Mariæ Vallis Lucent...communi custodiæ traditus ;
quis que fur fuerit vel Scripturarum hanc raserit anathema sit.
Amen.*"

H 2

858 LONGUS. Longi Pastoralium de Daphniæ et Chloe, Liber
Quattuor. Ex recensione & cum animadversionibus Johan.
Baptistæ Cosparis d'Ansse de Villoison, Regiæ Inscriptionum
Academiæ Paris. Regiæ Lond. nec non & Antiquariæ, Regiæ
Berolinensis, Gotting. Manhem. Upsal. Matrit. Massil. Corton.
Romæ. &c. Societatem Socii. Excudebat Franc. Ambr. Didot
Parisiis, Sumptibus Guill. De Bure natu majoris, Bibliopolæ,
MDCCLXXVIII (1778), LARGE PAPER, *engraved title after Coypel,
by Audran, and the series of engravings after Philippe d'Orleans
(le Régent), by Audran, with borders by Fokké,* 2 vol. A MOST
BEAUTIFUL COPY, *red morocco, the backs richly tooled with a
pastoral figure in each of the panels, g. e.* by DEROME   1778

859 LOVELACE. The Libertie of the Imprisoned Royalist, &c. VERY
FINE LARGE COPY, *half calf*   n. p. or d. *(London,* 1647)
  *** *The only other copy known* is in the British Museum. This
tract contains a short series of poems, of which the authorship is unknown, except that the one which is named above,
and which forms a head-line on sig. A, the volume having
been printed without a title-page, bears every mark of having
proceeded from the pen of Lovelace himself, and of being the
original production, which suggested the "Ode to Althea," in
his *Lucasta,* 1649.

860 Ludlow (Edmund) A Letter from General Ludlow to Dr. Hol-
lingworth, *Amsterdam,* 1692—A Letter from Major-General
Ludlow to Sir E. S. (Edmund Seymour), *ib.* 1691, *name cut
from title, a cut copy*   *in* 1 *vol.*

861 Mantuanus (Baptista) De Vita Beata, Opusculus, *initials painted
sine nota, R. Paffrœt, between* 1500-6
  *** Ascribed by a former owner to Theodore Martens of Alost
(1490-1510).

862 Mantuanus (B.) Carmina de Beata Virgine (Prima Parthenice),
wants last blank leaf, Daventriæ (R. Paffrœt), 1502—Carmina
de Beata Catherina, Secunde Parthenices, opus. *ib.* 1502—
Parthenice Tertia, *ib.* (*circa* 1502) *cut on title and mark at end,
but wants last leaf containing colophon*   *all* 3 *in* 1 *vol.*

863 Marbeck (J.) A Booke of Notes and Common Places, with their
expositions, collected and gathered out of the Workes of
divers singular Writers, **black letter,** *a few leaves slightly
injured by damp, and piece off title, half vellum*   *T. East,* 1581

864 Marguerite de Valois (Reine de Navarre) L'Heptameron remis
en la vray Ordre confus au paravant en la première impression
et dédié à la Princesse Jeanne de Foix (Jeanne d'Albret) par
Claude Gruget, *woodcuts and ornamental initials, title facsimile,
mended fragment of an original title from a later edition inserted;
corner of last leaf mended, otherwise a good copy of a rare edition*
          sm. 4to. *Paris, B. Prevost,* 1559
  *** Second edition of the Heptameron, but the first containing
72 Novels, the edition of 1558 having 67 only.

865 Maxwell (James) Carolanna, that is to say a Poeme in Honour of
Our King Charles James, Queene Anne and Prince Charles,
old morocco extra, gilt leaves   *Imprinted by Edw. All-de* (1619)
  *** Probably the largest and best copy in existence of this rare
volume of poetry.

866 M[ay] (T[homas]) The Heire, a Comedy, as it was acted by the
Company of the Revels, 1620, FIRST EDITION, *calf extra, g. e.*
1633

*** "The demand of the King that Leucothoë shall yield to his
desires, as the sole condition upon which he would spare the
life of her lover, *appears to be borrowed from Shakespeare's
Measure for Measure ;* as the constable and watch who seize
Eugenio seem to have had their language and manners from
those in the same author's *Much Ado About Nothing ;* and the
enmity of the two houses reminds us of *Romeo and Juliet.*"
There was a copy in Halliwell's Sale Catalogue, May, 1856.

867 Meagar (Leonard) The English Gardener; or a Sure Guide to
Young Planters and Gardeners, in three parts, FIRST EDITION,
24 *plates, new mottled calf extra, by Zaehnsdorf*
sm. 4to. P. Parker, 1670

868 Meagar (L.) The English Gardner ; in three parts (another and
later edition), 24 *plates, original calf, good copy*
sm. 4to. J. Rawlins for M. Wotton, 1688

869 Milton (John) Doctrine and Discipline of Divorce, FIRST EDI-
TION, FINE COPY, *calf extra, g. e. by Riviere* 1644

*** The first edition, although the title reads " Now the second
time revised."

870 MILTON (JOHN) PARADISE LOST: a Poem, written in Ten Books,
FIRST EDITION, *and first title page, with the fourth title-page of
the first edition, dated* 1668 ; *and 7 preliminary leaves, which
appeared here for the first time at end of the vol. fine copy in the
original calf Peter Parker,* 1667

871 MILTON (JOHN) PARADISE LOST: a Poem in ten Books, FIRST
EDITION, *seventh title, with the five line address, the Printer to the
Reader, Argument and Errata, very fine tall copy, with the bottom
margins of many leaves, including the whole of the sheets* O *and* T
uncut and in the original rough state, $7\frac{5}{16}$ *by* $5\frac{1}{8}$ *in. russia, with
joints, blind tooled, g. e. by Hering Printed by S. Simmons,* 1669

872 Milton (John) Paradise Lost, FIRST EDITION, *with the seventh title-
page, original calf binding, with many uncut leaves* 1669

873 Milton (John) History of Britaine, *portrait by Faithorne (backed),*
FIRST EDITION, *calf, first three leaves damaged*
sm. 4to. 1670

874 Milton (John) The History of Britain, that part especially now
called England. From the first Traditional Beginning continued to the Norman Conquest ; collected out of the antient
and best authors thereof, *brilliant impression of the portrait by
Faithorne, old calf* 1671

875 Missale Romanum summa revisum diligentia, *printed in double
columns in red and black* 𝔤𝔬𝔱𝔥𝔦𝔠 𝔩𝔢𝔱𝔱𝔢𝔯, *numerous woodcuts, borders
and initial letters and square musical notes, with the Giunta mark
on title, a few leaves damp stained and loose in binding, sold not
subject to return, oak boards covered with leather (no back)*
Venetiis, 1560

876 Montaigne. Essais de Michael Seigneur de Montaigne, FIRST
COMPLETE EDITION, *engraved title-page*, VERY FINE LARGE
COPY, *original calf* *Paris*, 1588

⁎ A full account of Shakespeare's indebtedness to Montaigne is
given by Mr. Hazlitt in his Life of the Poet, pp. 155-164.
This is a most rare edition, Brunet's copy having sold for
3,050 francs.

877 Months (The) of the Year, *a series of twelve very curious old woodcuts, inlaid, some are a little disfigured by names, &c. being written
in (in ink), morocco gilt, g. e.*

878 MULCASTER (RICHARD). POSITIONS wherein those primitive
circumstances be examined, which are necessary for the
training up of children, either for skill in their Booke, or
health in their bodie, FIRST EDITION, *morocco extra, g. e.* 1581

⁎ Mulcaster was ridiculed by SHAKESPEARE under the guise of
" Holofernes " (*Love's Labour Lost*). There was a copy in
Halliwell's Sale Catalogue, 1856. Refer to Mr. Hazlitt's
" Shakespeare," p. 252.

879 Music. BERARDI (D. Angelo) Docvmenti Armonici, *half vellum,
Bologna*, 1687—Bibliotheca Musico Liturgica : a Hand-list of
the Musical and Latin-Liturgical MSS. of the Middle Ages
preserved in the Libraries of Great Britain and Ireland, by
W. H. FRERE, *fascicule I, wrappers*, 1894 (2)

⁎ The music in the Berardi is printed in the old moveable types,
specimens of which are now rare.

880 Music. Haydn's Fifteen Quartettes, 4 parts—Mozart's Seventeen Quartettes, 4 parts—Mozart's Ten Quartettes, 4 parts—
Mozart's Trio, 1 part, *in wrappers* *Leipzig, Peters*

881 Navigation. Linton (Athonie) Newes of the Complement of the
Art of Navigation, and of the mightie Empire of Cataia,
together with the Straits of Anian, *morocco extra, g. e.*
F. Kyngston, 1609

882 Newcastle (Duke of) The Humorous Lovers, a Comedy, *unbound,
with name of " Will. Cavendish," on title* 1677

883 Newcastle (Duke of) The Triumphant Widow, or the Medley of
Humours, *with name of " Will. Cavendish," on title, unbound,*
1677

⁎ Has references to Shakespeare and Ben Jonson at pp. 60-61.

884 Norden (John, *of Hart Hall, Oxford*) Vicissitudo Rerum, an
Elegiacall Poeme, of the interchangeable courses and varietie
of things in this world, *green morocco extra, g. e. (by Charles
Lewis)* 1600

⁎ A singular Poem in 157 stanzas of seven lines each ; upon
change in all things with information of the most miscellaneous kind. It is dedicated to Lord Howard of Effingham, and consists of 24 leaves, the last leaf blank. The only
copy described by Mr. Hazlitt is one in the Bodleian, which,
according to him, consists of 22 leaves only. The Bibliotheca
Anglo-Poetica copy of this rare Elizabethan volume was priced
£12 12s.

885 Norden (John) The Labyrinth of Man's Life, or Vertues Delight
     and Envies opposite, by Jo. Norden, *morocco extra*   1614
     *** Dedicated to the notorious Robert Carr, Earl of Somerset.
     These poems are extremely rare. The British Museum copy
     is very much mutilated. This volume, printed within the
     Shakespearian era, is even rarer than the *Vicissitudo Rerum*.

886 Ovidius. Metamorphoses, with Variorum Notes, *cut on title and
     to each book, title torn and copy poor, wants three leaves of folio xv*
                                         Lugduni, Mareschal, 1519

887 Ovid. Le Metamorfosi ridotte da GIO. AND. DELL' ANGVILLARA
     in ottava rima, *engraved title and* 15 *copperplates, half vellum,*
     Venet. Giunti, 1584—Le Transformationi (di Ovidio) di
     LODOVICO DOLCE, *engraved title and woodcuts, Venetia, G.*
     Giolito, 1553   (2)

888 Pamphlets. Wycherley (Wm.) The Idleness of Business, a Satyr,
     second edition, *B. Bragg*, 1705—Stubbes (Geo.) The Laurel
     and the Olive, *E. Sanger*, 1710—Satire in the Manner of
     Persius by a Person of Quality (John Lord Hervey), *J. Clarke*,
     1739—Imitation of the Sixth Satire of the Second Book of
     Horace, the first part, done in the year 1714, by Dr. Swift,
     &c. *B. Motte, &c.* 1738—The Seven Wise Men, from a correct
     copy, 1704—The Sixteenth Epode of Horace Imitated,
     J. Standen, 1739 ; *all unbound*   *sm. fol.*

889 PENN FAMILY BIBLE. The Holy Bible, *King James's or Authorised
     Version*, with Speed's Genealogies, Downame's Concordance,
     Whole Book of Psalms in metre with Notes (*imperfect*), *old
     calf binding loose*
                   sm. 4to. R. Barker and Assigns of John Bill, 1654
     *** This Bible belonged to the PENNS of BUCKINGHAMSHIRE, a
     branch of the family of William Penn the founder of Penn-
     sylvania. It has the following contemporary entries (thrice
     over) :—" *Thomas the Son of Thomas Penn was born August* 12*th,*
     1660 ; *Mary the Daughter of Thomas Penn was born October* 30*th,*
     1662 ; *Francis the Son of Thomas Penn was born June* 5*th,*
     1666 " ; and there are notes of other Buckinghamshire families
     in the volume.

890 PETTIE (George) A Petite Palice of Pettie his Pleasure. Con-
     teyning many pretie Histories, by him set foorth in comely
     colours, and most delightfully discoursed, *title within woodcut
     border*, black letter, *half bound*   *London, R. W.* (1576)
     *** FIRST EDITION (of which but two other copies are recorded).
     To these "Pretie Histories," Shakespeare and the other
     Elizabethan dramatists were much indebted. An indifferent
     (but complete) copy of an excessively rare book.

891 Phillips (Stephen) Eremus : a Poem, *the very rare privately printed
     edition, in the original wrapper*   "*The Lillie Press*," *n. d.*

892 Photographs. Imperial Quarto Album, containing Fifty large
     Photos. of noted French Cathedrals, interior and exterior
     views, *all on stout leather-guarded mounts, black morocco, g. e.*
                                                          (187—)

893 Pitcairn (Rob.) Criminal Trials in Scotland from 1488 to 1624, compiled from Original Records and MSS. with Historical Notes and Illustrations, 3 vol. in 4, *sprinkled calf, m. e.*
Edinb. W. Tait, 1833

894 Pittoni (Bat.) Impresse di diversi Principi, Duci, Signori, &c. *engraved title and* 52 *plates of seals, all within elaborate borders, half vellum, Venetia,* 1562—Scrap Book containing 19 Original Drawings in water-colour, in the manner of Rowlandson, *diamond calf* (2)

895 Plates and Vignettes to Tasso's la Jérusalem Délivrée, 67 *engravings from the designs of Gravelot, wants plate* 16, *Parigi,* 1771 ; and another, *the lot with all faults* (2)

896 Porter (Thomas) The Carnival : a Comedy, as it was acted at the Theatre Royal, &c. *unbound* 1664

897 PRAYER. A BOOKE OF CHRISTIAN PRAIERS, collected out of the Ancient Writers and best learned in Our Time, worthie to be read with an earnest minde of all Christians, &c. QUEEN ELIZABETH'S PRAYER BOOK (*the fifth and last of the old editions*), *every page, including title, printed within woodcut borders of figures and ornaments, after designs by Holbein, A. Dürer, &c. figure of the queen kneeling on reverse of title, brown morocco extra, richly ornamented in imitation of old Lyonnese binding, g. e. by F. Bedford,* FINE COPY, VERY RARE. *Printed for the Company of Stationers,* 1608

898 PRECIS SANCTÆ BRIGITÆ. ENGLISH MANUSCRIPT, *written in large* 𝔤𝔬𝔱𝔥𝔦𝔠 𝔩𝔢𝔱𝔱𝔢𝔯𝔰, *in red and black, on* 95 *leaves of vellum, long lines of* 19 *to the full page, numerous large and bold painted capitals and initials, original oak boards covered with stamped calf*
SÆC. XV

  *** A curious Manuscript, containing some remarkable Indulgencies.

899 Prynne (William) The Unloveliness of Love Lockes; or, a Summarie Discourse, prooving : The wearing and nourishing of a Locke, or Love-Locke, to be altogether unseemely, and unlawfull unto Christians. In which there are likewise some passages collected out of Fathers, Councells, and sundry Authors and Historians, against Face-painting, &c. FIRST EDITION, *calf extra, g. e.* 1628

  *** Refer to Halliwell's folio Shakespeare, vol. IV.

900 PSALTERIUM DAVIDIS cum glossa Ordinaria, MANUSCRIPT ON VELLUM (130 *ll.* 10 *by* 7 *in.*), *finely written in* 𝔤𝔬𝔱𝔥𝔦𝔠 𝔩𝔢𝔱𝔱𝔢𝔯𝔰, *the text in a larger character than the gloss, in double columns, with numerous painted initials, probably an English work (portions of several leaves have been cut away),* XIV*th Century (English?), binding, oaken boards, leather, stamped in small compartments of acorns, flowering fleurs de lis, rosettes, &c.* SÆC. XI-XII

  *** An English hand of the XVIIth Century has added the variations from the Psalms contained in the Latin Primer of Henry VIII.

901 PSALTERIUM DAVIDIS Latinè, cum Credo Apostolorum, Letania,
Canticis, Hymnis et Orationibus una cum Calendario Martio
ad Decembrem (*wants Jan.-Feb.*) MANUSCRIPT ON VELLUM
(141 *ll.* 8½ *by* 5½ *in.*), *written in bold* gothic characters, *in red
and black, long lines, 21 to a full page, calendar within illuminated borders, the first page occupied by a large painted initial* B
*of scroll flower ornaments, 8 other similar but smaller initials in
the text, capitals painted in red, the Litany in double columns
within painted arches, modern boarded velvet doublé with white
morocco, in purple morocco lined silk case*   SÆC. XI-XII

    *** This very interesting and valuable Codex, probably of English
origin, has an inscription in gold letters in the first cover as
follows : " *This came from the Isle of Wight and was always con-
sidered as having belonged to Charles the First while at Carisbrooke
Castle.*" Some of the entries in the calendar have been erased,
and there are later MS. additions in the margins.

902 Pulci (Luigi) Il Morgante, nuovamente corretto et ristampato,
*fine figured initials and ornaments (a few ll. neatly repaired), half
bound*   *Fiorenza, B. Sermartelli,* 1574

903 Purchas (Sam.) A Theatre of Politicall flying Insects, wherein
the Nature &c. of the Bee is discovered and described, &c.
original calf   *R. I. for T. Parkhurst,* 1657

904 PYRAMUS AND THISBE. La Historia de Piramo et Tisbe, dove
s'intende Il Ragionamento d'Amore, con la morte loro, *most
curious woodcut on title, boards*
           In Milano, per Pandolfo Malatesta, senza data

    *** This EXTRAORDINARILY RARE Poem appears to have eluded
the researches of Capel, Malone, Steevens, and all subsequent
editors of Shakespeare. It consists of but 4 leaves, so its
extinction is easily understood. Its SHAKESPEAREAN interest
is very great as illustrating the Pyramus and Thisbe story in
A Midsummer Night's Dream. THE LARGE WOOD ENGRAVING
IS REMARKABLE, AND WAS EVIDENTLY DESIGNED SPECIALLY
FOR THIS POEM. In the foreground, Thisbe in the act of
stabbing herself with the sword, by the side of Pyramus.
Close by are the tomb, the mulberry-tree, and the fountain.
The lion and a girl running away from it are seen in the
background ; far off is a city on hills.

The Property of C. B. Hurst, Esq.

OCTAVO ET INFRA.

905 AMERICA. PSALTERIUM AMERICANUS. The Book of Psalms in
a Translation exactly conformed to the original, but all in
Blank Verse ; fitted unto the Tunes commonly used in Our
Churches, which Pure Offering is accompanied with Illustra-
tions digging for Hidden Treasures in it, &c. [by DR. COTTON
MATHER], ORIGINAL EDITION (*perfect, but sheets Dd to end
washed), calf extra, g. e. by Riviere,* EXTREMELY RARE
Boston in N.E. Printed by S. Kneeland for B. Eliot, &c. 1718

906 AMERICA. Mather (Dr. Increase, of New England) Κομηγογραφια ;
or a Discourse concerning Comets ; wherein the Nature of
Blazing Stars is enquired into, with an historical account of
all the Comets unto this present year 1683 ; also two Sermons
occasioned by the late Blazing Stars, &c. THE EXTREMELY
RARE ORIGINAL EDITION, *some margins close, those of title and
another leaf mended, somewhat soiled by age, but generally in fair
condition, American MS. notes in margins and fly-leaves at end,
half red morocco gilt, g. e.*
*Boston in New England, printed by S. G. for S. S. and sold by
J. Browning at the Corner of the Prison Lane next the Town
House,* 1683

907 Bonaventura (Card. S.) Meditationes devotissimæ totius vitæ
Domini nostri Jesu Christi, **lit. goth**. *double columns, 32 lines,
with signs. and Roman numerals,* Papiæ, Jacob de Burgofranco,
1490—S. Augustini Sermones ad Heremitas, **lit. goth**. *double
columns, 32 lines, with signs.*
Venet. Paganinus de Paganinis, 1487, *in 1 vol. new vellum*

908 Pote (Wm. *Junior*) Journal of Capt. William Pote, Jr. during
his Captivity in the French and Indian War, from May 1745
to August 1747, *plan and Morris map bound separately, one of
350 copies on Holland hand-made paper (No. 113), 2 vol.*
De Vinne Press, New York, Dodd, Mead & Co. 1896

QUARTO.

909 Decretalium libri Gregorii IX. Pont. Max. *a neat transcript on
paper*—P. F. Galli Wagner Ord. S. Bened. Principia Juris et
Actionis Canonicæ, *Bilinguæ,* 1641 ; *in 1 vol. oaken boards,
stamped ornamental pigskin, clasps*

910 HORÆ BEATÆ MARIÆ VIRGINIS cum Calendario, ILLUMINATED
MANUSCRIPT ON VELLUM (211 *ll.* 8 *by* 5¾ *in.*), *written in bold*
gothic letters, *with rubrics, long lines,* 15 *to a page, by a French
(or Anglo-French) scribe and illuminator, the Calendar in French,
in blue, red and gold, the* XV *Joys, &c. in French,* EVERY PAGE
decorated with light and elegant floreate scroll borders, 14 *fine*
PAINTED AND ILLUMINATED MINIATURES *of the usual subjects,
within rich borders connected with large illuminated ornamental
initials, and numerous smaller initials and decorative details, old
French brown morocco, line tooled, g. e.*   SÆC. XV
*** MS. entries of the marriage of Jehan Esperit of Chatillon
and Marie le Grant, and the births of their four children,
1552-60, written on fly-leaf at end.

911 HULSIUS (LEVINUS) COLLECTION OF VOYAGES, 23 Parts (out of
26), 1-19, 21, 22, 23 and 25, in 3 vol. *pigskin. Parts 1 to 19,
in 2 vol. are* ABSOLUTELY PERFECT (*see the following collation*),
*and are in the finest possible original condition, in blind stamped
pigskin binding. Parts 21, 22, 23 and 25 are inserted in a
similar pigskin binding, the text quite perfect, but a few plates
missing, as the collation given below shows, but the lot will be sold
not subject to return,* EXTREMELY RARE

   I.   Erste Schiffart, *fifth edition,* 13 *maps and plates*   *Franckfurt,* 1625
  II. Ander Schiffart, *second edition,* 15 *maps and plates*   *ib.* 1605
 III. Dritter Theil, *third edition,* 32 *maps and plates*   *ib.* 1612

Lot 911—Hulsius, *continued.*

IV.   Vierdte Thiel, *third edition, map in two portions, portrait of Schmidel and 15 plates*   *Franckfurt,* 1612
V.   Die Fünffe, *fourth edition, map and 6 plates*   *ib.* 1612
VI.   Sechster Thiel, *second edition, 6 maps and 9 plates*   *ib.* 1618
VII.   Siebende Schiffahrt, *third edition, map and 18 plates*   *ib.* 1624
VIII.   Achte Schiffart, *second edition, map and 6 plates*   *ib.* 1608
IX.   Neundte Schiffart, *second edition, map and 4 plates*   *ib.* 1612
X.   Zehende Schiffart, *second edition, map and 4 plates*   *ib.* 1613
XI.   Eylffte Schiffart (first part), *second edition, 6 plates, Franckfurt,* 1623
   —Eylffte Schiffart ander Theil, *only edition, 4 plates, ib.* 1613
XII.   Zwölffte Schiffahrt, *first edition, 3 maps, with 4 plates in text*   *Oppenheim,* 1614
XIII.   Dreyzehente Schiffahrt, *first edition, 4 plates*   *Hanaw,* 1617
XIV.   Viertzehende Schiffart, *first edition, map and 1 plate*   *Franckfurt,* 1617
XV.   Fünffzehende Schiffart, *first edition, requires no plates*   *Hanaw,* 1617
XVI.   Sechtzehende Schiffart, *only edition, 9 maps and plates Franckfurt,* 1619
XVII.   Siebenzehende Schiffart, *only edition, 8 plates*   *ib.* 1620
XVIII.   Achtzehende Theil, *only edition, 14 maps*   *ib.* 1623
XIX.   Neuntzehende Schiffart, *only edition, 6 plates*   *ib.* 1626
XXI.   Ein und zwantzigs te Schiffahrt, *only edition, portrait in photograph and 4 plates (the 2 folding from De Bry)*   *ib.* 1629
XXII.   Zwei und zwantzigste Schiffart, *only edition, 5 plates (Nos. 1. 2 defective) 5, 6 and 7), should be 8, two or 3 leaves slightly cut in headlines*   *Franckfurt,* 1630
XXIII.   Drey und zwantzigste Schiffahrt, *only edition, 1 plate (Puteoli), should be* 8   *ib.* 1632
XXIV.   Fünff und zweyntzigste Schiffahrt, *only edition, 3 maps, but wants plate of camel*   *ib.* 1649

912   Hulsius (Levinus) Voyages, parts I-X : part I, fifth edition, 1625, part II, third edition, 1615, part III, third edition, 1612, part IV, third edition, 1612, part V, FIRST EDITION, 1612, part VI (*no edition mentioned*), 1626, part VII, 1624, part VIII, 1640, part IX, 1612, and part X, 1613, *numerous maps and plates, some partly coloured, and some maps backed, otherwise excellent copy, but sold as usual not subject to return, bound in 3 vol. crimson morocco extra, inside dentelles, g. e. by W. Pratt,* RARE   *sm. 4to.   Franckfort A. M.* 1612-40

913   Whittinton (Robert) Various Grammatical Works, viz. : De Octo Partibus Orationis, 14 *ll. the last having De Worde's device and the verso, the recto being blank, title within woodcut border, slightly mended, as are the margins of three other ll.* Wynkyn de Worde, 1529 ; Grammatice Primæ Partis Liber Primus, nuperrime recognitus (14 *ll.*) *woodcut title and large device at end, ib.* ; Grammaticæ Prima Pars nuperrime recensita liber quintus, et liber sextus (20 *ll.*) *title within woodcut border, ib.* ; Lucubrationes, De Synonimis et de Epithetis, &c. (28 *ll.*) *device on last, ib.* 1527 ; Syntaxis (34 *ll.*) *title within woodcut border, large device on verso of last leaf, recto blank, ib.* 1529 ; De Heteroclitis Nominibus, Grammaticæ liber tertius (8 *ll.*) *title within woodcut border, ib.* 1526 ; Grammaticæ Liber Secundus Nominum Declinationes (14 *ll.*) *title within woodcut border, device on verso of last leaf, ib.* 1525 ; Secunda Grammaticæ Pars de Syllabarum quantitate (58 *ll. wanting E* 1), *title within woodcut border, ib. n. d.* ; De Accentibus (16 *ll.*) *ib.* 1528 ; Vulgaria, et de Institutione Grammaticulorum Opusculum (47 *ll.*) *title within woodcut border, large device on recto of last leaf, ib.* 1527, A VERY RARE COLLECTION, *all in excellent condition,* in 1 vol. *calf, m. e.*   *sm. 4to*

FOLIO.

914   Antiphonale Romanum (?), MANUSCRIPT ON VELLUM (180 *ll.*
      13½ by 10 in.) written in bold gothic letters, *red and black, with
      old shaped musical notes by a French or Anglo French scribe, with
      4 fine large illuminated ornamental scroll initials, with marginal
      decorations ending in grotesques, birds, &c. numerous ornamental
      pen letters and painted capitals (imperfect), oaken boards, stamped
      ornamental pigskin (rebacked)*   SÆC. XIV

915   Antiphonarius Ordinis Fratrum Minorum Secundum Consue-
      tudinem Romanæ Curiæ, MANUSCRIPT ON VELLUM (177 *ll.*
      20 by 13 in.) written in very large Italian gothic letters, *in red
      and black, square-shaped musical notes, contemporary oaken boards,
      leather, metal bosses and rims, &c.*   *large folio.* SÆC. XV

916   Psalterium.   Ordo Psalterii secundum Morem et Consuetudinem
      Romanæ Curiæ (cum Hymnis et Litaniis et Notis Musicis),
      MANUSCRIPT ON VELLUM (196 *ll.* 22 *by* 15 *in.) written in very
      large* gothic letters, *red and black, long lines,* 18 *to a full page
      (Italian), a very large painted and illuminated initial of David
      playing a lute, before the first Psalm, contemporary oaken boards,
      leather, metal rims, &c.*   *very large folio.* SÆC. XV

The Property of A. Fortescue, Esq.

QUARTO.

917   Augustinus (S.) De Civitate Dei, lit. goth. *double columns,* 50 *lines
      with signs. (Tabula stained and first leaf mended)*
                                      Venet. Bonetus Locatellus, 1486

918   Bernardus (S. Abbas Clarev.) Opuscula (castigata per P. de
      Brixia), lit. goth. *double columns,* 40 *lines with signs.*
                                      8vo. *Venet. Sim. Bevilaqua,* 1495

919   Cicero.   De Natura Deorum lib. III, MANUSCRIPT ON PAPER
      (48 *ll.* 9 *by* 6½ *in.) written in neat* gothic letters, *long lines,* 35 *to
      a page, rubricated, half bound*   *sm.* 4*to.* SÆC. XV

920   Formularium diversorum Contractuum noviter impressum, *lit.
      rom. title in red* gothic, *with Giunta device, oaken boards, half
      leather, clasp, sm.* 4*to. Venet. per L. A. de Zontis (Giunta),* 1523

921   Grapaldi.   Silva Francisci Marii Grapaldi in deditione Parme S.
      Julio II. Pont. Max. (2 *ll.) fine ornamental woodcut title, half
      morocco*   *sm.* 4*to.* [15—]

922   Hieronymus (S.) Vitas Patrum Sanctorum, partes IV, &c. lit. goth.
      double columns, 47 *lines, with signs. rubricated, capitals painted
      in blue and red (wants a j, blank), half vellum*
                                      sm. 4*to. Venet. O. Scotus,* 1483

FOLIO.

923 Biblia Sacra Latina, Editio Vulgata cum prologis S. Hieronymi et Interpret. Heb. Nom. lít. gotí). *double columns, 51 lines, with signs. two fine large illuminated ornamental initials, capitals painted in blue and red, a few head-lines shaved (and wants a j), but a clean and sound copy, bound in niger morocco, antique style, plain edges (by Douglas Cockerell)*
    sm. folio.   Venet. Fr. de Hailbrun et Nic. de Frankfordia, 1476

924 Bonaventura (S.) Speculum beate Marie Virginis compilatum ab humili fratre Bonaventura, EDITIO SECUNDA, *printed in a small* semi-gotíjíc *type, with ornamental woodcut initials in outline,* 50 ll. *long lines, 38 to a full page, without marks, half morocco, good copy,* RARE *(Hain 3567)*
    sm. folio.   Anthonius Sorg Civis Augustensis impressus 1477

925 Casali (Ubertus de) Arbor Vite Crucifixe Jesu, lít. gotí). *double columns, with signatures, vellum*
    sm. folio.   Venet. And. de Bonettis de Papia, 1485

926 DANTE.   Comedia di Danthe Alighieri Poeta divino col Espositione di Christophoro Landino, nuovamente impressa . . . revista y emendata, colle nuovissime postille, *lit. rom. title in red* gotíjíc *within woodcut border in compartments of heads of Italian Poets, Giunta device below, full-page bust of Dante on reverse, full-page cut before the Inferno, numerous small cuts in text, and ornamental initials, a few leaves slightly stained, but a good copy of a* RARE EDITION, *half bound*
    Venet. Jacob de Burgofranco ad Instantia di L. A. Giunta, 1529

927 Lactantius.   Opera; De Divinis Institutionibus, &c. *finely printed in roman letter, long lines, 38 to a full page, without marks, 8 fine large painted and illuminated ornamental initials, margin of first page of text decorated, rubrications, &c. in blue and red, some ll. slightly wormed and discoloured, otherwise good, old russia gilt, rough edges*
    Romæ in Domo Petri de Maximo, per Conradem Sweynheym et Arnoldum Pannartz, 1468

    *** Second edition of Lactantius; VERY RARE and a fine and early specimen of the Press of the First Printers in Rome.

928 Lombardus (Petrus de) Magister Sententiarum, lít. gotí). (*few ll. slightly wormed*), *oaken boards, half stamped leather*
    Venet. Opera et impensis O. Scoti, 1489 (*with device*)

929 Ordinarius Ecclesiæ Romanæ [begins fol. 1a] "Ordo ad Communicandum infirmum Secudum Ordinem Romane Curie"; &c. cud fol. 74 b "*Pretendo Domini famulis et famulabus tuis dexteram celestis auxilii,*" &c. MANUSCRIPT ON PAPER (11 *by* 7½ *in.*) *written in bold* gotíjíc lcttcrs (*Italian*) *in red and black with square musical notes, long lines, 22 to a full page, contemporary oaken boards, leather, stamped in ornamental diagonal compartments* (*Venetian*)   *sm. folio.*   SÆC. XV

930 Thomas Aquinas. Liber de Veritate Catolicæ Fidei contra Errores
      Gentilium, lit. **goth**. *double columns with signatures, contemporary
      MS. notes in margins (first leaf of table mounted), old calf
      (rebacked)*   *sm. folio. Venet. Nicolaus Jenson*, 1480

   ₊ Probably the last book printed by this celebrated printer at
      Venice as he died in the same year.   He was most renowned
      for his fine founts of Roman type.

931 Voragine (Jac. de) Legenda Aurea, lit. **goth**. *parva, double columns,
      49 lines CCLXXIX numbered ll. with signatures (Aj, a blank,
      wanting), old calf,* RARE
      *sm. folio.   Coloniæ ; "Finit anno XXCCCC LXXXII, XIII.
      Kl. Junii in Sancta Colonia"*

   ₊ Wm. Morris's copy, with his Kelmscott Press label.

Other Properties.

---

932 MARTIAL ACHIEVEMENTS of Great Britain and her Allies, from
      1799 to 1815, *numerous beautifully coloured plates by W. Heath,*
      with Text, *original half binding, uncut*   *imp. 4to.*   (1814)

933 Martialis (M. Valerius) Epigrammatum, cum commento Dom.
      Calderini, *roman letter, old vellum (Hain, *10185)*
                              Venetiis, Joa. Mocenico duce felic. vivente, 1482

934 Martyrologium Usuardi Monachi, MANUSCRIPT *of the XIIIth
      century,* ON VELLUM, *in large* **gothic characters**, *with ornamental
      initials, half calf*

   ₊ Usuardus was a French monk, who, under the patronage of
      Charles the Bold, composed this Martyrology.   He died
      about 877 A.D.

935 Merigot (J.) Select Collection of Views and Ruins in Rome and
      its Vicinity, LARGE PAPER, 62 *aquatint plates, coloured,* with
      Descriptions in English and French, *in the original binding*
                                                                     1797-8

936 Meyrick (Dr. R.) Engraved Illustrations of Antient Arms and
      Armour, after the Drawings of Dr. Meyrick, by Jos. Skelton,
      2 vol. *plates 74-150, uncut*   *imp. 4to.   Oxford,* 1830

937 Meyrick (S. R.) and C. H. Smith.   The Costume of the Original
      Inhabitants of the British Islands, from the Earliest Periods
      to the Sixth Century, *finely coloured plates,* with Descriptive
      Text, *red morocco gilt, g. e.*   1821

938 Military Costume.   Ten Engravings, after Holbein, of Sixteenth
      Century Swiss Military Costume, 1790—Eleven Lithographs
      (*coloured*) of German Military Costume, 1830   (21)

939 MISSALE SECUNDUM ORDINARIUM ECCLESIE HILDENSEMENSIS, *missal type*, *double columns, in red and black, two first leaves mended, affecting a few letters and figures of the Calendar, otherwise* FINE, SOUND AND LARGE COPY *in binding of stamped pigskin, after an ancient design*
Nurnberge, Georius Stöchs de Sulczbach, 1499

*** EXCESSIVELY RARE, THERE BEING BUT TWO OTHER COPIES KNOWN, BOTH OF WHICH ARE IN PUBLIC LIBRARIES AT HILDESHEIM. Hain was not aware of its existence, and Dr. Copinger derives his collation from Mr. Weale's *Bibliographia Liturgia*, which is very different from this copy. The 354 leaves are thus accounted for: 8, 16, clxxiv, xviij, 8 and 130. First of all there is only one group of Roman numeral foliations, viz.: i to ccxcix. Then there are 6 unnumbered Calendar leaves, 34 of Music, some, but not all, of which are numbered (Roman) *seriatim* in bottom right-hand corner. Five other unnumbered leaves of Table, &c. follow folio ccxcix, making in all 344 leaves. Furthermore the Music and other unnumbered leaves read straight on, and begin and end properly. There may have been two issues the same year, but the date given in the colophon (Sept. 17th), agrees with that given by Mr. Weale. As far as it is possible to ascertain, the present is the first occasion on which a copy has been offered for sale.

940 Missale Cartusiani Ordinis ex Ordinatione Capituli Generalis A.D. 1677, celebrati sub R. D. P. Innocentio le Masson Priore Cartusiæ ac Ordinalis Generali, *lit. rom. red and black, with musical notes, fine full-page engravings, chiefly by Caspar Huberti, ornamental and figured woodcut initials ; oaken boards, red velvet, with embroidered ornaments and silk threads of a large fleur-de-lis at each corner, coroneted shield in centres containing the letters* B N O *on upper cover and* A N A *on the under, g. e. clasps, in baize cover*
Fauralii in Sabaudia typis Ludov. du Jour, sumtibus Maioris Cartusiæ, 1679

941 Missale Romanum ex Decreto Concilii Trident restitutum, Pii V. jussu editum, **lit. goth**. *red and black, double columns, musical notes, 4 full-page woodcuts, with borders in compartments of Saints, those before the Proprium and Commune Sanctorum being very fine, numerous small cuts and ornamental initials, oaken boards, leather, with blind stamped ornaments, metal corners, centre-pieces and clasps, in good condition* *Venet. ap. Juntas*, 1578

942 MORLAND. Blagdon (F. W.) Authentic Memoirs of George Morland, with Remarks on his Abilities and Progress as an Artist, a variety of Anecdotes never before published, a facsimile of his writing, &c. *earliest issue, original and brilliant impressions of the 21 large and beautifully coloured plates, in the original half binding, with label on side* *E. Orme*, 1806

943 Morton (John) The Natural History of Northamptonshire, with some Account of the Antiquities, *folding map and plates, calf*
1712

944   MUNICH GALLERY. Gemälde Saal zu München und Schleissheim,
2 vol. *numerous large and finely executed lithographic plates on
india paper, by Strixner, Piloty, Hohe, &c. half crimson morocco
gilt, g. e.*   *München*, 1817-36

945   Munster (Sebastian) Cosmographia das ist Beschreibung der
gantzen Welt, darinnen aller Monarchien Kenserthumben
Konigsreichen Furstenthumben Graff-und herzschafften, Lan-
deren, Statten und Gemeinden, &c. ... Dreskgleichen aller
deren bender Standen Regenten ; Kensern, Konigen, ... so
dann aller Volctker in gemein Religion Gesatz, Sitten, Nah-
rung, klendung unnd Ubungen, wie auch aller Landern
sonderbare Thier, Vogel, Fisch, &c. *engraved frontispiece, numerous maps and woodcuts*, 2 vol. *original calf*   *Basel*, 1628
   *** Mentioned by Douce in his Illustrations of *The Merry Wives
of Windsor*.

946   Mystere des Actes Apotres et Apocalypse Sainct Jehan Zebedee.
Les Catholiques Œuvres et Actes des Apotres redigez en escript
par Saint Luc, avecques plusieurs hystoires en icceluy inserez
des Gestes des Cesars, &c. **black letter**, *with woodcuts*, 3 vol. *red
morocco gilt, g. e. (Derome)*   *Paris*, 1541
   *** A very fine copy of one of the rarest and most interesting
collections of old French Miracle Plays. The Brunet copy
sold for 1250 francs ; the Solar copy for 2450 francs.

947   Nash (Jos.) Mansions of England in the Olden Time, Series I-II,
ORIGINAL EDITION, 52 *fine lithographs*, 2 vol. *half morocco*
                        imp. folio. M'Lean, 1839

948   Naunton (Sir Robert) Fragmenta Regalia, or Observations on
Queene Elizabeth, her tymes and ffavourites   (1605)
   *** A highly interesting contemporary Manuscript of 104 pages,
with terse biographies of the Earls of Leicester and Sussex,
William Cecil Lord Burleigh, Sir Philip Sidney, Sir Francis
Walsingham, Lord Willoughby, Sir Nicholas Bacon, Sir
Francis Knowles (Knollys), Sir Henry Morris, Sir John
Perrot, Sir Christopher Hatton, Earl of Nottingham, Sir John
Parkington, Lord Hunsdon, Sir Walter Raleigh, Sir Fulke
Greville, Earl of Essex, Lord Buckhurst, Lord Monjoy
(Mountjoy), Robert Cecill Earl of Salisbury, Sir Francis Vere
and Lord Worcester. An account of " Fragmenta Regalia "
will be found in Dr. Hunter's *New Illustrations of Shakespeare*.

949   Norton (Robert) The Gvnner, shewing the whole practice of
Artillery : together with the Making of Extraordinarie Arti-
ficiall Fire-works, *engraved title, folding and other woodcuts (one
plate and two or three headlines cut into and title shaved on fore-
edge), good clean copy, with many rough edges and blank ll. at
beginning and end, original calf, broken*
               A. M. for Humphrey Robinson, 1628
  *** Probably the only complete copy in existence of this rare
book ; undescribed by any bibliographer. The British
Museum copy of the same date has an entirely different
engraved title-page, and contains only 17 entire plates out of
the 29 ; as in this, 7 of the double folding plates, containing
distinct sets of the illustrations, have been divided and placed
to suit the text.

953 Noehden (Dr.) Ancient Coins of Magna Græcia and Sicily, selected
from the Cabinet of Lord Northwick, 20 *plates by Henry Moses,
crimson morocco extra, g. e.* 1826

954 Ovid. Les Metamorphoses d'Ovide, en Latin et François, de la
Traduction de Pierre Du-Ryer, *with fine impressions of the
numerous engravings, title and last leaf defective, a few stained,
half bound, sold not subject to return* Brux. 1677

955 Paoli (P. A.) Rovine della Città di Pesto detta ancora Posidonia
(Ital. et Lat.) LARGE PAPER, *fine plates by Volpato, Bartolozzi,
&c. old French red morocco extra, full gilt back and broad ornamental side borders, large crowned initial C. with " Napoleone " in
the curve, g. e.; ex-libris of the Bibliothèque de Rosny and the
Duke of Hamilton; the* DUCHESSE DE BERRI'S COPY
imp. folio. Romæ, 1784

956 Perrier (F.) Eigentlyke Afbeeldinge van Hondert der Alderner-
maerdstle Statuen, of Antique-Beelden Staande binnen Romen,
engraved title and 100 plates by C. Van Dalen, old calf
Hagen, n. d.

957 Philips (Mrs. Katherine) Poems : to which is added Monsieur
Corneille's Pompey and Horace, Tragedies, with several other
translations out of French, *with fine impression of the portrait by
Faithorne,* FIRST GENUINE EDITION, *tall and clean copy in full
morocco extra, by Riviere* 1667

958 PLAYBILLS. A Collection of 104 Playbills : Drury Lane, Covent
Garden, Brighton, Margate, Liverpool, Carlisle, Watton, Walsingham, Eastbourne, and other provincial places, including
in the casts : Mrs. Jordan, Bannister, Quick, Braham, Barrymore, C. Kemble, Miss de Camp, Mrs. Mattocks, Munden,
Macready, Incledon, Widdicomb, C. Mathews, &c. ; there are
also in the collection 13 rare AMERICAN PLAYBILLS (Federal
Street Theatre, Boston, 1801-2), and two 4to Autograph
Letters of Barrymore, *in 1 vol.* 1781, &c.

959 Plumier (Charles) L'Art de Tourner, ou de faire en perfection
toutes sortes d'ouvrages au Tour, *numerous plates, original calf*
Lyon, 1701

960 Plutarchus. Vite di quattordici Nomini illustri Græci e Romani
colle loro Comparazioni volgarizzate. [*Begins folio 1 b*] : " In
questo libro si contengono le infra scripte Vite composte da
Plutarcho famosissimo Scriptore appresso di Græci & seguitano
le dette Vite chome furone composte, uno imperadore greco
& uno latino comparati insieme," MANUSCRIPT ON PAPER
(227 *ll.* 13½ *by* 9 *in.*) *finely written in roman letters by an Italian
scribe, long lines, 39 to a full page, historiated initial and 3 illuminated ornaments on first page, new boarded brown morocco gilt, by
Thompson of Paris* SECOLO XV

961 Pope (Alex.) Sober Advice from Horace to the Young Gentlemen
about Town, FIRST EDITION, *very fine uncut copy (size* 14½ *by*
9¾ *in.) half morocco* T. Boreman, n. d. (1735)
*** Extremely rare in this state, probably large paper.

I

963   POLE (Reginald Cardinal) Ad Henricum VIII pro ecclesiasticæ
Unitatis Defensione Libri IV, FIRST EDITION, *old half calf*
Romæ, A. Bladus (Typis Aldiniis), s. a. (sed circa 1536)

    *** This excessively rare and most important book for the
ecclesiastical history of this country was PRIVATELY PRINTED
by Cardinal Pole, who distributed *only a few copies as presents*
to the Pope and Cardinals. Pole promised Henry VIII
not to distribute the work, and the King tried in vain to
obtain a copy from the Cardinal. On obtaining one, Henry
ordered Archbishop Cranmer and the other bishops to draw
up an answer. Bishop Latimer preached against the work,
and Henry tried to inveigle the Cardinal into England,
offered 50,000 crowns for his head, and caused his brother
to be arrested and executed. The Pope, fearing for Pole's
danger from assassins employed by Henry, assigned him a
guard for his protection. *So great is the rarity of this original,
that even Sir Robert Harley, Earl of Oxford, so famous for his
Bibliomania, was never able to procure a copy, and had to be
contented with the reprint made in Queen Mary's reign. George III
also could never obtain a copy;* and even the British Museum
was without it until presented with the Grenville Library.

964   Post (Pieter) en Pieter Nolpe. Begraeffenisse van syne hoogheyt
Frederick Henrick, Prince van Orange, *coloured engravings of
the Funeral Procession, the flags and armorial bearings emblazoned,
vellum, g. e.*   *Amst.* 1651

965   Printing. Histoire de l'Invention de l'Imprimerie par les Monuments, *border designs by J. J. Grandville, coloured and illuminated portrait of Gutenberg, facsimiles of early woodcuts, printing,
&c. limp boards*   *Paris,* 1840

966   Pugh (E.) Cambria Depicta, *frontispiece and 70 beautifully coloured
plates engraved by E. Cartwright, half bound, uncut oblong.* 1813

967   Pyne (W. H.) The Costume of Great Britain, 60 *beautifully coloured
plates,* with Descriptions, *morocco, g. e.*   1808

968   ROBERTS (DAVID) Views in the Holy Land, Syria, Idumæa,
Arabia, Egypt and Nubia, 4 vol. *numerous large and beautiful
plates and vignettes,* with Historical Descriptions by Croly and
Brockedon, *half red morocco, g. e.*   *F. G. Moon,* 1842-9

969   ROMMANNT DE LA ROSE. Cy est le romant de la rose, ou tout lart
damours est enclose (par G. de Lorris et J. de Meun), lit.
goth. *(lettres bâtardes), double columns, 43 lines to a full column,
with* 86 SPIRITED WOODCUTS *and large device on title, Z 1 wanting,
last leaf slightly defective and small piece torn from blank margin
of title, remarkably large copy with some rough edges, unbound*
Imprime a Paris par Nicholas Despres (pour M. le Noir), vers 1505

    *** An extremely rare edition, remarkable for its fine woodcuts,
among which is a very curious representation of a Coursing
Scene on the reverse of Q 6.

971 Rosini (Giov.) Storia della Pittura Italiana, esposta coi Monu-
      menti, the Atlases only, bound in 2 vol. *comprising 254 large
      and elaborate plates of the masterpieces of Italian painters, half
      crimson morocco gilt, t. e. g.*   *Pisa,* 1839-45

972 RUSKIN (JOHN) "Does the perusal of Works of Fiction act
      favourably or unfavourably on the Moral Character?" 8 *pp.
      folio,* IN RUSKIN'S AUTOGRAPH, *very closely written, and signed
                                                  in a portfolio*

      *** An essay consisting chiefly of a glowing description of the
      writer's favourite authors—Scott, Lytton and Byron, written
      in 1836, when he was only 16 or 17 years of age. It was dis-
      covered in the desk of his tutor, Dean Dale, after his death,
      and was purchased by the late owner from Miss Dale.

973 St. Clair (Major T.) A series of views of events in the Campaigns
      of the Allied English and Peninsular armies in Spain and Por-
      tugal, 12 *large and beautiful plates, engraved in aquatinta and
      coloured by C. Turner, half bound oblong. Turner, Colnaghi,* 1812

974 Salmon (N.) History of Hertfordshire, with the rare second
      Appendix, *map, interleaved, with a few MS. additions, bound in
      2 vol. half calf, title written on*   1728

975 Salmon (N.) History of Hertfordshire, *interleaved and illustrated
      with about 100 additional views, engravings (fine view of Moor
      Park), portraits (Sir F. Bacon, by W. Marshall, &c.), water-colour
      drawings, including a large view (17 by 12 in.) of St. Albans,
      &c. half russia, covers loose*   *roy. folio.* 1728

976 Scotland. Charles I, a Large Declaration concerning the Late
      Tumults in Scotland from their first originalls, together with
      a Particular Deduction of the Seditious Practices of the prime
      Leaders of the Covenanters collected out of their owne foule
      Acts and Writings, *fine portrait of Charles I, tiny hole in p.* 163,
      *very large copy, with leaf of imprint at end, original stamped calf
      gilt, back damaged,* RARE
                  R. Young, His Majesties Printer for Scotland, 1639

977 Scotland. In the Current Parliament haldin at EDINBURGH the
      XXII day of Maii, the zeir of God 1584, theis Lawis,
      Statutis and constitutions ar devisit, ordinet, and concludit,
      be the richt excellent richt Heich and Michtie Prince Jame VI,
      black letter, *imperfect at end, title within border, with printer's
      mark, unbound, very rare*
                  Imprintit at Edinburgh be Alexander Arbuthnet, n. d. (1584)

978 SELECT MUSICALL AYRES AND DIALOGUES, In Three Bookes :
      First Book, contains Ayres for a Voyce alone to the
      Theorbo or Basse Violl ; Second Book, contains Choice Dia-
      logues for two Voyces to the Theorbo or Basse Violl ; Third
      Book, containes short Ayres or Songs for three Voyces, so
      Composed, as they may either be sung by a Voyce alone, to

Lot 978—*continued.*

an Instrument, or by two or three Voyces, *engraved vignette on title*, FIRST EDITION, *morocco extra, g. e.*

Printed by T. H. for John Playford, and are to be sold at his Shop, in the Inner Temple, near the Church doore, 1653

*** The composers of the songs in this most rare volume are John Wilson, Dr. Charles Coleman, Henry Lawes, William Lawes, William Webb, Nicholas Lanneare, William Smegergil, Edward Colman and Jeremy Savile. The words are by Shakespeare, Ben Jonson, Herrick, Suckling and other famous poets of the day. This is a most interesting Shakespearian volume, so many of the songs being by " Jack " Wilson, who sang, " Sigh No More, Ladies." A beautiful copy with several UNCUT leaves.

FIFTH DAY'S SALE.

OCTAVO ET INFRA.

Lot 979.

ROSSETTI (D. G.) Verses, FIRST EDITION, *printed on hand-made paper, in the original wrapper, uncut, in case*
privately printed, 1881

*** Contains " At the Fall of the Leaf" and "Sonnet after the French Liberation of Italy." The last-named has never been printed elsewhere.

980 Rowlandson (T.). Fielding's History of Tom Jones, a Foundling, 3 vol. FIRST EDITION, *with* 12 *plates by T. Rowlandson, clean copy, in old calf, very scarce* 1792

981 Rowlandson (T.). Sterne (L.) Sentimental Journey through France and Italy, *coloured plates by Rowlandson, clean copy, in original boards, uncut* *Tegg,* 1809

982 Rowlandson (T.). Surprising Adventures of the Renowned Baron Munchausen, *folding frontispiece and plates by T. Rowlandson, clean copy, uncut* *ib.* 1811

983 Rowlandson (T.). The Tour of Doctor Syntax in search of the Picturesque, a Poem, *engraved title and* 30 *coloured plates, clean copy, half calf* *Ackermann,* 1813

984 Rowlandson (T.). The Grand Master, or Adventures of Qui Hi ? in Hindostan, a Hudibrastic Poem by Quiz, 28 *coloured plates, including folding frontispiece, half calf gilt* *Tegg,* 1816

985 Rugby Press. Wratislaw (Theodore) Caprices, ONLY 20 COPIES *printed for sale, on Japanese vellum paper* 1893

986 Ruskin (John) Lectures on Art, delivered at Oxford in 1870— Three Letters and an Essay, 1836-1841, found in his Tutor's desk, 1893 ; *original cloth* (2)

987 RUSKIN (J.) The Nature and Authority of Miracles, 16 *pages, for private distribution* 1873

988 RUSKIN (J.) Samuel Prout, 10 *pp. printed for private circulation only, in the original wrapper* *Oxford,* 1870

989 Ruskin (J.) "The Future of England," a Paper read at the R.A. Institution, 14th December, 1869, 14 *pp. folded, not cut open, very scarce*

990 Ryley (S. W.) The Itinerant, or Memoirs of an Actor, vol. I and III, also vol. I and VII of The Itinerant in Scotland, 4 vol. *calf and half calf* 1808-27

*** Interesting 3 pp. 4to autograph letter from the author inserted, in which references are made to financial difficulties and this publication.

992   RYMER (Thomas) A Short View of Tragedy, its Original Excellency and Corruption, with some Reflections on Shakespeare and other Practitioners for the Stage, *old calf*   1693

　　　⁎ Contains the extraordinary essay on Shakespeare's *Othello.* This copy has been read and annotated in manuscript by a contemporary Critic.

993   St. John (Charles) A Tour in Sutherlandshire, with extracts from the field-books of a Sportsman and Naturalist, 2 vol. FIRST EDITION, *plates, clean fresh copy in original cloth, uncut*
Murray, 1849

994   Saint-Pierre (J. B. H.) Paul et Virginie, FIRST EDITION, "*Papier vélin d'Essone,*" FINE COPY, *with beautiful plates after Moreau and Vernet, engraved by Girardet, Halbon and Longueil, green morocco extra, g. e. by Derome*
Paris, de l'Imprimerie de Monsieur, 1789

995   Sandys (Geo.) A Paraphrase upon the Psalmes of David, and the Hymnes of the Old and New Testaments, FIRST EDITION, *fine copy, morocco gilt, by Riviere*   1636

996   Satirist (The) or Monthly Meteor, vol. I, 6 *coloured folding caricatures, half calf gilt,* 1808—The History and Origin of Fairlop Fair, *plate,* 1808—Trial of Richard Patch for the Murder of Mr. Bright, *portraits, &c.* 1806, in 1 vol. ; and another   3 *vol.*

997   Scotland.   [LOCKHART (Geo.)] Memoirs concerning the Affairs of Scotland from Queen Anne's Accession to the Throne to the Commencement of the Union in May, 1707, *russia super-extra, by Bedford,* FINE COPY, 1714—TANNAHILL (Robt.) Poems and Songs, chiefly in the Scotch dialect, *signature of Sir Walter Scott's daughter (Miss Ann Scott) on title, calf,* 1815 ; and another   (3)

　　　⁎ The Lockhart has the rare " Key " bound in at the end.

998   Scot (Thomas) Philomythie, or Philomythologie, wherein Outlandish Birds, Beasts and Fishes are taught to speak true English plainly, *engraved title by Elstracke, woodcuts, some side-notes cut into, morocco gilt*   1622

　　　⁎ Includes the rare " Second Part of Philomythie, containing certaine Tales," 1625.

999   Scott (Sir Walter) The Field of Waterloo, a Poem, FIRST EDITION, *uncut*   *Edinb.* 1815

1000   SCOTT (SIR W.) THE ANTIQUARY, with the Glossary at the end of vol. III, 3 vol. *all the half titles,* FIRST EDITION, *fine clean copy in the original boards,* UNCUT, *with the labels,* VERY RARE IN THIS STATE   *ib.* 1816

1001   Scott (Sir W.) Tales of my Landlord, third series, 4 vol. FIRST EDITION, *original boards, uncut*   1819

1002   Scott (Sir W.) The Monastery, a Romance, 3 vol. FIRST EDITION, *original boards, uncut*   1820

1003   Scott (Sir W.) Kenilworth, a Romance, 3 vol. FIRST EDITION, *original boards, uncut*   1821

1004   Scott (Sir W.) Peveril of the Peak, 4 vol. FIRST EDITION, *with half titles and slip of errata in vol. III, original boards, uncut, one cover missing*   *Edinb.* 1822

1005   Scott (Sir W.) Peveril of the Peak, 4 vol. FIRST EDITION, *original boards, uncut*   *Edinb.* 1822

1006   Scott (Sir W.) The Pirate, 3 vol. FIRST EDITION, *original boards, uncut*   *ib.* 1822

1007   Scott (Sir W.) St. Ronan's Well, 3 vol. FIRST EDITION, *with half titles, original boards, uncut*   *ib.* 1824

1008   Scott (Sir W.) Redgauntlet, a Tale of the Eighteenth Century, 3 vol. FIRST EDITION, *original boards, uncut*   1824

1009   Scott (Sir W.) Tales of the Crusaders, 4 vol. FIRST EDITION, *original boards, uncut*   1825

1010   Scott (Sir W.) Woodstock, 3 vol. FIRST EDITION, *uncut*, 1826 ; Quentin Durward, 3 vol. FIRST EDITION, *uncut*, 1823   (6)

1011   Scott (Sir W.) Woodstock, or The Traveller, a Tale of the Year Sixteen Hundred and Fifty-one, 3 vol. FIRST EDITION, *original boards, uncut*   1826

1012   SECCHI (N.) Gl' Inganni Comedia del Sig. N. S. Recitata in Milano l' Anno MDXLVII (1547), dinanzi alla Maesta del Re Filippo II   *In Vinegia,* 1602

     **** One of the foundation stories of Shakespeare's *Twelfth Night.*

1013   Selby (P. J.) History of British Forest Trees, 200 *illustrations, original cloth, Van Voorst,* 1842—Hewitson (W.) Eggs of British Birds, vol. 1 (*erased from title*), *numerous coloured plates, sold not subject to return, ib.* 1846—Moore (T.) British Ferns and their Allies, *coloured plates, &c.* 1861   *3 vol.*

1014   Shelley (P. B.) History of a Six Weeks' Tour through France, Switzerland, Germany and Holland, with description of the Glaciers of Chamouni, FIRST EDITION, *with Brooks' substituted title-page, uncut,* 1829—Byron (Lord) Lara, a Tale, Jacqueline, a Tale, FIRST EDITION, *with half title, original boards, uncut, with label,* 1814   *2 vol.*

1015   Shelley (P. B.) Declaration of Rights (contained in no. V, vol. I of " The Republican," published Sept. 24, 1819), VERY RARE, and other nos. of the Republican, in 1 thick vol. *half bound*   *R. Carlile,* 1819-20

1016   Shenstone (William) The School Mistress, a Poem, in imitation of Spenser, with the rare Index, FIRST EDITION, *sprinkled calf gilt, y. e.*   1742

1017   SHERIDAN (R. B.) THE RIVALS, A COMEDY, as it is Acted at the Theatre Royal in Covent Garden, FIRST EDITION, *morocco extra, t. e. g.* UNCUT   1775

     **** A presentation copy, with inscription in Sheridan's autograph " From the Author." On the last leaf (which has been mended), containing the mis-printed catchword " Epi-," Sheridan has written the word " Finis," and crossed out the catchword. Inserted is the original playbill of the performance at Covent Garden on February 27, 1775. An uncut presentation copy is extremely rare.

1018   Shakspeare's Sonnets, edited by Edward Dowden   1881

     **** With a long and interesting autograph letter by Dowden, relating to the Sonnets inserted.

1019 Sherwill (M.) Ascent to the Summit of Mont Blanc, 25th, 26th
and 27th of August, 1825, 1826—Colton (C. C.) Thoughts in
Rhyme, *Paris*, 1832; *in 1 vol. calf gilt*—The Traveller's Guide
to St. Petersburg by way of Sweden, *calf gilt*, 1818   (2)

1020 Sidney (Sir Philip) A Continuation of Sir Philip Sidney's
Arcadia, wherein is handled the Loves of Amphialus and
Helena, Queen of Corinth, Prince Plangus and Erona, with
the Historie of the Loves of Old Glaius and Young Strephon
to Urania, written by a young Gentlewoman, Mris. A. W. *old
half calf*   1651

1021 Six (The) Cuts in the Sword Exercise of the Cavalry, accompanied with instructions for making them, 6 *coloured plates*,
1799—Astley (P.) Remarks on the Profession and Duty of a
Soldier, *frontispiece*, 1794, *in 1 vol. old marbled calf gilt*

1022 Smith (H. and J.) Rejected Addresses, or the New Theatrum
Poetarum, FIRST EDITION, *with half title, original boards, uncut,
J. Miller*, 1812 (*the publisher paid £1000 for the copyright of this
small vol.*)—A Sequel to the Rejected Addresses, by another
Author, FIRST EDITION, *original boards, uncut*, 1813   2 *vol.*

1023 Smith (W.) A New Voyage to Guinea, *plates*, 1744—Bradley
(R.) A Treatise of Agriculture, displaying the Arts of Husbandry and Gardening, *plates, old calf*, 1757 ; &c.   4 *vol.*

1024 SMOLLETT (TOBIAS) The Adventures of Telemachus, the son of
Ulysses, translated from the French of Messire François
Salignac de la Mothe-Fenelon, Archbishop of Cambray, FIRST
EDITION, 2 vol. *calf extra, t. e. g.* UNCUT   1776
        ₊ An uncut copy is extremely rare.

1025 Songs. The Vocal Companion, or Songster's Delight, 1759—
Cunningham (G.) The Cheerful Companion, *Bath*, 1797—
Sweet Robin, or the Children in the Wood, a collection of
the Choicest Songs, Ancient and Modern, *frontispiece, uncut*,
1794—Encyclopædia of Wit, *frontispiece, calf, Tegg*, 1811 4 *vol.*

1026 SONGS OF THE CHACE, containing an extensive collection relative
to the Sports of the Field, including Hunting, Racing,
Shooting, Angling, Hawking, Coursing, &c. *frontispiece and
engraved title by Scott, contemporary red morocco extra, with emble-
matic gold tooling on sides, back, and inside borders, by T. Gosden,
with his book-plate, g. e. with a* WATER-COLOUR DRAWING OF A
FOX HUNT *on the fore-edges under the gilding, a very fine specimen*
                                                                    1811

1027 Southey (Robert) Wat Tyler, a Dramatic Poem, FIRST EDITION,
with half title, uncut, 1817—Byron (Lord) Manfred, a Dramatic
Poem, FIRST EDITION, *with half title, uncut*, 1817   (2)

1028 SOUTHEY (R.) ORIGINAL AUTOGRAPH MS. Collections and
Remarks on the Reform Bill, *with a few newspaper cuttings,
half morocco, uncut*   (1832)

1029 Southey (R.) Catalogue of his Valuable Library, sold by Sotheby
& Co. 16 *days' sale*   1844

1030 SOWERBY (JAMES) ENGLISH BOTANY, or coloured Figures of
British Plants, FIRST EDITION, 36 vol. *complete in* 267 *parts,
with all titles and indexes, and index to the whole work, numerous
beautifully coloured plates, in the original wrappers as issued, in*
3 boxes   1791-1814

1031   Sportsman's Directory **or** Park and Game Keeper's Companion,
       by J. Mayer, *Colchester*, 1815—Gent (T.) History of Rippon,
       curious woodcuts (wants folding plates), York, 1733 —Walker (T.)
       The Original, *half calf*, 1836 ; and others   5 *vol.*

1032   Sportsman's Magazine (The), or Chronicle of Games and Pas-
       times, *coloured and plain plates*, 3 vol. *complete in the original
       21 parts, with the wrappers, exceedingly rare in this fine state*
                                                                1823-5

1033   S(print) (J.) The Experienc'd Fowler, or the Gentleman, Citizen
       and Country Man's pleasant and profitable Recreation, *frontis-
       piece, old green morocco extra, g. e.*   1697

1034   Standish (John) A Discourse wherein is debated whether it be
       expedient that the Scripture should be in English for al men
       to reade that wyll, *Robert Caly*, 1555—Smyth (R.) Seconde
       Parte of the Book called a Bucklar of the Catholyke Fayeth,
       ib. 1555, 2 vol. in 1, **black letter**, FINE COPIES, *calf extra* 1555

   ₊ The volume by Smyth is not in the British Museum catalogue.
       The first article is also an extremely rare and interesting
       book.

1035   Stead (J.) Description and Natural History of English Song
       Birds, *coloured plates*, 1797—Thompson (W.) The New and
       Complete Bird Fancier, *frontispiece, n. d.* in 1 vol. *calf gilt—*
       The Oracle of Rural Life, *plates, calf gilt*, 1839 ; &c.   (3)

1036   STEEVENS (GEORGE) THE PLAYS OF WILLIAM SHAKSPEARE, in
       15 vol. with the corrections and illustrations of various com-
       mentators, to which are added Notes by Samuel Johnson and
       George Steevens...with a Glossarial Index, by the editor of
       Dodsley's Collection of Old Plays, *view of New Place, engraved
       by Birrell, after J. Jordan, facsimiles of the autograph of the Poet,
       and four folding plates entitled* " *The Plott of the Secound parte
       of the Seven Deadlie Sinns,*" " *The Plott of the deade man's fortune,*"
       " *The Plott of the first parte of Tamar Cam,*" " *The Plott of
       Ffrederick and Basilea,*" 15 vol. *russia extra gilt, marbled leaves,
       with the ex-libris of George Steevens*   1793

   ₊ This is George Steevens' own copy of his famous edition of
       Shakespeare.

1037   Stephens (Thomas) An Essay upon Statius, or, the Five First
       Books of his Thebais, done into English Verse, *fine portrait by
       Marshall*, FIRST EDITION, *original calf*   1648

1038   Sternhold and Hopkins. The Whole Booke of Psalmes with
       the Prose on the margin, collected into English Meeter, with
       apt notes to sing them withall, *fine copy in calf extra by Riviere*
                                                                1623

1039   STEVENSON (ROBERT LOUIS) THE STORY OF A LIE, 80 *pages, uncut*
                                              Hayley and Jackson, 1882

   ₊ This is the rarest of all the first editions of Stevenson's
       writings. It was suppressed before publication, and only some
       half dozen copies are believed to have been preserved.

1040   Stevenson (R. L.) A Child's Garden of Verses, FIRST EDITION,
       in the original blue cloth, uncut, t. e. g. scarce   1885

1041   Stevenson (R. L.) The New Amphion, by R. L. Stevenson,
       Andrew Lang, Robert Browning, &c. FIRST EDITION, LARGE
       PAPER COPY, *the plates printed on Japan paper, original vellum,
       uncut*
                                                      Edinb. 1886

1042   Stevenson (R. L.) Works, EDINBURGH EDITION, including the
       Appendix, containing facsimile reprints of rare little pieces,
       printed at Davos Platz, 28 vol. *portrait, uncut, t. e. g. limited
       issue*   *ib.* 1894-98

1043   Stewart (Wm.) The Bulk of the Chronicles of Scotland, or
       Metrical version of the History of Hector Boece, edited by
       W. Turnbull, 3 vol. *facsimile, half morocco,* UNCUT   1858

1044   Storer (T.) Life and Death of T. Wolsey, Cardinall (in Verse),
       FINE LARGE COPY, *morocco extra, g. e.*   *T. Dawson,* 1599

   ₊ To this excessively rare poem Shakespeare was probably
       indebted for his character of Wolsey in his play of *King
       Henry VIII.*

1045   Storer (J.) and J. Greig.   Views in North Britain illustrative
       of the Works of Robert Burns, *plates, old tree calf gilt,* 1805
       —Stothard (Mrs. C.) Memoirs of the late C. A. Stothard,
       portrait, calf gilt, m. e. 1823—Price (R.) Works of the late
       Dr. Benjamin Franklin, consisting of his Life, written by
       himself, together with Essays, &c. *portrait,* 2 vol. *calf gilt,*
       1802 ; and others   (6)

1046   Storer (J. and H.) and J. N. Brewer.   Histrionic Topography,
       or the Birth Places, Residences and Funeral Monuments of
       the most distinguished Actors, *plates, calf gilt,* 1818—Cowper
       (W.) Poems, with Life by J. Johnson, 3 vol. *old calf gilt,* 1800-
       17—Scott (Sir W.) Lay of the Last Minstrel, 1816—Bower
       (J.) Description of the Abbey of Melrose, *frontispiece,* 1816,
       in 1 vol. *calf gilt;* and another   (6)

1047   Stothard.   Langhorne (Dr.) The Fables of Flora, FIRST EDITION,
       illustrations by Stothard, clean copy in the original boards, uncut
                                                                   1794

1048   Strickland (Agnes) Demetrius, and other Poems, FIRST EDITION,
       PRESENTATION COPY, *with autograph inscription on title, "Robert
       Shields, from his Friend the Author," uncut*   *J. Fraser,* 1833

1049   SUCKLING (SIR JOHN) FRAGMENTA AUREA, a Collection of all the
       Incomparable Peeces, written by Sir John Suckling, and pub-
       lished by a Friend to perpetuate his Memory, printed by his
       owne Copies, *portrait by Wm. Marshall,* FIRST EDITION, *in the
       original sheepskin,* FINE TALL COPY   1646

1050   Suckling (Sir John) Poems, printed by his owne Copy, *with the
       scarce portrait (part torn off), original calf*   1648

1051   Sulpitius Severus.   Opera Omnia quæ extant ex optimis
       Editionibus accurate recognita, FIRST AND BEST ELZEVIR
       EDITION, *large copy in original vellum Lugd. Bat. Elzevir,* 1635

1052   Surtees (E.) Handley Cross, or the Spa Hunt, FIRST EDITION,
       3 vol. *half calf extra, t. e. g. uncut*   1834

1053   SWIFT (DEAN) Travels into several Remote Nations of the
World, in 4 parts, by LEMUEL GULLIVER, 2 vol. FIRST EDI-
TION, *with continuous pagination, portrait and maps, in the original
calf*   *B. Motte,* 1726

1054   Swift (Dean) Travels by Lemuel Gulliver, 4 parts in 3 vol.
second edition, *portrait of Gulliver, and maps*   *ib.* 1727

1055   [Swift (Dean, &c.)] A Tale, being an Addition to Mr. Gay's
Fables, *Dublin,* 1728—The Coachman's Wish, a Dialogue be-
tween Thomas and Grizel, *ib.* 1729—An Apology to the Lady
C—r—t, on her inviting Dean S—f—t to Dinner, *ib.* 1730—
An Epistle to a certain Dean, *London, Dublin reprinted,* 1730—
A Satyr on the Times, and some of the Modern Plays, viz.
Beggars Opera, Timoleon, Humours of Oxford, Cheshire
Comicks, 1730—The Pheasant and the Lark, a Fable, *Dublin,*
1730; &c. *half morocco, g. t. very curious collection*   *in* 1 *vol.*

1056   Swift. An Essay upon the Life, Writings and Character of
Dr. Jonathan Swift, &c. by Deane Swift, Esq. FIRST EDITION,
uncut, scarce in this state   1755

1057   Swinburne (A. C.) Unpublished Verses [1866], *two leaves*
**** Very scarce, only 20 copies are said to have been printed,
most of which were destroyed.

1058   Swinburne (A. C.) An Appeal to England against the Execution
of the Condemned Fenians, *original wrapper, extremely scarce*
Manchester, reprinted from the "Morning Star," 1867
**** This reprint was given away, or, in some instances, sold in
the streets of Manchester before the execution of Allen, Larkin and Gould for the murder of Sergeant Brett near that
city.

1059   Swinburne (A. C.) Siena, FIRST PUBLISHED EDITION, *original
wrappers, uncut,* VERY SCARCE   1868

1060   Swinburne (A. C.) Songs before Sunrise, FIRST EDITION, *one of
25 copies printed on* LARGE PAPER, *for private circulation only,
original cloth, uncut*   *F. S. Ellis,* 1871

1061   Swinburne (A. C.) Auguste Vacquerie, par Swinburne, FIRST
EDITION, *original wrapper, uncut*   *Paris,* 1875
**** Very rare, originally published in the *Examiner,* but never
reprinted in England. "Le grand poëte Swinburne vient de
publier dans une des principales revues anglaises, l'Examiner,
l'étude suivante, que nous sommes empressé de traduire,
comme ayante le double intérêt d'être d'un écrivain illustre
et de montrer comment les écrivains français sont appréciés
en Angleterre."

1062   Swinburne (A. C.) Tristram of Lyonesse, and other Poems,
FIRST EDITION, *original cloth*   1882
**** A Presentation Copy to Frederic Sandys, with signed inscrip-
tion in the author's handwriting.

1063   Swinburne (A. C.) Dolorida, a Poem (in French), written in the
album of Adah Isaacs Menken   1883
**** This beautifully printed little leaflet is of exceeding scarcity.
It was never published, and only 50 copies were printed. "In
spite of Mr. Swinburne's apparent disclaimer in the *Pall Mall
Gazette,* of December 28, 1883, the lines are indubitably his,
and are still extant in his autograph and over his signature
in the album referred to."—*Swinburne's Bibliography.*

1064 Swinburne (A. C.) For the Album of Adam Menken, 2 *leaves,*
containing verses in French, scarce

1065 S(ylvester) (Joshua) Certaine Worthy Manuscript Poems of
great Antiquitie, reserved long in the Studie of a Northfolke
Gentleman ; The Northern Mother's Blessing ; The Way of
Thrift, written nine years before the death of G. Chaucer,
FIRST EDITION, *having also the blank E 2 frequently missing, text*
printed within ornamental top and bottom borders, morocco extra
gilt, g. e. TALL COPY, VERY SCARCE   1597

1066 SYLVESTER (J.) PARLIAMENT OF VERTUES, Royal, Panaretus,
Bethulians Rescue, Little Bartas, Map of Man, Epigramms,
Lachrymæ for Prince Henry and Funerall Elegie on Sydneys,
1614—THE SECOND SESSION of the Parliament of Vertues,
Reall, containing Job Triumphant, Memorials of Mortalitie,
Henrie the Great, St. Lewis the King, A Hymn of Alms,
The Battaill of Yvry, Honor's Farwel, &c. 1615 : 2 vol. in 1,
VERY FINE COPIES, *calf extra, g. e. by F. Bedford*
*** The two parts are rarely found together. The present copies
have *all the separate titles and blank leaves so often wanting.*
The pieces composing this volume appear to have been separately printed at intervals, during the years 1614-15, and
scarcely two copies exactly correspond in the contents. The
present one, in unusually fine state, possesses the two Sessions
and some of the supplementary forms subsequently added,
and has *certain blank leaves, not in most copies, necessary to com-*
plete the sheets. See the long account in the Grolier Club's Cata-
logue of Early English Literature (no. 241).

1067 Tate (Nahum, Poet Laureate) Poems, FIRST EDITION, *dark blue*
morocco extra   1677
*** A fine copy, with the leaf A 1 which contains the " License."
Autograph of Charles Cotton on title-page.

1068 Tate (N.) Poems by Several Hands, and on Several Occasions,
FIRST EDITION, *full red morocco extra, g. e.*   1685

1069 Tate (N.) Elegies on Her late Majesty, late Archbishop of Canterbury, Duke of Ormond, Countess of Dorset, &c. *old purple*
morocco, delicately gold tooled on both sides, crowned monogram of
William III (TO WHOM THE BOOK IS DEDICATED) *at corners,*
g. e.   1702
*** DEDICATION COPY.

1070 Taverner (Richard) THE FLOWERS OF SEN[TEN]CIES, gathered
out of sundry wryters by Erasmus in Latine and Englished,
black *and roman letter,* A LARGE AND BEAUTIFUL COPY, *morocco*
extra, g. e.   imprynted at London by Wyllyam Myddylton, 1547
*** Exceedingly rare, the British Museum copy is the only other
known ; it is in fact a *very early school book,* and its great
rarity is thus explained. Collation A to B 4 in eights, the last
leaf entirely occupied by the printer's mark.

1071 [Taylor (Thomas, *the Platonist)*] The Hymns of Orpheus, with a
Dissertation on the Life and Theology of Orpheus, *vignette on*
title, uncut, scarce   1792

1072 Tennis (a Treatise on) by a Member of the Tennis Club, FIRST
EDITION, *folding plan, half calf, scarce*   1822

1073   Tennyson. Poems, by Two Brothers, *the very rare* FIRST EDI-
            TION, *red morocco extra, uncut, t. e. g. (title repaired)*   1827

1074   TENNYSON (Alfred Lord) Poems, chiefly Lyrical, FIRST EDITION
            (*a few inner margins stained*), *uncut, scarce*   1830

1075   Tennyson (Lord) Poems, 2 vol. FIRST EDITION, *uncut, with the
            original boards and paper labels*   *Moxon,* 1842

1076   Tennyson (Lord) The Princess, a Medley, FIRST EDITION, *with
            half-title, in the original cloth, uncut*   1847

1077   Tennyson (Lord) Ode on the Death of the Duke of Wellington,
            ORIGINAL EDITION, *unbound*   *Moxon,* 1852

1078   Tennyson (Lord) Maud, and other Poems, FIRST EDITION, *original
            cloth*   1855

1079   Tennyson (Lord) A Welcome, FIRST EDITION, *scarce, Moxon,* 1863

1080   Tennyson (Lord) The Passing of Arthur, FIRST EDITION, *in the
            original wrappers as issued*   1884
      ₊ Only a few copies were issued for examination purposes, very
            scarce.

1081   Tennyson (Lord) To H.R.H. Princess Beatrice, *an Ode consisting
            of 22 lines printed on one side, composed by the Poet Laureate on
            the occasion of the marriage of Her Royal Highness, uncut*   1885

      ₊ Only a few copies were printed for private circulation ; ex-
            cessively scarce.

1082   TENNYSON (LORD) Life and Works, 12 vol. " édition de luxe,"
            portraits and frontispieces, silk binding, uncut   1898-99

1083   Tennyson (Lord) A Memoir, by his Son, 2 vol. *portraits and
            illustrations, original cloth, uncut*   1897

1084   Terentius (Pub.) Comœdiæ sex, acced. Ælii Donati Comment.
            integer accurante C. Schrevelio, *old calf, arms of Louis Henry
            Comte de Loménie on both sides, Lugd. Bat.* 1657—Les Comédies
            de Terence avec la traduction, &c. de Madame Dacier, 3 vol.
            frontispieces, &c. old calf, Rotterdam, 1717 — Virgile, les Géor-
            giques, trad. par Delille, *frontispiece by Casanova, and plates by
            De Longueil, after Eisen, French mottled calf gilt, Paris, Bluet,*
            1770   (5)

1085   Testament (New) both in Latin and English, after the vulgare
            Text, which is red in the Churche, translated and corrected
            by Myles Coverdale, **black letter** (*the Latin in roman letter*), *fine
            copy, but title, dedication, one leaf of the calendar, to the reader,
            and folios* I *and* VIII *admirably facsimiled by E. Offor, blue morocco
            extra, gilt gaufré edges, very rare*   *Paris, F. Regnault,* 1538
      ₊ This edition, according to Fox, was printed by Bishop Bonner
            whilst English Ambassador in France, and its excessive rarity
            is easily accounted for, as after the distribution of a few copies
            as presents to the Council and Officers of State by Bonner, to
            procure himself the See of London, the whole impression was
            seized by the Inquisition and destroyed.

1086   Testament. The New Testament of Our Lord and Saviour
            Jesus Christ published in 1526, being the first translation from
            the Greek into English by William Tyndale, reprinted with a
            Memoir by George Offor, *portrait, purple morocco extra, sides
            covered with gold tooling, g. e.*   *Bagster,* 1836

1087   Testament (Das New) so durch L. Emser salige verteutscht
        anno 1529 (*a translation correcting Luther's version*), lit. goth.
        register in red and black, woodcuts (*title and next 2 ll. mended*),
        vellum   *Leyptzich*, 1529

1088   Thackeray (W. M.) Essay on the Genius of George Cruikshank,
        numerous illustrations by G. C. original cloth   1840

1089   Thackeray (W. M.) The Irish Sketch-Book, by Mr. M. A. Tit-
        marsh, *frontispieces and numerous illustrations in the text*, FIRST
        EDITION, 2 vol. *original cloth, uncut*   1843

1090   THACKERAY (W. M.) THE SNOB, a Literary and Scientific Jour-
        nal, not "Conducted by Members of the University," *numbers
        III to VI with title-page, dedication, preface and index, Cambridge,*
        1829—The Snobs Trip to Paris, or the Humours of the Long
        Vacation (*in verse*), *ib. n. d.*—The Fellow, *no. XI*, 1856—The
        Tripos, *no. I, n. d.*—Granta, a Fragment by a Freshman, edited
        by the Rev. J. Snodgrass, 1841—A Few more Words to Fresh-
        men by the Rev. T. T. *Cambridge, for the author*, 1841 ; *in
        1 vol. half cloth*

1091   Thackeray.   Notes of a Journey from Cornhill to Grand Cairo,
        coloured frontispiece and woodcuts by the author, FIRST EDITION,
        very fine clean copy, in the original cloth, uncut   1846

1092   The Innocent Epicure, or the Art of Angling, a Poem, *calf extra,
        with symbolical tooling in blind and gold on the back and sides, by
        T. Gosden, g. e. scarce*   1713

1093   THE SPORTING REPOSITORY : Horse-racing, Hunting, Cocking,
        &c. Anecdotes on Sporting Subjects, *beautifully coloured plates
        by H. Alken* (4 *wanting*), *in the original half binding, very scarce,
        sold not subject to return*   *Mc Lean*, 1822

1094   Thomas Aquinas.   Compendium Theologiæ, *Italian MS. on* 269
        leaves of vellum, in red and black, with illuminated capitals
                                            thick sm. 8vo.   SÆC. XIV

1095   Thomson (J.) Alfred : a Masque, represented before their Royal
        Highnesses the Prince and Princess of Wales at Cliffden, on
        the First of August, 1740, FIRST EDITION, FINE LARGE COPY,
        calf extra, g. e.
                *printed for A. Millar, over-against St. Clement's Church in the
                                                        Strand*, 1740

    ⁎ Contains the first edition of "Rule Britannia."   "From 1740
        dates one of Thomson's most famous compositions—the noble
        ode known as 'Rule Britannia,' destined to be the political
        hymn of this country as long as she maintains her political
        power."—SOUTHEY.

1096   Thornton (A.) Don Juan in London, 2 vol. FIRST EDITION,
        *coloured engravings, red levant morocco extra, by Riviere & Son,
        rough g. e. fine copy*   1821-2

1097   Tobacco.   Traité de la Culture, Fabrication, et Vente du Tabac,
        folding plates, 1791 — Lovedan (A.) Tratado de los usos, y
        Abusos del Tabaco, Café, Té, y Chocolate, *calf, Madrid*, 1796
        —Buc'hoz, Dissertations sur l'Effets du Tabac, du Café, du
        Cacao et du Thé, *folding plates*, 1788   (3)

1098 Tobacco. Meisner (L. F.) de Caffe, Chocolatae, Herbae Theo ac
        Nicotianae : Natura, Usu, et Abusu, *plates, Norimb.* 1721—
        Schoon (T.) De Cultur van de Tabak, &c. *plates, old calf,*
        1692   (2)

1099 Tobacco. Tatham (W.) Essay on the Culture of Tobacco, 1800
        —Jennings (J.) Practical Treatise on the Cultivation of
        Tobacco, *plates,* 1830 — Prescott (H. P.) Strong Drink and
        Tobacco Smoke, *illustrations,* 1869 ; and others   (8)

1100 Tobacco. Thorius (R.) Tobacco : a Poem, in two Books, *un-
        bound,* 1716 — Code des Fumeurs et des Priseurs, *coloured
        frontispiece, uncut,* 1830   (2)

1101 Tobacco. Tiedemann (F.) Geschichte des Tabaks, *plates, uncut,*
        1854 — Saint-Aubin, Le Monopole des Tabacs, *uncut,* 1819 ;
        and others   (6)

1102 Tom Thumb. The Travels of Tom Thumb over England and
        Wales, containing Descriptions of whatever is most remark-
        able in the several Counties, interspersed with many pleasant
        Adventures that happened to him personally during the Course
        of his Journey, *with a folding map, calf*   1746

   ⁂ At page 45 is a very curious notice of Shakespeare. " The
        famous *Shakespear,* whose plays the people are so fond of in
        London, was born and died at Stratford-upon-Avon in this
        County. The following lines are upon his grave-stone, which
        I venture to say were not made by himself " (*here follow the
        verses*). Most copies of this juvenile book have been " thumbed
        out of existence."

1103 Tracey (Richard) A Bryef and Short Declaracyon made, where-
        bye everye Chrysten Man may knowe what is a Sacrament,
        of what partes a Sacramente consysteth and is made, for what
        intent Sacramentes were instituted, and what is the pryncypall
        effect of Sacraments, and finally of the abuse of the Sacrament
        of Chrystes body and bloud, black letter, LARGE AND BEAUTI-
        FUL COPY, *morocco extra, g. e.*   *Robert Stoughton,* 1548

   ⁂ Not in the British Museum. Examples of Stoughton's press
        are exceedingly rare.

1104 TRACTS. Price (R.) On the Importance of the American Revo-
        lution, 1785 — Young (Arthur) The Example of France a
        Warning to Britain, 1793—Moore (Thos.) Letter to the
        Roman Catholics of Dublin, 1810 — Plan of the New Con-
        stitution for the United States of America, 1787—Paine (T.)
        Letter to the Marquise of Lansdowne, respecting the ac-
        knowledgment of American Independence, *portrait,* 1791—
        Godwin (Wm.) Letters of Verax to the Editor of the Morn-
        ing Chronicle, 1815 — Talleyrand, Memoir concerning the
        Commercial Relation of the United States with England,
        1806 ; and numerous other Tracts on Political Affairs, the
        Army, Agriculture, East India Trade, Currency, Napoleon
        Bonaparte, &c. ; and others   *in 33 vol.*

1105 Trials for Adultery, &c. including " Memoirs of Mrs. Harriet
        Er——g——m " (175—), *bound in 3 vol. some curious plates, old
        calf*   1732-1789

1106   Tyndall (Wyllyam) A Briefe Declaration of the Sacraments,
       expressing the fyrst oryginall how they came up, and were
       institute with the true and moost syncere meaning and under-
       standing of the same, **black letter**, *fine large copy, morocco
       extra, g. e.*
               *Imprinted at London by Robert Stoughton dwellynge within
               Ludgate, at the sygne of the Bishoppes Miter (about* 1548)
   *** Very rare.   " This is the *only* edition of the Treatise which,
       although an admirable piece of English prose, was yet not
       sufficiently dogmatic on the subject of the Real Presence to
       please either party in the Church of England."

1107   Vanbrugh (Sir John) La Maison Rustique, or the Country House,
       a Farce, *frontispiece, calf gilt*, 1835 — Itard (E. M.) Historical
       Account of the Discovery and Education of the Young Savage
       caught in the woods near Aveyron, *frontispiece, calf gilt*, 1802
       —Okes (T. V.) Account of the Providential Preservation of
       Eliz. Woodcock who survived a Confinement under the snow
       of nearly eight days and nights, *portrait inserted, half calf*,
       1799 ; and another   (4)

1108   Veneres uti observantur in Gemmis Antiquis, 70 *plates*, with
       Descriptive Text in English, *red morocco gilt, g. e.*
                                                   Lugd. Bat. n. d.

1109   Veneres uti observantur in Gemmis Antiquis, *the* 70 *plates in
       bistre*, with Descriptive Text in English, *red morocco gilt, g. e.*
                                                   ib. n. d.

1110   Veneres uti observantur in Gemmis Antiquis, 69 *plates only*, with
       Descriptive Text in English and French (*no title to part II*),
       half bound, sold not subject to return

1111   Vere (Marquis de) Life and Adventures of the Prince of Salermo,
       and Amour with an Ottoman Princess, &c. *old calf*, 1770 —
       The Captivity, Sufferings, and Escape of James Scurry who
       was detained ten years in the Dominion of Hyder Ali, and
       Tippoo Saib, *portrait, uncut*, 1824 ; and others   *4 vol.*

1112   Victorian Portraits.   Album containing Fifty-eight Cabinet and
       Carte-de-visite Photographs of Royalty, including several of
       her late Majesty, the Princess of Wales, Princess Beatrice,
       Dukes of Cambridge, Connaught, &c. *red morocco, g. e.*

1113   Villon.   The Poems of Master Francis Villon of Paris, now
       first done into English Verse, by John Payne, *issue limited to
       157 copies, printed for private distribution, gilt parchment, uncut,
       t. e. g.*   1878

1114   VOLTAIRE.   La Pucelle, Poëme en XXI Chants, avec les Notes
       et les Variantes, édition conformé à l'Originale, publiée en
       1784, 2 vol. *portraits and beautiful plates after Moreau, engraved
       by Baquoy, Dambrun, Lemire, &c. a series of "planches libres"
       (neatly inlaid) inserted, fine copy in morocco extra, watered silk
       linings, joints, g. e. by Bozérian*   1789

1115   Vyner (R. T.) Notitia Venatica, a Treatise on Fox Hunting,
       embracing the General Management of Hounds, &c. *coloured
       plates, calf extra, t. e. g. by Riviere & Son, uncut, Ackermann's
       Catalogue of Sporting Prints bound in at end, scarce*   1847

1116   Wake (Isaac) Rex Platonicus: sive de potentissimi principis
       Jacobi Regis, ad Illustrissimam Academiam Oxoniensem ad-
       ventu, Aug. 27, Anno 1605, *vellum*   *Oxoniæ*, 1635
       „ An account will be found in Hunter's New Illustrations of
       Shakespeare. "*Macbeth* was certainly one of Shakespeare's
       latest productions, and it might possibly have been suggested
       to him by a little performance on the same subject at Oxford,
       before King James, 1605.   I will transcribe my notice of it
       from *Wake's Rex Platonicus:* 'Fabulæ ansam dedit antiqua de
       Regiâ prosapiâ historiola apud Scoto-Britannos celebrata, quæ
       narrat tres olim Sibyllas occurrisse duobus Scotiæ proceribus,
       Macbetho & Banchoni, & illum prædixisse Regem futurum, sed
       Regem nullum geniturum; hunc Regem non futurum, sed
       Reges geniturum multos.   Vaticinii veritatem rerum eventus
       comprobavit.   Banchonis enim è stirpe potentissimus Jacobus
       oriundus.' "—Dr. FARMER.   There was a copy in Halliwell's
       Sale Catalogue, May, 1856.

1117   WALKINGTON (Thos.) The Optick Glasse of Humours, or the
       touchstone of a golden temperature,…Wherein the foure
       complections Sanguine, Cholericke, Phlegmaticke, Melancho-
       licke, are succinctly painted forth, &c. *woodcut title, frontispiece,
       calf*   *Oxford (about* 1605)
       „ Refer to Dr. Farmer's "Essay on the Learning of Shak-
       speare."   It contains the well-known story from Scaliger of
       one who could not endure the playing on the bagpipe alluded
       to by Shakespeare in "The Merchant of Venice."   There was
       a copy in Halliwell's Sale Catalogue, May, 1856.

1118   Waller (Edmond) Poems, &c. Written upon several occasions
       and to several persons : never till now corrected, and published
       with the approbation of the author, FIRST AUTHORISED
       EDITION, *calf*   1664

1119   Waller (E. and others) Examen Miscellaneum, consisting of
       Verse and Prose, of Verse by Marquis of Normanby, Lord
       Rochester, Waller, Wolseley, and Mrs. Wharton, with Satires
       and Fables, *original calf*   1702
       „ Shakespeare and other English Poets are alluded to at p. 63.

1120   Walpole (Horace) Catalogue of Royal and Noble Authors of
       England, FIRST EDITION (with the scarce postscript printed
       in 1786, of which only 40 copies were taken), *plates,* 2 vol.
       straight grained crimson morocco, line tooled, g. e. by Mackenzie
                                    Printed at Strawberry Hill, 1758-86

1121   Walton (Izaak) Lives of Dr. John Donne, Sir H. Wotton, R.
       Hooker, G. Herbert and Dr. R. Sanderson, edited, with
       notes, by John Major, *portraits and plates on india paper, and
       woodcuts, morocco gilt, g. e.*   *Major,* 1825

1122   Walton (Izaak) Lives of Donne, Wotton, Hooker, Herbert and
       Sanderson, with Index and Illustrative Notes, *portraits, plates,
       india proofs, and woodcuts,* LARGE PAPER, *old straight grained
       green morocco extra, g. e.*   *ib.* 1825

1123   Walton and Cotton's Complete Angler, Notes, &c. by Sir John
       Hawkins (and Sir Henry Ellis), *portraits and other plates,
       uncut, back broken*   *Bagster,* 1815

1124 Walton (I.) and C. Cotton. The Complete Angler, with an Introductory Essay and Illustrative Notes, *plates, india proofs, and woodcuts,* LARGE PAPER, *old straight grained green morocco extra, emblematically tooled back, g. e. wants the original portrait, but one engraved by C. Rolls, in proof state, substituted, Major,* 1833

1125 Walton. Herne (S.) Domus Carthusiana: An Account of the Foundation of the Charter House, portrait of Thos. Sutton, *with the autograph of Izaak Walton on the title-page, and that of his son, " Is. Walton, 1683-4," on the flyleaf, original calf* 1677

1126 WASHINGTON. A COLLECTION OF FORTY VERY RARE PAMPHLETS ISSUED DURING THE LIFETIME OR IMMEDIATELY AFTER THE DEATH OF GEORGE WASHINGTON. The whole printed in different cities of the United States. *Uniformly bound in green cloth, many uncut*

1. Tribute to Washington (in verse), *Troy*, 1800. 2. The Last Official Address of General Washington to the Legislatures of the United States, *Hartford*, 1783. 3. Holmes (A.) Sermon on the Death of George Washington (presentation copy from the author), *Boston*, 1799. 4. Foster (J.) Discourse on the Death of George Washington, *ib.* 1800. 5. Hart (L.) Discourse occasioned by the Death of George Washington, *Norwich*, 1800. 6. Harris (T. M.) Discourse on the Death of George Washington, *Charlestown*, 1800. 7. Kirkland (J. T.) Discourse on the Death of George Washington, to which is added his Valedictory Address to the people of the United States, *Boston*, 1800. 8. Morris (Gouverneur) Oration upon the Death of George Washington, *New York*, 1800. 9. Strong (N.) Discourse upon the Death of George Washington, *Hartford*, 1800. 10. Willard (J.) Address in Latin, and David Tappan's Discourse in English on the Death of George Washington, *Boston*, 1800. 11. Thacher (P.) Sermon on the Death of George Washington, *ib.* 1800. 12. Stillman (S.) Sermon on the Death of George Washington, *ib.* 1800. 13. Taggart (S.) Discourse on the Death of George Washington, *Greenfield*, 1800. 14. Trumbull (B.) Discourse on the Death of George Washington, with a Portrait, *Newhaven*, 1800. 15. White (D. A.) Eulogy on George Washington, *Haverhill*, 1800. 16. Stearns (E.) Eulogium on George Washington, *East Windsor*, 1800. 17. Tomb (S.) Oration on the Death of George Washington to which is annexed two Odes and an Acrostic, *Newburyport*, 1800. 18. Abbot (A.) Eulogy on the Life and Character of George Washington, *Haverhill*, 1800. 19. Bascom (J.) Oration on the Death of George Washington, *Boston*, 1800. 20. Boddily (J.) Sermon on the Death of George Washington, *Newburyport*, 1800. 21. Bigelow (T.) Eulogy on the Life, Character, and Services of Brother George Washington, *Boston*, 1800. 22. Bartlett (J.) Oration on the Death of George Washington, *Charleston*, 1800. 23. King (W.) Discourse on the Death of George Washington, *Norwich*, 1800. 24. Lewis (E.) Eulogy on the Life and Character of George Washington, in verse, *Pittsfield*, 1800. 25. Dwight (T.) Discourse on the Character of George Washington, *Newhaven*, 1800. 26. Isham (J.) Oration Commemorative of George Washington, *New London*, 1800. 27. M'Clure (D.) Discourse on the Death of George Washington, presentation copy from the author, *East Windsor*, 1800. 28. Moseley (J. O.) Oration on the Death of George Washington, *Hartfield*, 1800. 29. Mycall (J.) Funereal Address on the Death of George Washington, *Boston*, 1800. 30. Lee (H.) Funeral Oration on the Death of George Washington, *ib.* 1800. 31. Carroll (Bp.) Discourse on George Washington, *Baltimore*, 1800. 32. Cumings (H.) Eulogy on George Washington, *Amherst*, 1800. 33. Davis (J.) Eulogy on George Washington, *Boston*, 1800. 34. Dana (J.) Discourse on the Death of George Washington, *Newburyport*, 1800. 35. Everett (O.) Eulogy on George Washington, *Charlestown*, 1800. 36. Flint (A.) Discourse on the Death of George Washington, *Hartford*, 1800. 37. Porter (E.) Eulogy on George Washington, *Boston*, 1800. 38. Parish (E.) Oration on the Death of George Washington, *Newburyport*, 1800. 39. Russell (J. M.) Funeral Oration on George Washington, *Boston*, 1800. 40. Story (J.) Eulogy on George Washington, presentation copy from the author, *Salem*, 1800.

1127   Watson (William) Excursions in Criticism : being some prose recreations of a Rhymer, FIRST EDITION, *original boards, uncut, one of 50 copies*   1893

1128   Watts (Isaac) Horæ Lyricæ : Poems, chiefly of the Lyric kind, in 2 books, FIRST EDITION, *soiled throughout, first and last leaves mended, and title cut round and mounted, morocco, sold not subject to return*   1706

1129   [WATTS (ISAAC)] THE CHILD'S PSALTER, containing (i) Morning and Evening Prayer ; (ii) The Church Catechism Explain'd ; (iii) Select Psalms, and other parts of Holy Scripture ; (iv) Graces before and after Meat.   To which is added many Profitable and Delightful Instructions for Youth, *original sheep*   London, 1711

    **** THE CHILD'S PSALTER, which we have excellent reasons for believing to be a little volume of the first order of rarity (*no other appears to have occurred for sale*) seems from the title-page to belong to that large and singular family of literature especially dedicated to juvenile learners or readers.   Internal evidence points to Isaac Watts as the probable author of this practically unknown little volume.

1130   Watts (Isaac) The Psalms of David, imitated in the Language of the New Testament, FIRST EDITION, *contemporary blue morocco, g.e.*   1719

1131   WATTS (ISAAC) CATECHISMS OR INSTRUCTIONS IN THE PRINCIPLES OF THE CHRISTIAN RELIGION, AND THE HISTORY OF SCRIPTURE, COMPOSED FOR CHILDREN AND YOUTH, according to their different Ages.   To which is prefix'd a Discourse on the Way of Instruction by Catechisms, and the best manner of composing them, FIRST EDITION, *in the original sheep-skin binding, fine large copy*   1730

    **** Presentation Copy to the Revd. Dr. Curteis, with signed inscription in Watts' autograph.   Lowndes cites *no* copy as having occurred for sale, and the example in the British Museum is the only other one that can be traced.   It is probably quite as rare, therefore, as the famous " Divine Songs," a copy of which sold in these rooms recently for £155.   The excessive difficulty of obtaining first editions of books of the 18th Century which have enjoyed a world-wide reputation is now beginning to be better understood. Watts' Preface, directed to the Congregation usually assembling in Berry (? Bury) Street, Hertfordshire, explains the object of the work, which is conceived in a sufficiently broad and liberal spirit, and advises teachers of various denominations how they should instruct children in the elementary knowledge of Christianity.

1132   Wesley (J.) An Extract of the Life of the late Rev. David Brainerd, Missionary to the Indians, *original sheep*, 1800—Vigne (G. T.) Six Months in America, *plates*, 2 vol. *calf gilt, m. e.* 1832—A Discours of Dunkirk, with some reflexes upon the late surrender thereof, *old calf*, 1664   (4)

1133 WEBBE (GEORGE) A POSIE OF SPIRITUALL FLOWERS, TAKEN OUT OF THE GARDEN OF THE HOLY SCRIPTURES, consisting of these sixe sortes : Heart's Ease, True Delight, The World's Wonders, The Soules Solace, Times Complaint, The Doom of Sinners, &c. *dark brown morocco extra, t. e. g. uncut* 1610

*** *Probably unique in uncut state.* Lowndes simply gives the title of this excessively rare little volume, but no indication of the whereabouts of a single copy. *No other Bibliographer mentions it. Not in the British Museum.*

1134 Wellington (Duke of) A. L. signed Wellington, $2\frac{1}{2}$ pp. 8vo, *with directed franked wrapper and seal, dated Jan.* 12, 1823 (1)

1135 Westall (Richard) A Day in Spring, and other Poems, *bound in white silk, with a water-colour drawing on each cover, and a painting of a river scene on the fore-edge under the gold* 1808

1136 Westmacott (C. M.) THE ENGLISH SPY . . . . Portraits of the Illustrious, Eminent, Eccentric and Notorious, drawn from the Life by " Bernard Blackmantle," vol. I, FIRST EDITION, *coloured plates and woodcuts by Robert Cruikshank, many leaves soiled, front. and title slightly defective, half bound, sold not subject to return* 1825

1137 Weston (Jas.) Stenography Compleated, or the Art of Short-Hand brought to Perfection, 3 parts, *portrait and 2 engravings by J. Cole, old calf* n. d.

1138 Whistler (J. McNeill) Mr. Whistler's " Ten o'Clock," FIRST EDITION, *original wrapper, uncut* 1888

1139 WHITTINGTON (ROBERT). A Frutefull Worke of Lucius Anneus Senecæ, called THE MYRROUR OR GLASSE OF MANNERS AND WYSSEDOME, bothe in latin and englysshe, black letter, *woodcut on title, a* LARGE AND FINE COPY, *morocco extra, g. e.* *Imprynted at the Sygne of Saynt George by W. Myddylton,* 1547

*** An extremely rare *school book ;* there are copies in the British Museum and Bodleian Libraries, but *no others are recorded.* This was designed as an educational manual by Robert Whittington, an Oxford man, and the master and predecessor of the famous William Lily. He was the first person who compiled a systematic grammar for use in schools.

1140 Whyte Melville (G. J.) General Bounce, or The Lady and the Locusts, 2 vol. FIRST EDITION, *clean copy, in original cloth* 1855

1141 Wilde (Oscar) Lady Windermere's Fan, a Play about a Good Woman, FIRST EDITION, *original cloth, uncut* 1893

1142 Wilde (Oscar) Salomé : Drama en un Acte, FIRST FRENCH EDITION, *original wrapper, uncut* Paris, 1893

1143 Wilde (Oscar) Salomé : a Tragedy in one Act, translated from the French, pictured by Aubrey Beardsley, FIRST ENGLISH EDITION, *uncut* 1894

1144 Winston (C.) Inquiry into Ancient Glass Paintings . . . . with
      Hints on Glass Painting, 2 vol. *numerous coloured and other
      plates, original cloth, t. e. g.*   *Oxford,* 1847

1145 Wither (George) Hymns and Songs of the Church, translated
      and composed by G. W. 1623—The Psalms of David, trans-
      lated by G. W. *wants title and a few headlines are shaved,* 1623,
      morocco gilt, g. e. uniform   (2)

1146 Wither (George) Vox Pacifica : a Voice tending to the Pacifi-
      cation of God's Wrath, FIRST EDITION, *with the curious wood-
      cut map of England, Scotland, and Ireland, calf*   1645

1147 Wit's Interpreter : The English Parnassus, THIRD EDITION,
      with many New Additions by J. C. *frontispiece by Gaywood,
      morocco, g. e.*   1771

1148 Wollstonecraft (Mary) Original Stories from Real Life, FIRST
      EDITION, *frontispiece and plates by W. Blake, original sheep*
                                                   J. Johnson, 1791

1149 Wordsworth (William) Lyrical Ballads, with a few other Poems,
      FIRST EDITION, *title damaged and mounted, original calf* 1798

1150 Wordsworth (W.) Poems, 2 vol. FIRST EDITION, *with both the half
      titles, in the original boards, uncut, very scarce in this state* 1807
   ⁎ Presentation copy, with the author's autograph inscription on
      half title, "To Mrs. Fermer from William Wordsworth."

1151 Wordsworth (Wm.) The Waggoner, a Poem, to which are added
      Sonnets, FIRST EDITION, *original wrapper, uncut*
                                                   Longman, 1819

1152 Wordsworth. Thomson (Jas.) Poetical and Dramatic Works, 2
      vol. (*vol. I,* 1768, *vol. II,* 1763) *calf, one title a little damaged*
   ⁎ Purchased at the sale of Wm. Wordsworth's library at Rydal
      Mount, July 21, 1859, and bears the poet's autograph signa-
      ture in each volume.

1153 Wordsworth. Eikon Basilike, *old calf, no title*   (1648)
   ⁎ Wm. Wordsworth's copy, with his autograph on the first
      page. Purchased at the sale at Rydal Mount in 1859.

1154 World in Miniature, edited by F. Shoberl, 43 vol. *numerous
      coloured engravings of costume, &c. calf*   *R. Ackermann, n. d.*

1155 Worlidge (J.) Vinetum Britannicum : Treatise on Cider and
      other Wines and Drinks extracted from fruits growing in
      this Kingdom, FIRST EDITION, *with "Licensed" leaf, original
      sheep*   1676

1156 Worth of a Penny, or Friendly Advice how to Value Money,
      the Many Uses that a Penny may be put to, &c. *printed and
      sold at Stamford, in Lincolnshire, and at St. Edmund's Bury,
      Suffolk, n. d.*—Sowter (J.) The way to be Wise and Wealthy,
      or The excellency of Industry and Frugality, recommended
      to the Gentleman, Scholar, Soldier, Sailor, Husbandman, &c.
      Exon. P. Bishop, 1716, and 12 Sermons on the Education of
      Children, 1719-33, *half calf*   *in 1 vol.*

1157 Wright (W.) The Complete Fisher, or The True Art of Angling,
      frontispiece, old calf extra, g. e.   1740

1158 WYCLIFFE. ENGLISH NEW TESTAMENT, WITH CAL-
ENDAR, &c. ILLUMINATED MANUSCRIPT on THIN VELLUM
(341 *ll.* 6½ by 4½ *in.*) *finely written in English* black letter,
*endings and headings of chapters in red, double columns of 21 lines,
calendar, &c. in red and black,* 27 *of the pages have* VERY FINELY
ILLUMINATED BORDERS *of flower decorations connected with a
beautiful ornamental initial, and there are many other separate
initials with short marginal decorations, and numerous ornamental
pen letters also with marginal decorations, bound in boarded purple
velvet with brass lacquered ornaments and clasps, in modern oak
box with lock and key*   SÆC. XV. [*c.* 1425]

*** An EXCEEDINGLY VALUABLE AND INTERESTING WYCLIFFE
TESTAMENT. It commences with a Table to find Easter for
40 years from 1424, on reverse of which is a leaf to find the
movable feasts for ever. The Calendar follows, occupying
twelve pages. Then come 27 pages containing a Table of
Lessons, Epistles, and Gospels: "*Here bigyneth a rule yet
tellith in whiche chapitris of ye bible ye mai fynde ye lessoñs,
pistlis & gospels yat be rad in ye chirche after ye Uss of Salisburi marked with lettris of ye a. b. c.*" &c. The Prologue to St.
Matthew follows. There are two Prologues to each book.
The epistle Jude is divided into two chapters at "Woe to
them." After the Apocalypse begins "*Ye Lessoñs and Pistlis
of ye Oold Lawe yet ben red in ye chirche in al ye yeer after ye
Uss of Salisburi.*" The MS. finishes with a leaf headed "*Here
suen Õ (other) Lessons ye whiche ben not in Salisberie Uss.*" In
the Calendar for July 2 are Processus and Martinian instead
of the Visitation. This latter began to be observed in England in 1431. At the end of the Lessons and Epistles is a
Rhymed Prayer to the Virgin against the Pestilence, in a
later hand, beginning "*O heavenly Queen of Grace our lode
Ster.*" On the first leaf are the following inscriptions:
"*Guilielmo Lambardo dedit Rudulphus Rokebius Hospitalis Sctæ
Catherinæ Magister atqz Serenissimæ Reginæ Elizabethæ a Sup-
plicñ Libellus Jul.* 1591." In the margin of the same page,
"*Ante Annos* 166 (*nempe circiter initium Regni Regis II.* 6)
*scriptum fuisse hoc exemplar ex hac Tabella conjecturam facio
W. Lambarde* 1591." Below this is written "*Script. Anno
Xti* 1425." The "Ralph Rokeby" by whom the Manuscript
was presented to Wm. Lambarde (the first Kentish Historian)
was Master of the Old Foundation of St. Katherine's Hospital,
which originally was located near the Tower. The MS. was
also formerly in the possession of Wm. Herbert, the Historian
of English Typography, in 1773. The MS. came afterwards
into the possession of Charles Mayo, M.A.,F.R.S. (1767-1858),
first Rawlinson Professor of Anglo-Saxon at Oxford, and was
inherited by the present owner.

1159 Yarrell (William) History of British Fishes, 2 vol. LARGE PAPER,
with two Supplements, nearly 400 *woodcuts, morocco extra, g. e.*
Van Voorst, 1836

1160 Zoological Society's Proceedings for 1861 to 1885, 25 vol.
numerous coloured and other plates, calf gilt, g. e.   1861-1885

1161 Zouch (T.) Life of Isaac Walton, including Notices of his Con-
temporaries, *plates, proofs, original boards, uncut*
S. Prowett, 1823

QUARTO.

1162   [Raynsford (John)] The Yong Souldier | Instructing the Right
       Use of Arms, Distances, Motions, and Firings, &c.] (8 *ll.*) *top
       of title shaved, half calf, scarce*
                          sm. 4to.   *J. E. for Jos. Hunscott,* 1642

1163   Roman Emperors.   Huttichus (J.) Imperatorum et Cæsarum
       Vitæ, *numerous woodcut portraits in white on black backgrounds
       within figure borders by Holbein (one leaf missing), calf, Argent.*
       1534—An Earlier Issue of the same, *woodcut borders to titles
       only, Argent.* 1533   (2)

1164   Roman de la Rose.   Cy commence le Rommans de la Rose.
       Ou lart damoars est tout encloze (By Guillaume de Lorris
       and Jehan de Meun).   Begins
                  "Maintes gens dient qui en songes
                   Na se fables non et menconges
                   Mais len peut telz songes songier
                   Qui ne sont mie mensongier."
   ₊ MS. of the Fifteenth Century, on vellum, ff. 145 (11 *by* 10
       in.) written in neat lettres bâtardes in double columns of 37
       lines, *rubricated, with* 11 *illuminated historiated miniatures,* 2½ *in.
       square (some rubbed), and several hundred small illuminated orna-
       mental initials, modern red morocco gilt.*   From the Ashburnham-
       Barrois Collection, where it sold for £110.

1165   Rowe (John) Tragi-Comœdia, Being a Brief Relation of the
       Strange and Wonderfull hand of God discovered at Witney,
       in the Comedy Acted there February the third, where there
       were some Slaine, many Hurt, with severall other remarkable
       passages, Together with what was Preached in three Sermons
       on that occasion from Rom. i, 18.   Both which may serve
       some check to the Growing Atheisme of the Present Age,
       half calf   *Oxford,* 1653
   ₊ The Comedy was Mucedorus, one of those attributed to
       Shakespeare.   (Halliwell-Phillipps's Shakespearian Rarities).
       Refer to Mr. Hazlitt's "Shakespeare," pages 6 and 7.

𝕽𝖔𝖝𝖇𝖚𝖗𝖌𝖍𝖊 𝕮𝖑𝖚𝖇 𝕻𝖚𝖇𝖑𝖎𝖈𝖆𝖙𝖎𝖔𝖓𝖘.

1166   A Roxburghe Garland, PRINTED ON VELLUM   1817
   ₊ Presented by James Boswell.

1167   Vox Populi Vox Dei, a Complaynt of the Commons against
       Taxes, *half bound morocco, uncut*   1821
   ₊ This was printed by Sir Joseph Lidderdale as his contribution
       to the Club, but for some reason Skelton's Magnificence was
       substituted.   After his death, in accordance with his request,
       it was presented to the members.   This was Mr. Lloyd's
       copy, and has the dedication and list of members.

1168   Cuck-Queanes and Cuckolds Errants: a Comœdye.   The Faery
       Pastorall by W(illiam) P(ercy), edited by J. Haslewood,
       PRINTED ON VELLUM, *half bound morocco, uncut*   1824
   ₊ Only two copies were printed on vellum.   Presented by Mr.
       Lloyd.   This was his copy.

Roxburghe Club Publications, *continued.*

1169   Parlyament of Deuylles. *Emprynted by Wynkyn de Worde* 1509,
       facsimile Reprint by R. Weber, half bound morocco, uncut, VERY
       RARE
   ⁎ Only 33 copies printed (about 1825) by Mr. Richard Heber,
       as his contribution to the Club, but for some reason it was
       never issued.

1170   Roxburghe Revels and other relative Papers, including Answers
       to the Attack on the Memory of Joseph Haslewood, with
       Specimens of his Literary Productions (edited by James
       Maidment), *only 50 copies printed, uncut*   *Edinb.* 1837

1171   Powis (Earl of) Speech in the House of Lords, May 29, 1843,
       half bound morocco, uncut   1843
   ⁎ Presented by the Earl of Powis.

1172   Forrest (W.) History of Grisild the Second : a Narrative in
       Verse of the Divorce of Queen Katherine of Arragon, edited
       by W. D. Macray, LARGE PAPER, *half bound morocco, uncut,
       presentation copy from Baron Heath, who presented this book to
       the Club*   1875

1173   Harington (Sir J.) Tract on the Succession to the Crown (1602),
       with Notes and Introduction by C. R. Markham, *portrait,
       half bound morocco, uncut*   1880
   ⁎ Mr. Ouvry's copy, with autograph letters from the Earl of
       Carnarvon, Earl Cawdor, Earl Powis, Lord Houghton, J.
       Payne Collier, and others, thanking him for the portrait of
       Sir J. Harington, which he presented to the Club.

1174   The Ayenbite of Inwyt, edited by the Rev. J. Stevenson, 1855
       —A Fragment of Partenope of Blois, from a MS. at Vale
       Royal, 1873, *half bound*   (2)

1175   The Pilgrimage of the Lyf of the Manhode, from the French of
       Guillaume des Deguileville, edited by W. A. Wright, *half
       bound*   1869

1176   Le Mystère de Saint Louis, Roi de France, publié pour la pre-
       mière fois, d'après un Manuscript, par Francisque-Michel,
       half bound   1871

1177   Royal Academy Exhibition Catalogues, from the First to the
       One Hundred and Twenty-Seventh, reprinted by the Royal
       Academicians, and bound in 8 vol. *half russia, m. e.* 1769-1875

1178   Scotland. WALLACE (James) Ane Account off the Ancient and
       Present State of Orkney, by Mr. James Wallace, Minister
       of Kirkwall, Anno 1684. THE ORIGINAL AUTOGRAPH
       MANUSCRIPT of 42 leaves, *with numerous pen and ink drawings,
       one being a full-page sketch of St. Magnus's Kirk, bound in the
       original limp vellum*   1684
   ⁎ The Original Autograph Manuscript of the printed work,
       which was first published in 1693 by Wallace's son. The
       MS. differs slightly from the printed book, and a list of
       functionaries which appears at the end of the above MS. is
       omitted in the publication. This MS. was formerly in the
       possession of Dr. Thos. Stewart Traill, late Editor of the
       "Times," to whom it was presented by "his affectionate
       friend, Jas. Baikie," on the 15th October, 1833. A presenta-
       tion inscription in the autograph of Baikie to this effect is on
       the first page. The ex-libris of Dr. Traill is pasted on the cover.

1179   Sacro Busto (Johannes de) Spheræ Mundi compendium fœliciter inchoat . . . . *curious engravings on title, and large numbers of cuts throughout, old limp vellum,* FINE COPY
Venetiis, Jacobus de Leucho, 1510

1180   SCOTT (Sir Walter) The Lady of the Lake, a Poem, FIRST EDITION, *portrait, presentation copy, with inscription on fly-leaf :* "James Skene, Esq. of Rubislaw, from his affectionate friend WALTER SCOTT," *and book-plate of James Skene, to whom the fourth Canto of Marmion was dedicated, half calf*   *Edinb.* 1810

1181   Scrap Book, containing a large variety of scarce and curious prints, including : The Mother's Duty, *coloured,* Pictorial Alphabets, *plain and coloured,* Eccentric Characters, Trades, Twelfth Night Characters, *coloured,* Sporting Prints, *coloured,* Pantomimic Characters, *coloured,* Curious Coloured Woodcuts, Scriptural Prints, *coloured,* The Cabin Boy, Little Bess, A Welsh Love Song, Children's Games, Greenwich Park, *coloured,* Theatrical Characters, *coloured,* Military Prints, *coloured,* Mrs. Mary Ann Clarke, *coloured,* St. George for England, Whittington and His Cat delineated, Astley's Amphitheatre, Broad Sword Exercise, Characters in Valentine and Orson, Robinson Crusoe, The Golden Fish, The White Cat, Virgin of the Sun, &c. *all coloured,* and numerous other old and scarce engravings, *half bound*

1182   Sea-Mans (The) Grammar, **black letter,** *vellum, wants title-page*
(1653)

1183   Sermónes Dominicales, &c.   MANUSCRIPT ON PAPER (178 ll. 8½ by 6 in.) *written in minute cursive letters much contracted, long lines, 42 to a full page, by an English Scribe, unbound,* SÆC. XIV-XV

*** AN INTERESTING ENGLISH MANUSCRIPT.   It contains several Carols and Songs in English, one of which in eight lines begins—

"Lullay, Lullay thou lytil child slep and be wel stylle,
The Kynge of Blys thy fader is, as yt was his wille
Thys other nyzcht I saw a syghte a made a cradel keep,
Lullay sche songe & scyde amonge, by stille my childe & slepe."

Nine leaves are occupied with a Part Song in English, with Musical Notes diamond shaped ; and there are several other old English Notes in the volume.

1184   Settle (E.) The World in the Moon, an Opera, FIRST EDITION, 1697—Fatal Love, a Tragedy, FIRST EDITION, 1680 (*two or three margins cut into*)—Motteux (P.) Love's Triumph, FIRST EDITION, 1708 (*one leaf cut into*)   (3)

1185   Shadwell (Thos.) The Royall Shepherdess : A Tragi-Comedy, FIRST EDITION, *calf gilt*   1691

1186   Shakespeare (William) Sonnets, *woodcut borders, and numerous initial letters, by B. G. Goodhue, parchment, uncut, one of* 750 *copies*   *University Press, Copeland & Day, Boston, U.S.A.* 1897

1187   Sheraton (Thomas) The Cabinet-Maker and Upholsterer's Drawing-Book, with Appendix, second edition, *with additional plates,* bound in 2 vol. *some leaves soiled, several of the plates wrongly placed, sold not subject to return, half bound*   1794-6

1188 SHIRLEY (James) The Young Admirall, as it was presented by her Majesties Servants, at the private house in Drury Lane, FIRST EDITION, *calf extra, gilt leaves*   1637

1189 Skelton (Sir John) Charles I, JAPANESE VELLUM PAPER, *with a duplicate series of the full-page illustrations, numerous vignette engravings in the text, crimson morocco extra, gold and blind tooling on back and sides, the large centre design on each side enclosing the Tudor rose, repeated, doublé with brown morocco, with inlaid floral ornaments at corners, joints, silk linings, uncut, t. e. g. by de Sauty*   *Goupil & Co.* 1898

1190 SMITH (Henry) The Sermons of Maister Henrie Smith, gathered into one volume, printed according to his corrected copies in his life-time, *engraved title, original calf*   1594

    *** An interesting account of this rare volume is given in Hunter's New Illustrations by Shakespeare. There was a copy in Halliwell-Phillipps' sale catalogue, July, 1899.

1191 Spanish Mandevile of Miracles (The) or, the Garden of Curious Flowers; whereupon are handled sundry points of Humanity, Philosophy, Divinitie and Geography, beautified with many strange and pleasant Histories, translated from the Spanish by Lewis Lewkenor, FIRST EDITION, *calf (short copy)*   1600

    *** A book which appeared just in time to afford Shakespeare information on points connected with foreign opinion and sentiment, as it contains a store of marvellous narrations of various kinds. Refer to Mr. Hazlitt's *Shakespeare*, p. 125.

1192 SPENSER (EDMUND) THE FAERIE QUEENE; disposed into twelve Books fashioning XII Morall Vertues; FIRST EDITION *of the First Three Books*; A FINE CLEAN, PERFECT AND GENUINE COPY THROUGHOUT, *panelled calf, rebacked (18th cent.)* VERY RARE   *printed for Wm. Ponsonbie,* 1590

1193 SPENSER (E.) THE FAERIE QUEENE; disposed into twelve Books fashioning XII Moral Vertues, FIRST EDITION OF THE SIX BOOKS, 2 vol. *short but fair copy; margins of several ll. at end of vol. I repaired, russia, with blind ornaments, g. e. Birket Foster's copy, with his ex-libris*   *ib.* 1590-96

1194 Spinola (Geo.) Rules to get Children by with Handsome Faces; or Precepts for the contemporary Sectaries which preach and pray, and get children without Book to consider and look on before they leape, &c. (4 *ll.*) *fine copy, in new half calf*
printed for R. H. 1642

    *** A VERY RARE and singular tract. Lowndes could only quote Bliss's damaged copy.

1195 STAGE-PLAYERS. A Declaration of the Lords and Commons assembled in Parliament, for the appeasing and quietting of all unlawfull Tumults and Insurrections in the severall Counties of England and Dominion of Wales. Also an Ordinance of both Houses for the Suppressing of Stage-Playes, *unbound*
1642

    *** An excessively rare tract of 4 leaves only. Not mentioned by Lowe in his *Bibliographical Account of English Dramatic Literature*.

1196 STAGE-PLAYERS.   Coke (Lord) Speech and Charge at Norwich
      Assises.   With a Discoverie of the Abuses and Corruption of
      Officers, *half morocco*   *printed for Nathaniell Butter*, 1607
   *** Mr. J. O. Halliwell-Phillipps' copy, with the following note in
      his autograph on the fly-leaf: "The cur(ious) entry about
      playes has been collated in my provincial volume." The entry
      referred to will be found on H 2 obverse, and reads as fol-
      lows : "The abuse of STAGE PLAYERS, wherewith I find the
      Countrey much troubled, may easily be reformed. They
      having no Commission to play in any place without leave ;
      and therefore, if by your willingnesse they be not entertained
      you may soone be rid of them." The present copy has the
      very rare blank leaf A 1.

1197 Stamp Album, containing about 750 old used and unused Eng-
      lish, Colonial and Foreign Postage Stamps

1198 Stevenson (Robert Louis) Underwoods, FIRST EDITION, LARGE
      PAPER (*only* 50 *printed*), *original cloth*   1887

1199 STOW (JOHN) The Annales of England, faithfully collected out
      of the most authenticall Authors, Records and other Monu-
      ments of Antiquitie, from the first inhabitation untill this
      present yeare 1592, *engraved title*, black letter, *old calf*
                                      London, by Ralfe Newbery, 1592
   *** This edition was unquestionably used by Shakespeare. Refer
      to Boswell-Stone's *Shakespeare's Holinshed.*

1200 STOW (JOHN) A Survey of London, conteyning the Originall,
      Antiquity, Increase, Moderne Estate, and description of that
      City, written in the yeare 1598... increased, with divers rare
      notes of Antiquity, and published in the yeare 1603. Also
      an Apologie (or defence) against the opinion of some men,
      concerning that Citie, the greatnesse thereof. With an Ap-
      pendix, &c. *woodcuts*, black letter, *calf extra, gilt leaves*   1603
   *** The woodcuts in this volume were reproduced by Halliwell
      in his folio edition of *As You Like It.*

1201 Sykes (Sir Mark Masterman) Catalogue of his Highly Valuable
      Collection of Prints, *the five parts complete (42 days' sale), ruled
      in red, with neatly written prices and purchasers' names, portrait,
      a facsimile from old print of Oliver Cromwell lying in State in-
      serted*   *Sotheby*, 1824

1202 Sylvester (Josuah) Lachrimæ Lachrimarum, or the Distillation
      of Teares Shede for the untymely Death of the incomparable
      Prince Panaretus (Prince Henry), *title in white letters on a
      black ground, and heavy mourning borders to the pages, calf gilt*
                                                             1612

1203 Sylvester (J.) Lachrymæ Lachrymarum, or the spirit of Tears
      distilled by the un-tymely death of the incomparable Prince
      Panaretus (Henry Prince of Wales), with Funeral Elegies on
      the Death of Prince Henry by Severall Authors (Holland,
      Donne, Sir W. Cornwallis, &c.) *allegorical figures round the
      borders and black pages, several cut into, morocco extra*   1613
   *** Rare. This copy has the scarce elegy at the end on the death
      of Sir William Sidney, mentioned by Hazlitt, and usually
      missing.

1204 TASSO (TORQUATO) Godfrey of Bulloigne, or the Recoverie of
      Hierusalem.   An Heroicall poem written in Italian by Sig.
      Torquato Tasso, and translated into English by R. C.
      Esquire : And now the first part containing five Cantos,
      imprinted in both languages, *red morocco extra, g. e.*
                                        imprinted by John Windet, 1594

   *** The first English translation of Tasso, and earliest work of
      the poet Richard Carew.   Reprinted by the Rev. A. B. Gro-
      sart in 1881.   See *Grolier Club's Catalogue of Early English
      Literature* (no. 32).

1205 TESTAMENTUM NOVUM LATINUM. Order of contents: S. Mattheus,
      S. Marcus, S. Lucas, S. Johannes, Actus Apostolorum, Epistola
      S. Jacobi, Epistolæ Petri, Epistolæ Johannis, Epistola S. Jude,
      Apocalipsis Johannis, Epistola ad Laodicenses, Epistola ad Ro-
      manos, Epistolæ ad Corinthios, Epistola ad Galathas, Epistola
      ad Ephesios, Epistola ad Philippenses, Epistola ad Colosenses,
      Epistolæ ad Thessalonicenses, Epistolæ ad Timotheum, Epis-
      tola ad Titum, Epistola ad Philemonem, Epistola ad Hebreos,
      MANUSCRIPT ON VELLUM, *of the latter end of the XIIth or com-
      mencement of the XIIIth century, probably executed in Italy ; it
      is written upon 244 leaves (7⅝ by 4¾ in.) in double columns, with
      30 lines to a page, the initial letters and headlines being in blue
      and red ; each of the Books has a large illuminated initial, which
      in some cases extends far down the page, and in one or two instances
      contains the head of a Saint ; on the verso of fol. cxii, facing the
      Acts of the Apostles, is a fine full-page miniature of the Crucifixion,
      with the figures of St. Mary and St. John, beautifully executed in
      colours upon a gold ground, and in the four corners of the frame
      are circles containing the Emblems of the Four Evangelists ; this
      miniature and the other illuminations are executed in the Byzantine
      style, newly bound in oak boards, half niger morocco, clasps, by D.
      Cockerell*

1206 TENNYSON (ALFRED LORD) HELEN'S TOWER [Stanzas by Lady
      Gifford, with a Poem by Lord Tennyson], *vignette of the tower
      on the title, in the original light green wrapper, g. e.*
                                              Clandeboye, n. d.
   *** EXCEEDINGLY SCARCE, only a few copies having been printed
      for private distribution.

1207 Tour through Paris, 21 *beautifully coloured plates*, with Descrip-
      tive Letterpress, *half bound, g. e.*   *W. Sams,* 1822

1208 Tracts.   Reyner (W.) Babylon's Ruining—Earthquake, and the
      Restauration of Zion, 1644—Hill (T.) The Season for Eng-
      land's Selfe-Reflection, 1644—Gower (S.) Things Now-a-
      doing, or, The Churches Travaile of the Child of Reformation
      now-a-bearing, 1644—Harrison (A.) Sermon before the H. of
      Commons for the Success of the Forces, *neer* YORK, 1644—
      Vines (R.) Sermon for the Thanksgiving for the Great Victory
      of PRINCE RUPERT, *neere* YORKE, 1644—Caryl (J.) The Saints
      Thankful Acclamation, &c. . . . *for the* VICTORY OF LORD FAIR-
      FAX AT SELBY IN YORKE-SHIRE, 1644—Case (T.) The Root
      of Apostacy . . . . for the Great Victory to Sir Wm. Waller
      against Sir Ralph Hopton, 1644 ; and 23 others, *all fine clean
      copies, in original calf*   *in* 1 *vol.*

1209 Turberville (George) The Booke of Falconrie or Hawking, newly revised, corrected and augmented, 1611 ; The Noble Art of Venerie, or Hunting, 1611 ; **black letter**, *numerous curious woodcuts, large and sound copies, in the original limp vellum*
in 1 vol.

1210 Tusser (Thos.) Five Hundredth Points of Good Husbandrie, **black letter**, *one or two headlines shaved, calf* 1604

1211 Tusser (T.) Five Hundered Points of Good Husbandry (in Verse), with the properties of Winds, Plants, Hops, Bees, &c. **black letter**, *calf* 1672

1212 Vite de Filosofi cavate da Laertio et altri, 78 *fine woodcuts by G. Salviati, original vellum* *Vinegia, G. Brugnolo*, 1602

1213 Valiant Welshman (The), or, The True Chronicle History of the Life and Valiant Deeds of Caradoc The Great, King of Cambria, now called Wales. As it hath been sundry times Acted by the Prince of Wales his servants, *frontispiece (mounted), half bound* 1663

*** A very scarce play attributed to Robert Armin, the colleague of Shakespeare, and actor at the Globe Theatre. It is, in part, a plagiarism of Hamlet. Refer to Halliwell's Sale Catalogue, May, 1856.

1214 Viola Sanctorum, **lit. goth.** *long lines, with signatures, oak boards (wormed), half stamped vellum* *Argent. Jo. Prusz*, 1487

1215 Walpole (Horace) Historic Doubts on the Life and Reign of King Richard the Third, FIRST EDITION, *portraits*
Dodsley, 1768

1216 Watt (James) and Murdock. The Earliest Locomotive in England, *illustrations, calf extra, g. t.*
privately printed, Birmingham, n. d.

1217 Webster (John) Vittoria Corrombona ; or, The White Devil, a Tragedy, as it is acted at the Theatre Royal, by His Majesties Servants, *calf, g. e.* 1672

*** At an unascertained date between 1607 and 1612 he (Webster), for the first time, wrote a play (Vittoria Corrombona) single-handed, and there evidenced such command of tragic art and intensity as Shakespeare alone among English-men has surpassed. Detraction is the sworn friend to ignorance : for mine own part, I have ever truly cherisht my good opinion of other men's worthy labours ; especially of that full and heighten'd of Mr. Chapman ; the labour'd and understanding works of Mr. Johnson ; the no less worthy composures of the both worthily excellent Mr. Beaumont, and Mr. Fletcher ; and lastly (without wrong last to be named) the right happy and copious industry of *Mr. Shakespeare*, Mr. Dekker, Mr. Heywood, &c. wishing what I writ may be read by their light, protesting that, in the strength of mine own judgment, I know them so worthy, that though I rest silent in my own work, yet to most of theirs I dare (without flattery) fix that of Martial : Non novunt Haec monumenta mori. J. W."— *Extract from the Epistle " To the Reader."* Refer to Mr. Hazlitt's " Shakespeare," pp. xx and xxi.

1218 Whetstone (George) A Mirrour for Magestrates of Cyties representing the Ordinances, &c. of the Emperour Alexander (surnamed) Severus, to suppresse and chastise the notorious Vices noorished in Rome, by the superfluous Nomber of Dicing-houses, Tavarns and Common Stewes, with sundry grave Orations by the said noble Emperor concerning Reformation, and hereunto is added a Touchstone for the Time, contayning many perillous Mischiefes, bred in the bowels of the Citie of London, by the Infection of some of thease Sanctuaries of Iniquitie, VERY LARGE AND BEAUTIFUL COPY, *morocco, g. e.* 1584

  *** See the Grolier Club's Catalogue of Early English Literature (No. 257).

1219 Whitman (Alfred) The Print Collector's Handbook, *with* 80 *illustrations, uncut, t. e. g.* 1901

1220 WILLIAMSON (G. C.) RICHARD COSWAY, R.A. AND HIS WIFE, and Pupils, Miniaturists of the Eighteenth Century, *numerous beautiful illustrations, limited issue* 1897

1221 Williamson (G. C.) and H. L. D. Engleheart. George Engleheart (1750-1829) Miniature Painter to George III, *numerous beautiful illustrations, some in colours, hand-painted, one of* 53 *copies, privately printed, buckram, uncut, t. e. g.* 1902

1222 Woodward (G. M.) Every Body in Town, 6 *coloured plates*, and Every Body Out of Town, 6 *coloured plates, in* 1 *vol. half calf* 1796

1223 WORDSWORTH (WILLIAM) THE EXCURSION, being a portion of the Recluse, a Poem, FIRST EDITION, *a large and fine copy, in the original calf gilt, g. e.* 1814

  *** Presentation copy, with inscription on the flyleaf : " To John Davy, M.D., as a Token of grateful respect, from his Friend, Wm. Wordsworth, Rydal Mount, 28th Decr. 1843."

1224 Wordsworth (William) Ode performed in the Senate House, Cambridge, in 1847, at the first commencement after the Installation of H.R.H. the Prince Albert, FIRST EDITION, *Cambr.* 1847 ; and an illuminated copy of the same, of later date ; with other Cambridge Odes, by W. Smyth, Chr. Wordsworth, Rev. T. Whytehead, and C. Kingsley, in a 4to vol. *half bound*

1225 Worlidge (T.) Select Collection of Drawings from Curious Antique Gems . . . . etched after the manner of Rembrandt, *fine impression, including the head of Medusa, and Hercules slaying the Nemœan Lion,* with Descriptive Text, *calf gilt, m. e.* 1768

1226 WRIGHT (THOS.) The Passions of the Minde in Generall. Corrected, enlarged, and with sundry new discourses augmented. A Succinct and Philosophicall declaration of the nature of Clymactericall yeeres, occasioned by the death of Queene Elizabeth, *half calf* 1604

  *** A very rare volume, dedicated to Shakespeare's Lord Southampton, contains verses by Ben Jonson. Refer to Mr. Hazlitt's " Shakespeare," p. 192.

1227 WÜRTTEMBERG UNND TECKH (Friderich Hertzog zu) kurtze
      und warhaffte Beschreibung der Badenfahrt welche der
      durchleuchtig hochgeborn Fürst und Herr Friderich
      Hertzog zu Württemberg unnd Teckh Grave zu Mümppelgart
      . . . unnd Hosenbands in Engelland, &c. In negst
      abgeloffenem, 1592. Jahr von Mümppelgart ausz in das
      weitberümbte Konigreich Engellandt hernach im zuruck
      ziehen durch die Niderland bisz widerumb gehn Mümppelgart
      verrichtet hat, &c. &c. *Portrait of the Duke of Wirtemberg,
      arms of the Duke, and folding plates, vellum*   *Tübingen*, 1602
    ₊ FIRST EDITION. This volume is not only highly interesting
      as a description of England in 1592, but is also valuable to
      the *Shakespeare* collector. In the 4to edition of the MERRY
      WIVES OF WINDSOR, and only therein, occurs the word
      Garmombles, altered in the folio to *Jermons*. The meaning of
      Garmombles has puzzled Shakespearian annotators, and, as
      Mr. Rye, in his "England as Seen by Foreigners," suggests,
      was probably an allusion to the Duke of Wirtemberg, who
      had been travelling in England incognito as Count of Mump-
      pelgart. THE PRESENT IS A VERY FINE COPY IN THE
      ORIGINAL VELLUM BINDING, THE RARE FOLDING PLATES
      BEING INTACT. Mr. Turner's copy of the second edition sold
      in 1888 for £15.

1228 WÜRTTEMBERG UNND TECKH (Friderich Herzog zu) Besch-
      reibung zweyer Raisen in Engellandt (in 1592) unnd in
      Italien (1599), wol verrichtet. In Truck gefertiget durch E.
      Cellium, 2 vol. in 1, *woodcut portrait, large folding wood
      engravings, and 2 large folding tables descriptive of the College of
      Oxford and Cambridge, original vellum*   *Tübingen*, 1604
    ₊ A remarkably fine copy of the second and much enlarged
      edition. The plates of Oxford and Cambridge appear only
      in this edition.

FOLIO.

1229 Sherwood (Robert) A Dictionarie: English and French, compiled
      for the commoditie of all such as are desirous of both the
      Languages, *calf gilt (imperfect at end and title shaved in fore-
      margin, sold not subject to return)*   *A. Islip*, 1632

1230 Slatyer (W.) Palæ-Albion; the History of Great Britaine from
      the first peopling of this Iland to this present Raigne of our
      happy and Peacefull Monarke K. James, in verse, *engraved title*,
      FIRST EDITION, *calf*   (1621)

1231 Smirke. The Adventures of Hunch-Back, and the Stories con-
      nected with it, LARGE PAPER, *fine impressions of the plates by
      Daniel, after drawings by R. Smirke, R.A.* PROOFS ON INDIA
      PAPER, *uncut*   1814

1232 Spenser (Edmund) The Faerie Queen : The Shepheards Calendar,
      together with the other Works of England's Arch-Poet,
      collected into one volume and carefully corrected, *woodcut title
      and separate titles to each piece, numerous woodcuts, fine copy in
      old calf*   *H. L. for M. Lownes*, 1617

1233   SPORTING PRINTS: a collection of 20 large and beautifully coloured plates, comprising Coaching Scenes, Finding, Partridge, Hare and Woodcock Shooting, Coursing, Trying to Discover (2 *humorous illustrations*), Hunting (4 *illustrations*), *the whole neatly mounted on cardboards, half bound*   *in* 1 *vol.*

1234   Stage Plays. Philosophical Conference of the French Virtuosi, englished by J. Davies of Kidwelly, a curious old book treating on Tobacco Smoking, the Herb, Magic, STAGE PLAYS, Moles and Marks appearing on the Face, &c. 2 vol. *old brown calf*   1664-5

    *** Very scarce, most of the copies were burnt in the great Fire of London.

1235   SYRIAC MANUSCRIPT. Portion of an ancient Choral Service Book, probably Xth-XIth century, *on* 25 *ll. of vellum* (11½ *by* 7 *in.*) *written in bold characters in double columns,* 33 *lines, in red and black* (*much damaged*), *half bound,* VERY RARE
                                sm. folio. SÆC. X-XI

1236   Syriac Manuscript. The Four Gospels, Fragmentary of Different Dates, the old portion being dated A.G. 1052—A.D. 741, *written in bold characters on* 326 *ll. of paper* (10⅓ *by* 6½ *in.*) *with rubrications, long lines,* 20 *to a page, half bound,* VERY RARE
                                  sm. folio. SÆC. VIII, *&c.*

1237   Terentius. Ælii Donati Commentarius in Terentii Comœdias, *finely printed in Roman letter, long lines,* 41 *to a page, without marks* (7 *ll. supplied in contemporary MS.*), *old red morocco gilt, worn, an early and rare edition, Wm. Morriss's copy with his Kelmscott book label*   *Venet. Vindelin de Spira,* 1472 (?)

1238   THACKERAY (W. M.) A folded sheet of paper covered on three sides with pen and ink Sketches of heads and full length figures of soldiers, civilians, ladies, peasant women, grotesque groups, &c. *several have names and initials written under them, but apparently not in Thackeray's autograph, the sheet unfolded measures* 22 *ins. by* 17½ *ins.*

    *** These sketches were given to Mr. Weld, in whose presence they were done, by Thackeray, and from Mr. Weld they were inherited by his daughter, from whom the present owner obtained them.

1239   THACKERAY. The Britannia: a Weekly Journal of News, Politics and Literature, for the year 1841, *half calf*

    *** Contains: an Exhaustive Review of "The Second Funeral of Napoleon, by M. A. Titmarsh"; Loose Sketches, by Michael Angelo Titmarsh; Reading a Poem, a St. Philip's Day at Paris, and Rolandseck.

1240   Themistius, Opera Omnia; acc. Alex. Aphrodisiensis de Anima, et de Fato; Graece: "editio princeps"; *ornamental initials, that on the first page printed in red, vellum*   *Venet.* 1534

1241   Thomas de Hibernia. Manipulus Florum: Manuscript on vellum, written in small 𝔤𝔬𝔱𝔥𝔦𝔠 𝔩𝔢𝔱𝔱𝔢𝔯𝔰, with many marginal notes in a smaller hand, numerous ornamental pen letters, *morocco gilt;* (*at end*) "*Explicit Manipulus Florum compilata a Magistro Thoma de Ybernia quondam socio de Sorbona*"
                                      SAEC. XV

1242 THUCYDIDES. The History writtene by Thucydides the Athenyan of the Warre, which was betweene the Peloponesians and the Athenyans, translated oute of Frenche into the Englishe language by Thomas Nicolls, **black letter**, *woodcut title, old calf* 1560

 *** The first English translation. Refer to Johnson and Steevens' edition of Shakespeare, vol. II, p. 93. A VERY FINE LARGE COPY.

1243 Tracts. The Norfolk Congress, *n. d.*—The Silent Flute: a Poem, 1729—Estimate of the value of South-Sea Stock, 1720—Answer to the Depositions concerning the Birth of the Prince of Wales, 1689—Trials for High Treason, etc. Parliamentary Proceedings, and other items, *half bound in 1 vol.*

1244 Vallance (Aymer) The Art of William Morris : a Record, *with reproductions from designs and fabrics, printed in the colours of the originals, examples of the types, etc. used at the Kelmscott Press, and many other illustrations, one of 220 copies, uncut, t. e. g.* 1897

1245 Vander Meulen (F.) Tableaux du Roi (forming a portion of vol. I of the " Cabinet du Roi ") 15 *large and fine plates, only, morocco, the sides completely covered with fleurs de lys, the Royal Arms in centre of sides (rebacked), no title*   *n. d.*

1246 Vernet (Carle) Les Campagnes d'Italie sous Napoléon le Grand, 23 *fine plates, only, engraved by Duplessis Bertaux, a few extra engravings added*   *n. d.*

1247 Versailles. Sixty-two large and finely Engraved Views, Statues, Grottos, Fountains, Basreliefs, Pillars, Ornaments, etc. of Versailles, engraved by Israel Silvestre, F. Le Pautre, etc. ORIGINAL IMPRESSIONS, *bound in a vol. old French red morocco, line frame sides, fleurs-de-lys at angles and on back, Royal arms of France in centre* (*Louis XIV*)   [1675, *etc.*]

1248 Voragine (Jacob. de) Legenda Aurea [begins fol. 1a] "Missidua frm. postulatone de victus necnon et obediêcie Salutaris fructu Provocatus," etc. ; Explicit prologus ; Incipit legenda beatissimi Patris Anthonii" ; [ends fol. 114] "De Claudis Sanatis" ; MANUSCRIPT ON VELLUM (114 *ll.* 10½ *in.* × 7¼ *in.*) *written in* **gothic letters**, *double columns, 37 lines, with rubrics, painted ornamental initials, modern russia, g. e.*   SAEC. XIV

1249 VORAGINE (JAC. DE) LEGENDA SANCTORUM, **lit. goth**. *double columns, few small wormholes, some marginal notes, fine large copy, old half calf, s. e. et n. t. folio.* (*Coloniæ, U. Zell*), 1483

 *** EXTREMELY RARE. No copy in the British Museum, and the Bodleian only possesses an imperfect copy. It is the most complete of all the editions of this celebrated work, and contains a supplement of 200 lives of Saints not found in the earlier editions, and many of them do not appear in the editions published afterwards.

1250 Voragine (Jac. de) The Golden Legende (translated by William Caxton, **gothic letter**, *woodcuts, very imperfect and damaged, old binding, sold not subject to return* (*Wynkyn de Worde*, 1527)

1251   Walford (E.) Small Folio Scrap Book used by Mr. Walford for
       the preservation of critical notices and autograph letters re-
       lating to his "Tales of Our Great Families," *mostly loosely
       inserted*   (1877-82)

1252   Weever (J.) Ancient Funerall Monuments, within the United
       Monarchie of Great Britaine, Ireland and the Islands adjacent,
       with the Monasteries, &c. FIRST EDITION, *fine portrait, and en-
       graved title by Cecil, and woodcuts (no index), fine copy in original
       calf*   1631

1253   Windsor Castle.   Hollar's Views of the Castle, comprising (1)
       Prospect from the North (1667); (2) Prospect from the
       South East; (3) Prospects of the Castle and Towne from
       the South West, West South West, and West by South; all
       after Christopher Wren by Hollar—St. George's Chapel,
       Prospect from the South, with Ground Plan, *half calf*   1667
   *** Refer to Halliwell-Phillipps' Shakespearean Rarities 373.
       Valuable for their illustrations of "The Merry Wives of
       Windsor."

1254   YORKE (JAMES) THE UNION OF HONOUR, *the numerous coats of
       arms beautifully emblazoned, the engraved front. cut round and
       mounted, interleaved, and* EXTRA ILLUSTRATED *by the insertion of
       several hundred old engravings, consisting of portraits, plates of
       Palaces, Castles, Antiquities, Tombs, etc. many of which are very
       scarce, calf*   1640

1255   Young Student's Library (The) containing, Extracts and
       Abridgments of the Most Valuable Books printed in England,
       and in the Foreign Journals, from the Year Sixty Five to
       This Time.   To which is Added, A New Essay upon all sorts
       of Learning, wherein The Use of the Sciences Is Distinctly
       Treated on, *unbound*   1692
   *** Contains a reference to SHAKESPEARE; "We are pretty
       confident, it would not have been for the Disreputation of
       Sir *William Davenant*, if the World had never seen anything
       of his, but his *Gondibert*, and the much more Excellent
       Shakespear wou'd not have been less admir'd, if an abundance
       of these things which are Printed for his, were omitted, Mr.
       Cowly is of this Opinion, we are sure." (*Pages* xii *and* xiii).

SIXTH DAY'S SALE.

𝕾hakespeareana.

OCTAVO ET INFRA.
LOT 1256.

SHAKESPEARE. THE / HISTORY / OF / TIMON OF ATHENS / THE MAN HATER / FIRST WRITTEN BY MR. WIL. SHAKESPEAR / AND SINCE ALTERED BY MR. THO. SHADWELL / *ornament on title*
Printed for T. Johnson / Bookseller at the Hague / MDCCXII / (1712)

₊ Collation. Title, verso blank; To the most illustrious Prince George, Duke of Buckingham, &c. A 2 and A 3; Prologue to Timon, A 3 (verso) and A 4; Dramatis Personæ, A 4 (verso); Timon of Athens, A 5 to G 6 (recto); Epilogue, G 6 (recto and verso). This edition, printed for the use of the English Colony in Holland, seems to have ENTIRELY ELUDED THE NUMEROUS BIBLIOGRAPHERS AND BIOGRAPHERS OF SHAKE-SPEARE. Lowndes mentions *no edition whatever* as bearing the Hague imprint; moreover, there appears to be no record of any issue of this play between the years 1703 and 1732. Mr. Sidney Lee is equally reticent, for in his exhaustive account of foreign editions *supra* Holland (Life of Shake-speare, 1899, page 293) he simply remarks: "Two complete translations have been published in Dutch, one in prose by A. S. Kok (Amsterdam, 1873-1880), the other in verse by Dr. L. A. J. Burgersdijk (Leyden, 1884-8, 12 vol.)" He makes no reference to any English version with a Dutch imprint. THIS PERHAPS UNIQUE VOLUME IS IN BEAUTIFULLY CLEAN AND CRISP CONDITION.

1257   Shakespear (W.) The History of Timon of Athens, the Man-Hater, first written by Mr. Wil. Shakespear, and since altered by Mr. Tho. Shadwell, *a few leaves soiled, unbound*
Printed for T. Johnson, Bookseller at the Hague, 1712

1258   Shakespear. HAMLET / PRINCE / OF / DENMARK / a / Tragedy / written by / Mr. William Shakespear /
Dublin / Reprinted by George Grierson at the / Two Bibles in Essex Street, 1721 /

₊ [Collation. Title, with list of Dramatis Personæ on reverse, and pp. 3-107.]

1259   Shakespear. JULIUS CÆSAR / A / TRAGEDY / by Mr. William Shakespear /
Dublin / Printed by and for George Grierson at the / Two Bibles in Essex Street, 1721 /

₊ [Collation. Title, with list of Dramatis Personæ on reverse, and pp. 1-72.]

L 2

1260   Shakespear. THE / TRAGEDY / OF / MACBETH / written by Mr.
         W. Shakespear /
             *Dublin / Printed for George Ewing, Bookseller, at the / Sign of
                     the Angel and Bible, in Dames' Street / 1723 /*
     *** [Collation. On reverse of title is list of Dramatis Personæ,
         pp. 3-66, then leaf (blank on reverse) with list of publications.]
1261   SHAKESPEAR (William) THE TEMPEST : a Comedy, collated and
         corrected by the former editions, by Mr. Pope, *unbound*
                                                          Dublin, 1725
1262   Shakespear. THE / MERRY WIVES / OF / WINDSOR / a / Comedy /
         as it is acted at the / Theatres / by Mr. William Shakespear /
             *Dublin / Printed for A. Bradley, at the Golden Ball and / King,
                   opposite Sycamore Alley, in Dame Street, Book / seller*, 1730
     *** [Collation.   Title, with list of Dramatis Personæ on reverse,
         pp. 3-72.]
     N.B.—The above five volumes are of remarkable interest and im-
         portance to collectors and bibliographers of Shakespeare, they
         being of the greatest rarity, TWO OF THEM (*Macbeth*, 1723,
         and *Merry Wives of Windsor*, 1730) ARE PERHAPS UNIQUE,
         AND ARE HITHERTO UNDESCRIBED. Of *Hamlet*, 1721, and
         Julius Cæsar, 1721, only one other copy of each is known
         to have occurred for sale, viz. those which were sold, with
         Othello, 1721, in these rooms last December. The late Mr.
         J. O. Halliwell-Phillipps had none of the early Irish editions
         of Shakespeare's plays in his collection, and seems to have
         come across (in the Harrison collection) a solitary copy of the
         Tempest, 1725, which he thus describes : "THIS LITTLE
         VOLUME IS MOST RARE, IF NOT QUITE UNIQUE, AND IT IS THE
         EARLIEST KNOWN EDITION OF ANY OF SHAKESPEARE'S PLAYS
         PRINTED IN IRELAND ; UNNOTICED IN ALL LISTS OF SHAKE-
         SPEAREANA." It will be noticed that the wording of the
         five title-pages varies : "Hamlet" is "*Written by Mr. William
         Shakespear*"; "Julius Cæsar" simply "*By Mr. William
         Shakespear*"; "Macbeth," "*Mr. W. Shakespear*"; and "Merry
         Wives of Windsor," "*By Mr. William Shakespear.*"

<h2 style="text-align:center">QUARTO.</h2>

1263   SHAKESPEARE (W.) A MOST PLEASANT AND EXCELLENT CON-
         CEITED COMEDY OF SIR JOHN FALSTAFFE AND THE MERRY
         WIVES OF WINDSOR, with the swaggering vaine of Ancient
         Pistoll and Corporall Nym, *morocco gilt, joints, g. e. the lower
         corner of two leaves torn, otherwise* A FINE COPY, VERY RARE,
         28 *ll. without pagination ; sig.* A-G *in fours*
                                       Printed for Arthur Johnson, 1619
1264   Shakespear (W.) MACBETH, a Tragedy, with all the Alterations,
         Amendments, Additions, and New Songs, as it is now acted
         at the Dukes Theatre, *P. Chetwin*, 1674—The History of
         Timon of Athens, The Man-Hater, made into a Play by T.
         Shadwell, FIRST EDITION, 1678, *both slightly wormed in margin* (2)
1265   Shakespeare (W.) Julius Cæsar, a Tragedy, as it is now acted
         at the Theatre Royal, *fine copy, morocco extra, g. e. by Riviere*
             By H. H. Jun. for Hen. Herringman and R. Bentley, &c. n. d.
                                                       (*but date* 1680)
     *** Exceedingly scarce. The first separately published edition
         of this play. It originally appeared in the folio of 1623.

1266 Shakespear (W.) Othello, the Moor of Venice, a Tragedy, as acted at the Theatre Royal, *page* 68 *imperfect*, 1681—History of Timon of Athens, the Man-Hater, made into a Play, by Tho. Shadwell, *a leaf defective*, 1688—Griffith (Mrs.) The Morality of Shakespeare's Drama, *illustrated, portrait (8vo)*, 1775; &c. (8)

1267 Shakespear (W.) Othello, the Moor of Venice : a Tragedy, as it hath been divers times acted at the Globe, and at the Black-Friers ; and now at the Theatre Royal, by His Majestie's Servants, *calf extra*   1687

   *** A large copy of the fourth edition of "Othello." "A Catalogue of Plays printed for R. Bentley" follows the title in which "Henry the 6th, with the Murder of the Duke of Glocester in 2 parts," "King Lear," and "Othello, the Moor of Venice," are advertised.

1268 Shakespeare's Macbeth. The Original Songs, Airs and Choruses, which were Introduced in the Tragedy of Macbeth in score ; composed by Matthew Locke, Chapel Organist to Queen Catharine, Consort to King Charles II. Revised and corrected by Dr. Boyce ; dedicated to David Garrick, Esq.   *circa* 1750

1269 Shakespeare. Henry IV, Part II, *Chiswick Press*, 1817, 12*mo*, *William Dowton's copy, with pages 5 to 10 torn out and numerous passages scored and emended by him*—Two Gentlemen of Verona, *Oxberry's edition (Dowton's name on title, but no alteration)*—The Male-Coquette (*no title*), with Alterations by Dowton, 8vo—The Enchanted Island (The Tempest), 1669, by John Driden (*no title*) ; and 14 others   (18)

1270 Shakespeare. Shylock in the Merchant of Venice, for Mr. Wm. Ward, Doncaster, October 25th, 1772, *Manuscript of 16 pages, formerly the property of W. Dowton*

1271 Shakespeare. Sir John Falstaff in Henry IV, 2nd Part, *Manuscript of 36 pages, paper wrapper*   1794

   *** A Manuscript of the part of Falstaff with considerable differences, both in the way of alteration and omission, from the received text. On the cover is the inscription : "Sir John Falstaff in 2nd Part of Henry 4th—Mr. King, Novr 12th 1794," and inside cover : "This Part was the property of Mr. Wm. Dowton the Comedian and belonged to Thos. King in 1794—(*signed*) H. H. Dowton."

1272 Shakespeare. Sir John Falstaff in Falstaff's Wedding, Mr. Palmer, Theatre Royal, Drury Lane, 1803, *Manuscript on 15 leaves, formerly belonging to W. Dowton, paper covers*

FOLIO.

1273 Shakespeare's (Mr. William) Comedies, Histories, Tragedies, published according to the true Originall Copies, the first folio edition, *words of title and portrait from the Second Edition (T. Cotes for R. Allot, date cut off), cut down and mounted* ; " To the Reader B. J." *inlaid* ; *lower corners of many leaves mended, making some words defective* ; " Troilus and Cressida " *placed at the end instead of the usual place* ; *some preliminary ll. not in their proper order, but all are there* ; (*measures* 12¼ *by* 7⅝ *in.*), *modern boarded russia in cloth case, imprint at end of* " Cymbeline "   Printed at the charges of Mr. Jaggard, Ed. Blount, J. Smeth- wicke, and W. Apsley, 1623

   *** Notwithstanding its defects the body of this copy is, though

Lot 1273—*continued.*

> short, in fair condition, and contains every leaf genuine except those mentioned. Page 237 misprinted 233, which Lowndes mentions as exceptional. This copy is recorded in Mr. Sidney Lee's census.

1273* SHAKESPEARE (W.) Comedies, Histories, and Tragedies: being a reproduction in facsimile of the First Folio Edition, 1623, from the Chatsworth copy, in the possession of the Duke of Devonshire, with Introduction and Census of copies by Sidney Lee, *half buckram, "Census" in a separate cover, as issued*   *Oxford, Clarendon Press,* 1902

1274 Shakespeare. MR. WILLIAM SHAKESPEARE'S COMEDIES, HISTORIES, AND TRAGEDIES, published according to the true Originall Copies, THE SECOND IMPRESSION, *portrait by Droeshout very defective, wants the Verses by Ben Jonson, and lower margins of many leaves are damaged by damp, therefore the volume will be sold not subject to return, old calf, rebacked (date and most of the imprint are missing)*

Tho. Cotes for Robert Allot, 1632

1275 SHAKESPEARE (WM.) COMEDIES, HISTORIES AND TRAGEDIES, published according to the true Original Copies, THE SECOND IMPRESSION (*measures 13 by 8½ in.*) *the title containing portrait split and backed, and the leaf with verses backed; a few ink stains and rust spots, russia (18th cent.) y. e.*
Printed by Tho. Cotes for Robert Allot, and to be sold at the Blacke Beare in Pauls Church-yard, 1632

> *** A PERFECT AND VERY EXCELLENT COPY OF THE SECOND FOLIO, WITH ALL THE ORIGINAL BLANKS, every leaf being genuine throughout, and in sound state. The name and address of WILLIAM ARNALL of Whitchapel 1729, a political writer in Walpole's pay, is on reverse of last leaf.

1276 SHAKESPEARE. AN ARM CHAIR MADE FROM THE WOOD OF THE MULBERRY TREE planted by SHAKESPEARE IN NEW PLACE GARDEN, STRATFORD-ON-AVON

> *** The pedigree of this chair is complete from the destruction of the tree to the present time, and is as follows: After the tree was cut down it was acquired by Thomas Sharp and William Hurdis Harborne, who divided it. Thomas Sharp made his portion into table and fancy articles, many of which have since passed into well-known collections, though the tables are still in Stratford. William H. Harborne converted the greater part of his portion into chairs, of which the present one he kept for himself, and exhibited in the "Stratford Arms," of which house he was the proprietor. In 1845 he died, and his daughter, Mrs. R. Voisey, inherited the chair, and kept it in her possession in Shakespeare Street up to the time of her death in 1900, when, as an heirloom, it passed into the possession of the present owner, Mrs. Hillier, a direct descendant of William Hurdis Harborne, and niece of Mrs. R. Voisey. While in the possession of Mrs. Voisey the chair had been seen by many thousands of visitors, and since her death it has been on exhibition in the Public Museum, Weston Park, Sheffield.

1277 SHAKESPEARE. HENRY IV, *Act* II, *Scene* IV. FINE ORIGINAL
WATER-COLOUR DRAWING BY J. MASSEY WRIGHT of Sir
John Falstaff. "*Falstaff! Fast asleep behind the arras, and
snorting like a horse,*" with the Prince of Wales and Peto
searching his pockets, size 10½ by 9 in. oval, *signed on the
back by the artist, in gilt frame*   (1)

Another Property.

1278 SHAKESPEARE (WILLIAM) Versuch / einer gebundenen / Ueber-
setzung / des / Trauer-Spiels / von dem Tode / des / JULIUS
CÄSAR, / Aus den Englischen Wercke / des Shakespear /
Berlin, 1741

   *** [Collation : Title verso blank, Translator's Notice, dated
May 30, 1741, with Dramatis Personæ on the reverse, and
pp. 1-139 verso blank]. AN EXCESSIVELY RARE LITTLE VOLUME,
no copy of which can be traced as occurring for sale. This
edition of *Julius Cæsar* is not only the first translation of any
of Shakespeare's Plays published in Germany, but it is also
the first translation of any of Shakespeare's plays published
on the Continent of Europe. The first French translation
did not appear until 28 years' afterwards, when Ducis, in
1769, published his famous translation of *Hamlet.* The present
volume is in perfect preservation, with large margins.

1279 SHAKESPEARE (W.) TIMON VON ATHEN, / ein / Schauspiel / in
dreyen Aufzugen / von Shakespeare / Furs. Prager Theater
eingerichtet / von F. J. Fischer /   *Prag.* 1778

   *** [Collation : Title with list of Dramatis Personæ on reverse,
and pp. 1-62]. There is no record of the previous occurrence
of any copy of this little volume. No translation whatever
of *Timon of Athens* (published in Bohemia); occurs in the
British Museum catalogue, and Mr. Sidney Lee could only
refer to the collected edition of Shakespeare, published at
Prague in 1874. The present volume is in perfect preservation, with large margins.

1280 SHAKESPEARE (W.) Venus und·Adonis ;/ Tarquin und Lukrezia /
Zwei Gedichte / von / Shakespeare. / Aus dem Englischen
ubersezt. / Mit beigedruktem Original, / *original wrappers,*
UNCUT   *Halle,* 1783

   *** [Collation : Title verso blank : preface pages III to XVIII, the
title being counted as pp. I and II ; the Dedication to Henry
Wriothesley, Earl of Southampton, 3 leaves, the verso of the
third leaf, containing the commencement of *Venus and Adonis,*
the *Poem,* pp. 6 to 305, verso blank]. The text in English and
German, *the first German translation of Shakespeare's Poems.*
The British Museum possesses no German translation of *Venus
and Adonis anterior to that of* 1849. The present copy is in
its original binding and UNCUT. An uncut copy is perhaps
unique.

1281 SHAKESPEARE (W.) Hamlet, / Tragedie, / Imitée de l'Anglois par M. Ducis. / Représentée, pour la première fois par les / Comédiens François Ordinaires du Roi, / le 30 Septembre, 1769   *8vo. Paris,* 1770

  *** [Collation : Title verso blank; dedication, 2 pp. ; avertissement 1 leaf, with the list of Dramatis Personæ on the reverse, and pp. 1 to 68]. Ducis' own copy with his stamp on the title-page. Excessively rare, especially in the uncut state. The earliest edition in the British Museum is that of 1815. The present copy is UNCUT.

1282 SHAKESPEARE (W.) Macbeth, / ein / Trauerspiel / in / fünf Aufzügen   *8vo.* (1780)

  *** [Collation : Title, with list of Dramatis Personæ on the reverse, preface 2 leaves, and pp. 3 to 127, verso blank]. Very rare, apparently the first translation of *Macbeth* into German. The above copy has good margins, and is preserved in a blue wrapper.

1283 SHAKESPEARE (W.) Macbeth, / Tragédie, / en vers et en cinq Actes ; / Remise au Théâtre le premier Juin 1790, / Par M. Ducis, / Secrétaire ordinaire de Monsieur, l'un des / quarante de l'Académie Françoise /   *8vo. Paris,* 1790 .

  *** [Collation : Half-title, 1 leaf ; title, verso blank, 1 leaf ; avertissement, 2 leaves, the verso of the second leaf contains the list of Dramatis Personæ, and pp. 1 to 64]. Evidently an acting copy, annotated and corrected throughout in a contemporary hand. The British Museum has no earlier edition than that of 1827, in good preservation, with large margin.

The Property of the Hon. Richard C. Grosvenor.

OCTAVO ET INFRA.

1284 STEVENSON (ROBERT LOUIS) Complete Works, "EDINBURGH EDITION," 30 vol. *portrait and facsimiles, limited issue, original cloth, uncut, t. e. g.*   1894-99

1285 Yule (Colonel H.) The Book of Ser Marco Polo the Venetian, concerning the Kingdoms and Marvels of the East, newly translated and edited with Notes, *maps and illustrations,* 2 vol. second edition, *original cloth, uncut*   *Murray,* 1875

QUARTO.

1286 Froissart (Sir John) Chronicles of England, France, Spain, &c. translated by Lord Berners, reprinted from Pynson's edition of 1523 and 1525, 2 vol. *calf*   1812

1287 Verdizotti (Giov. Mar.) Cento Favola Morali, de i piu illustri antichi, e moderni autori Greci e Latini, *woodcut title and numerous beautiful woodcuts, some of which are after the designs of Titian,* FIRST EDITION, *morocco super extra, g. e. by De Coverly*   *Venetia,* 1570

FOLIO.

1288 Bell (Malcolm) Edward Burne-Jones: a Record and Review, LARGE PAPER, *one of* 27 *copies only, numerous beautiful illustrations, the frontispiece in two states, half parchment, t. e. g.* 1892

1289 BURNE-JONES. AN ORIGINAL DRAWING BY SIR E. BURNE-JONES : ONE OF THE DESIGNS FOR THE " SLEEPING BEAUTY " SERIES. Head of a girl asleep, the head resting on the right arm, exhibited by the artist at the New Gallery, *framed and glazed*

1290 Burne-Jones. HEAD OF A GIRL LOOKING TO THE LEFT : AN ORIGINAL DRAWING BY SIR E. BURNE-JONES, *framed and glazed*

1291 Burne-Jones. HEAD OF A GIRL LOOKING DOWNWARDS TO THE LEFT : AN ORIGINAL DRAWING BY SIR E. BURNE-JONES, *framed and glazed* ·

1292 Burne-Jones. HEAD AND BUST OF A FEMALE FIGURE HOLDING A BOOK IN HER RIGHT HAND : AN ORIGINAL DRAWING BY SIR E. BURNE-JONES, *on brown paper, framed and glazed*

1293 Burne-Jones. DESIGN FOR A STAINED GLASS WINDOW : FULL-LENGTH FIGURE OF ST.   , HOLDING A VESSEL IN THE RIGHT HAND, BY SIR E. BURNE-JONES, *framed and glazed*

   *** The purchaser of this design must give a written undertaking not to reproduce it in stained glass, or to allow any one else to do so.

1294 Gerarde (John) The Herball, or Generall Historie of Plantes, *engraved title and numerous beautiful woodcuts, a sound and clean copy, in the original russia* 1636

1295 Mantegna (A.) Oeuvre, reproduit et publié par Amand-Durand, texte par G. Duplessis, 27 *large and beautiful plates, in a portfolio* 1878

FAMOUS MODERN PRESSES.

The Kelmscott Press.

All Octavo et Infra unless otherwise mentioned.

1296 Morris (William) The Well at the World's End, *with four pictures designed by Sir Edward Burne-Jones, woodcut borders and numerous initial letters,* PRINTED UPON VELLUM, *only* 8 *copies issued, limp vellum, uncut* 1896

1297 Morris (William) The Water of the Wondrous Isles, *the borders and ornaments designed entirely by William Morris, except the initial words " Whilom " and " Empty," which were completed from his unfinished designs by R. Catterson-Smith,* PRINTED UPON VELLUM, *only* 6 *copies issued, limp vellum, uncut* 1897

1298 Morris (William) The Sundering Flood, the last romance written by William Morris, overseen by May Morris, *map, woodcut borders, and numerous initial letters,* PRINTED UPON VELLUM, *only* 10 *copies issued, uncut* 1897

KELMSCOTT PRESS—*continued.*

1299 Chaucer (Geoffrey) Works, now newly imprinted, edited by F. S. Ellis, *ornamented with pictures designed by Sir Edward Burne-Jones, beautiful woodcut borders, and numerous large and small initial letters, stamped pigskin, from a design by William Morris, clasps, g. e. by Cobden Sanderson, The Doves Bindery, 1896, in a case, book form* 1896

1300 Biblia Innocentium : being the Story of God's Chosen People before the Coming of Our Lord Jesus Christ upon Earth, written anew for children by J. W. Mackail, *woodcut border and numerous initial letters, vellum, uncut* 1892

1301 Caxton (William) The History of Reynard the Foxe, *elaborate woodcut borders, numerous large initial letters, and ornamental scroll work, limp vellum, uncut* *folio.* 1892

1302 Meinhold (William) Sidonia the Sorceress, translated by Francesca Speranza, Lady Wilde, *woodcut borders and numerous large and small initial letters, limp vellum, uncut* *folio.* 1893

1303 Morris (William) Gothic Architecture : a Lecture for the Arts and Crafts Exhibition Society, *woodcut initials, uncut* 1893

1304 Shakespeare (William) Poems, printed after the original copies, edited by F. S. Ellis, *woodcut borders and initial letters, limp vellum, uncut* 1893

1305 Psalmi Penitentiales, transcribed and edited by F. S. Ellis, from a Manuscript circa 1440, *woodcut borders and initial letters, uncut* 1894

1306 The Tale of the Emperor Constans, and of Over Sea, done out of ancient French into English by William Morris, *woodcut borders and initial letters, uncut* 1894

1307 Rossetti (D. G.) Hand and Soul, reprint from the German, *woodcut borders and initial letters, vellum, uncut* 1895

1308 Child Christopher and Goldilind the Fair, by William Morris, 2 vol. *woodcut borders and initial letters, uncut* 1895

1309 Biblia Innocentium : being the Story of God's Chosen People before the coming of Our Lord upon Earth, *woodcut borders and initial letters, vellum, uncut* 1892

1310 The History of Reynard the Foxe, *elaborate woodcut borders, scroll work and initial letters, limp vellum, uncut* 1892

1311 The Nature of Gothic, a Chapter of the Stones of Venice, by John Ruskin, *woodcut border and numerous initial letters, vellum, uncut* 1892

1312 Maud, a Monodrama, by Alfred Lord Tennyson, *woodcut borders, initial letters and other ornamentation, limp vellum, uncut* 1893

1313 CHAUCER (GEOFFREY) WORKS, now newly imprinted, edited by F. S. Ellis, *ornamented with pictures designed by Sir Edward Burne-Jones, elaborate and beautiful woodcut borders, initial letters, uncut, in a lined cloth case* *roy. folio.* 1896

1314 Morris (William) The Well at the World's End, with four pictures designed by Sir Edward Burne-Jones, *woodcut borders and initial letters, limp vellum, uncut* 1896

KELMSCOTT PRESS—*continued.*

1315   Laudes Beatæ Mariæ Virginis, *woodcut initial letters and scroll-work designs, uncut, in a lined cloth case*   1896

1316   Some German Woodcuts of the Fifteenth Century, *woodcuts, the blocks prepared by Walker and Boutall, under the direction of the late Wm. Morris, uncut*   1897

1317   A Note by William Morris on his aims in founding the Kelmscott Press, edited by S. C. Cockerell, *woodcut borders, &c. uncut*   1898

    . This was the last book printed at the Kelmscott Press.

1318   Gothic Architecture : a Lecture for the Arts and Crafts Exhibition Society, by William Morris, *woodcut initials, original boards*   1893

1319   Gothic Architecture ; another copy   1893

1320   Cavendish (G.) Life of Thomas Wolsey Cardinal Archbishop of York, *woodcut borders and initial letters, vellum*   1893

1321   Cavendish (G.) Life of Thomas Wolsey Cardinal Archbishop of York, *woodcut borders and initial letters*, PRINTED ON VELLUM   1893

1322   Rossetti (D. G.) Ballads and Narrative Poems, *woodcut borders and initial letters, vellum, uncut*   1893

1323   Sonnets and Lyrical Poems, *woodcut borders and initial letters, vellum, uncut*   1894

1324   The Tale of King Florus and the Fair Jehane, *woodcut borders and initial letters, original boards, uncut*   1893

1325   Shelley (P. B.) The Poetical Works, 3 vol. *woodcut borders and initial letters, original boards*   1895

    . Special copy, with the edges untrimmed.

1326   SOME GERMAN WOODCUTS OF THE FIFTEENTH CENTURY, for which the blocks (with one exception) were prepared by Walker and Boutall, under the direction of the late William Morris, now edited by S. C. Cockerell, PRINTED UPON VELLUM, ONE OF 8 COPIES, *numerous beautifully executed facsimile woodcuts, stained vellum, uncut*   demy 4to. 1897

1327   A Note by William Morris on his Aims in founding the Kelmscott Press, with a Description of the Press and a List of the Books printed Thereat, *woodcut borders and other ornamentation, original boards, uncut, an autograph of William Morris inserted at end of volume*   1898

    . This was the last book printed at the Kelmscott Press.

1328   Two trial pages of the projected edition of Lord Berners' translation of Froissart, printed at the Kelmscott Press in September, 1897, to preserve the designs made for the work by William Morris, PRINTED UPON VELLUM.

1329   MORRIS (WILLIAM) The Earthly Paradise, 8 vol. *elaborate woodcut borders and numerous large and small initial letters, vellum, uncut*   1897

1330   Ancoats Brotherhood, March, 1894, to March, 1895, two leaves, a poem by Tennyson, and extract from John Ruskin, *large woodcut with ornamental border, initial letters and scroll work*

KELMSCOTT PRESS—*continued.*

1331 Two trial pages of the projected edition of Lord Berners' translation of Froissart, printed at the Kelmscott Press, in September, 1897, to preserve the designs made for the work by William Morris, ON VELLUM, *in ebony frame, glazed*

1332 Morris (Wm.) Poems by the Way, *printed in red and black, woodcut border and ornamental initials, vellum*   1891

1333 Caxton (W.) The Golden Legend, edited by F. S. Ellis, 3 vol. *beautiful woodcuts the full size of the page, borders and initial letters*   *folio.* 1892

1334 Sidonia the Sorceress, translated from the German of William Meinhold, by Lady Wilde, *printed in red and black, woodcut borders and numerous initial letters, vellum*   1893

1335 Morris (W.) Gothic Architecture, a Lecture for the Arts and Crafts Exhibition Society, *woodcut initial letters, uncut* 1893

1336 Of the Friendship of Amis and Amile, done out of the ancient French into English by Wm. Morris, *woodcut borders, &c.* 1894

1337 Sulkhan-Saba Orbeliani. The Book of Wisdom and Lies, a Georgian Story, translated, with notes, by Oliver Wardrop, *woodcut borders and numerous initial letters, vellum*   1894

1338 Coleridge (S. T.) Poems chosen out of the Works of, edited by F. S. Ellis, *woodcut borders and initial letters, vellum*   1896

1339 Morris (W.) The Story of the Glittering Plain, *ornamented with 23 pictures by Walter Crane, woodcut borders and initial letters, vellum, arms on the sides*   *folio.* 1894

1340 Morris (W.) Poems by the Way, *vellum, arms on the sides*
                                                   sm. 4to. 1891

1341 The Order of Chivalry, *full-page woodcut borders, and initials, vellum, arms on the sides*   1893

1342 Mackail (J. W.) Biblia Innocentium : being the Story of God's Chosen People . . . written anew for Children, *woodcut border and numerous initial letters, vellum, arms on the sides, uncut*
                                                   W. Morris, 1892

1343 Morris (W.) Gothic Architecture for the Arts and Crafts Exhibition Society, *woodcut initial letters*   1893

1344 Of the Friendship of Amis and Amile, done out of the ancient French into English by W. Morris, *woodcut borders, &c.* 1894

1345 ORIGINAL DESIGN BY WILLIAM MORRIS for the title to the Poems by Percy Bysshe Shelley

1346 ORIGINAL DESIGN BY WILLIAM MORRIS for one of the frames round the Chaucer illustrations

1346* Leaf of the Well at the World's End, with ORIGINAL DESIGN BY WILLIAM MORRIS between the columns

1346**Proof of one of Walter Crane's illustrations to the Story of the Glittering Plain, with ORIGINAL DRAWING BY WILLIAM MORRIS for side ornament

1347 MORRIS (WILLIAM) A Tale of the House of the Wolfings, and all the Kindreds of the Mark, written in Prose and Verse, 1901—The Roots of the Mountains, 1901—The Story of Grettir the Strong, translated from the Icelandic by E. Magnússon and W. Morris, 1901—Volsunga Saga, translated

KELMSCOTT PRESS—*continued.*

LOT 1347—*continued.*

from the Icelandic by E. Magnússon and W. Morris, 1901—
The Odyssey of Homer, done into English Verse, 1901—
The Æneids of Virgil, done into English Verse, 1902—
Hopes and Fears for Art: Five Lectures, 1902—Architec-
ture, Industry and Wealth: collected papers, 1902; *original
boards*   4*to.* (8)

*** Reprinted at the Chiswick Press with the Golden type designed by William Morris for the Kelmscott Press; published
by Longmans, Green & Co.; the edition limited to 315 copies.

Caradoc Press.

1348 DE PROFUNDIS, MANUSCRIPT, *beautifully written in large semi-
gothic characters, in imitation of an early Service Book, in red
and black, on two leaves of pure vellum, the intitulation, capitals,
and finials, finely illuminated and heightened with gold, purple
polished levant morocco extra, joints, watered silk linings* CENT. XX

1349 STABAT MATER, MANUSCRIPT, *beautifully written in large semi-
gothic characters, in imitation of an early Service Book, in red
and black, on six leaves of pure vellum, the intitulation, capitals,
and finials finely illuminated, heightened with gold, purple
polished levant morocco extra, joints, uniform with the preceding*
                                                CENT. XX

*** These interesting specimens of modern caligraphy were
designed and executed by Hesba D. Webb, at Caradoc,
Bedford Park, Chiswick.

1350 " IN PRAISE OF WISDOM," PRINTED ON PURE VELLUM, *with the
initials and capitals* BEAUTIFULLY ILLUMINATED BY HAND, *in
imitation of early manuscripts, only one copy issued in this manner,
morocco super extra, appropriately tooled on sides and back, silver
clasps to an original design, g. e.*   1902

*** The initials and ornaments are designed and the whole
printed by H. D. and H. G. Webb, at Caradoc, Bedford
Park, Chiswick.

1351 QUIA AMOR LANGUEO, a XVth Century English Poem, *from a
manuscript at Lambeth Palace, printed on* PURE VELLUM, *bound
in vellum with silk ties; one of* 20 *copies so produced by H. D.
and H. G. Webb at Caradoc, Bedford Park, Chiswick*

Doves Press.

1352 CORNELII TACITI DE VITA ET MORIBUS JULII AGRICOLÆ
LIBER, Officina Columbarum excuderunt T. J. Cobden-San-
derson et Emery Walker textum recensuit, *one of five copies*
PRINTED UPON VELLUM, *limp vellum, uncut*   1900

1353 THE IDEAL BOOK, OR BOOK BEAUTIFUL: a Tract on Caligraphy,
Printing and Illustration, and on the Book Beautiful as a
whole, written by T. J. Cobden-Sanderson, and printed by
him and Emery Walker, PRINTED UPON VELLUM, *limp vellum,
uncut*   1900

DOVES PRESS—continued.

1354   WILLIAM MORRIS: AN ADDRESS DELIVERED THE XIITH NOVEMBER, MDCCCC, AT KELMSCOTT HOUSE, HAMMERSMITH, before the Hammersmith Socialist Society, by J. W. Mackail, printed by T. J. Cobden-Sanderson and Emery Walker, PRINTED UPON VELLUM, *limp vellum, uncut*   1901

1355   SEVEN POEMS AND TWO TRANSLATIONS, by Alfred Lord Tennyson, printed by T. J. Cobden-Sanderson and Emery Walker, PRINTED UPON VELLUM, *limp vellum, uncut*   1902

1356   PARADISE LOST, a Poem in XII Books, the Author John Milton, printed by T. J. Cobden-Sanderson and Emery Walker, PRINTED UPON VELLUM, *limp vellum, uncut*   1902

1357   THE IDEAL BOOK, or Book Beautiful, a Tract on Caligraphy, Printing and Illustration, and on the Book beautiful as a whole, written by T. J. Cobden-Sanderson, and printed by him and Emery Walker, *limp vellum, uncut*   1902

1358   Cornelii Taciti de Vita et Moribus Julii Agricolæ Liber, Officina Columbarum excud. T. J. Cobden-Sanderson et Emery Walker, *limp vellum*   4to. *Hammersmith*, 1900

1359   The Ideal Book, or Book Beautiful : a Tract written by T. J. Cobden-Sanderson, and printed by him and Emery Walker, *limp vellum*   4to. *ib.* 1900

1360   Paradise Lost, a Poem in XII Books, the Author John Milton, printed by T. J. Cobden-Sanderson and Emery Walker, *limp vellum*   4to. *ib.* 1902

1361   Tennyson (Alfred Lord) Seven Poems and Two Translations, printed by T. J. Cobden-Sanderson and Emery Walker, *limp vellum*   4to. *ib.* 1902

1361*   Cornelii Tacitii de Vita et Moribus Julii Agricolæ Liber, *vellum, uncut*   1900

1362   The Ideal Book, or Book Beautiful, a tract on Caligraphy, Printing and Illustration, and on the Book Beautiful as a whole, *vellum, uncut*   1900

1363   Mackail (J. W.) William Morris, an address delivered the XIIth November, 1900, at Kelmscott House, Hammersmith, before the Hammersmith Socialist Society, *vellum, uncut*   1901

1364   Mackail (J. W.) William Morris, another copy, PRINTED ON VELLUM (*one of* 15 *copies*), *vellum, uncut*   1901

1365   Milton (John) Paradise Lost, a Poem in XII Books, *vellum, uncut*   1902

1366   MILTON (JOHN) Paradise Lost, another copy, PRINTED ON VELLUM (*one of* 25 *copies*), *vellum, uncut*   1902

1367   Seven Poems and Two Translations, Alfred Lord Tennyson, *vellum, uncut*   1902

1368   SEVEN POEMS and Two Translations, Alfred Lord Tennyson, PRINTED ON VELLUM (*one of* 25 *copies*), *vellum, uncut*   1902

1369   Authorised Version of the English Bible, specimen page, *folio*   1901

1370   Complete set of a List of Books printed and in preparation by T. J. Cobden-Sanderson and Emery Walker, at the Doves Press, 1901-2   (3)

<DOVES PRESS—*continued*.>

DOVES PRESS—*continued*.

1371 The Ideal Book, or Book Beautiful, a Tract on Caligraphy, Printing and Illustration, and on the Book Beautiful as a whole, written by T. J. Cobden-Sanderson, and printed by him and Emery Walker, *limp vellum, uncut*
Hammersmith, 1900

1372 William Morris, an address delivered the XIIth November, 1900, at Kelmscott House, Hammersmith, before the Hammersmith Socialist Society, by J. W. Mackail, *limp vellum, uncut*   *ib.* 1901

1373 Seven Poems and Two Translations, by Alfred Lord Tennyson, printed by T. J. Cobden-Sanderson and Emery Walker, *limp vellum, uncut*   *ib.* 1902

1374 Paradise Lost, a Poem in XII Books, the author John Milton, printed by T. J. Cobden-Sanderson and Emery Walker, *limp vellum, uncut*   *ib.* 1902

1375 The Ideal Book, or Book Beautiful, a Tract on Caligraphy, Printing, and Illustrations, and on the Book Beautiful as a whole, written by T. J. Cobden-Sanderson, was printed by him and Emery Walker, *limp vellum, uncut*   *ib.* 1900

1376 Paradise Lost, a Poem in XII Books, the Author John Milton, printed by T. J. Cobden-Sanderson and Emery Walker, *limp vellum, uncut*   *4to.* 1902

1377 Tennyson (Alfred Lord) Seven Poems and Two Translations, *limp vellum, uncut*   *4to.* 1902

1378 Paradise Lost, a Poem in XII Books, the author John Milton, printed by T. J. Cobden-Sanderson and Emery Walker, *limp vellum, uncut*   *Hammersmith*, 1902

1379 Cornelii Taciti de Vita et Moribus Julii Agricolæ Liber ; Officina Columbarum, excuderunt T. J. Cobden-Sanderson et Emery Walker, *vellum, uncut*   *4to.* 1900

1380 Seven Poems and Two Translations by Alfred Lord Tennyson, printed by T. J. Cobden-Sanderson and Emery Walker, *limp vellum, uncut*   *Hammersmith*, 1902

1381 William Morris: an Address delivered the XIth November, 1900, at Kelmscott House, Hammersmith, before the Hammersmith Society, by J. W. Mackail, printed by T. J. Cobden-Sanderson and Emery Walker, *limp vellum, uncut*   *ib.* 1901

1382 William Morris ; another copy (*as preceding*)   *ib.* 1901

1383 William Morris ; another copy   *ib.* 1901

1384 Cornelii Taciti de Vita et Moribus Julii Agricolæ Liber ; Officina Columbarum, excuderunt T. J. Cobden-Sanderson et Emery Walker textum recensuit, *limp vellum, uncut*   *ib.* 1900

Elston Press.

1385 Langland (William) The Vision of William concerning Piers the Plowman, now newly done into type by Clarke Conwell, *with illustrations and initial words by H. M. O'Kane, uncut*
(*4to*) *New Rochelle, New York*, 1901

1386 Pope (Alex.) The Rape of the Lock, the text edited from the edition of 1714, *uncut, one of 160 copies*   *ib.* 1902

Essex House Press.

1387   The Poems of William Shakespeare, according to the Text of
       the Original Copies, including the Lyrics, Songs and Snatches
       found in his Dramas, edited by F. S. Ellis, *large woodcut and
       numerous initial letters, limp vellum, uncut, one of* 450 *copies* 1899

1388   The Praise of Folie : Moriæ Encomium, a booke made in Latin
       by that great clerke Erasmus Roterodame, Englished by Sir
       Thos. Chaloner, 1549, edited by Janet E. Ashbee, *woodcuts and
       ornamental borders, vellum, uncut, one of* 250 *copies sm. fol.* 1901

1389   The Psalter, or Psalms of David, edited from the Cranmer Bible
       of MDXL, by Janet E. Ashbee, *numerous large woodcut initials
       and other ornamentation by C. R. Ashbee, one of* 250 *copies, green
       vellum, uncut*   *folio.* 1902

1390   SHELLEY (P. B.) ADONAIS, *printed under the care of C. R. Ashbee,
       by whom also is the drawing of the grave of John Keats, in the
       Protestant Cemetery at Rome, one of* 50 *copies only and all on
       vellum, bound in vellum, with a rose stamped on the upper side*
                                                                   1900

1391   The Psalter, edited from the Cranmer Bible of 1540 by J. E.
       Ashbee, *numerous woodcuts, one of* 10 *copies printed entirely on
       vellum, limp vellum, with ties*   4*to.* 1902

1392   Record of an Endeavour towards the Teaching of John Ruskin
       and William Morris, being an Account of the Work and Aims
       of the Guild of Handicraft, by C. R. Ashbee, *one of* 350 *copies,
       woodcut and initial letters, vellum, uncut*   1901

1393   THE POEMS OF WILLIAM SHAKESPEARE, according to the Text
       of the Original Copies, including the Lyrics, Songs and
       Snatches found in his Dramas, edited by F. S. Ellis, *vellum,
       uncut, one of* 450 *copies*   1899

1394   Keats (John) The Eve of St. Agnes, *printed, with a frontispiece,
       by Reginald Savage, under the care of C. R. Ashbee, one of* 125
       copies only, and ALL ON VELLUM, *vellum binding, with a rose
       stamped on the upper side*   8*vo.* 1900

1395   Shelley (Percy B.) Adonais, *printed under the care of C. R. Ashbee,
       by whom also is the drawing of the grave of John Keats, in the
       Protestant Cemetery at Rome, one of* 50 *copies only, and* ALL ON
       VELLUM, *vellum binding, with a rose stamped on the upper side*
                                                              8*vo.* 1900

Roycroft Press.

1396   Ruskin (John) Sesame and Lilies, done into a book by Elbert
       Hubbard, *ornaments and initial letters in gold and colours, uncut,
       one of* 450 *copies*   *East Aurora, New York, U.S.A.* 1897

1397   Aucassin and Nicolete, a Love Story, translated out of the
       Ancient French by Andrew Lang, *initials in gold and colours,
       stained chamois leather, silk linings, uncut*   *ib.* 1899

1398   Stevenson (R. L.) Will o' the Mill, *portrait, ornaments and initials
       by S. Warner, stained chamois leather, watered silk linings, uncut,
       t. e. g.*   *sm.* 4*to. ib.* 1901

1399   Poe (Edgar A.) Poems, IMPERIAL JAPAN VELLUM PAPER, *one of*
       100 *copies, half morocco, t. e. g.*   *ib.* 1901

Yale Press Publications.

1400   Suckling (Sir John) Poems and Songs, edited by John Gray, *woodcut border and initial letters by C. Ricketts, ornamental boards as originally issued, uncut*   1896

1401   Suckling. Poems and Songs ; another copy, *as the preceding*   1896

1402   Spiritual Poems, chiefly done out of several Languages, by John Gray, *woodcut frontispiece and border by C. Ricketts, original boards, uncut*   1896

1403   Arnold (Matthew) Empedocles on Etna, *woodcut border and initial letters by C. Ricketts, original boards, uncut*   1896

1404   Campion (Thomas) Fifty Songs, chosen by John Gray, *woodcut border and numerous initial letters by C. Ricketts, ornamental boards, as originally issued, uncut*   1896

1405   Constable (Henry) Poems and Sonnets, edited by John Gray, *woodcut border and decorations by C. Ricketts, ornamental boards, as originally issued, uncut, one of 210 copies*   1897

1406   Apuleius. Marriage of Cupide and Psyche, translated by Wm. Adlington, 1566, *woodcuts by C. Ricketts, buckram, uncut, one of 210 copies*   1897

1407   Browning (E. B.) Sonnets from the Portuguese, *initials in red, original boards, uncut*   1897

1408   Blake (William) The Book of Thel, Songs of Innocence, and Songs of Experience, *woodcut and borders by C. Ricketts, original boards, uncut, one of 210 copies*   1897

1409   Laforgue (Jules) Moralités Légendaires, 2 vol. *woodcut borders and initial letters, ornamented boards, as originally issued, uncut, one of 220 copies*   *Epping (Essex)*, 1897-8

1410   Field (Michael) Fair Rosamund, *with woodcut border and initial letters by C. Ricketts, ornamented boards, as originally issued, uncut, one of 210 copies*   1897

1411   Shelley (P. B.) Lyrical Poems, *ornamented by C. Ricketts, original boards, uncut, one of 210 copies*   1898

1412   Sidney (Sir Philip) Sonnets, edited by John Gray, *borders and initial letters by C. Ricketts, ornamented boards, as originally issued, uncut, one of 210 copies*   1898

1413   Perrault (C.) La Belle au Bois Dormant, et le Petit Chaperon Rouge, *woodcuts, borders and initial letters, ornamented boards, as originally issued, uncut, one of 224 copies*   1899

1414   Rossetti (D. G.) Hand and Soul, *woodcut borders and initial letters by C. Ricketts, original boards, uncut*   1899

1415   Guérin (Maurice de) The Centaur, the Bacchante, translated by T. S. Moore, *woodcuts by Moore, buckram, uncut, one of 150 copies*   1899

1416   Blake (William) Poetical Sketches, *woodcut borders and other ornamentation by C. Ricketts, original boards, uncut*   1899

1417   Coleridge (S. T.) The Rime of the Ancient Mariner, in seven parts, *woodcut border and initial letters by C. Ricketts, original boards, uncut*   1899

VALE PRESS—*continued.*

1418 Rubaiyat of Omar Khayyam, translated by Edward Fitzgerald, *woodcut and borders, woodcut frontispiece and borders by C. Ricketts, original boards, uncut*   1901

1419 Rubaiyat of Omar Khayyam; another copy, PRINTED UPON VELLUM, *green morocco, t. e. g.*   1901

1420 Villon. Autres Poésies de Maistre François Villon et de son École, *woodcut frontispiece, border and initial letters, ornamented boards as originally issued, uncut, one of 226 copies*   1901

1421 Field (Michael) The Race of Leaves: a Play, *woodcut border and other ornamentation by C. Ricketts, ornamented boards as originally issued*   1901

1422 Perrault (C.) Histoire de Peau d'Ane, *woodcuts, borders and initial letters, ornamented boards as originally issued, uncut, one of 230 copies*   1902

1423 Constable (Henry) Poems and Sonnets, edited from early Editions and Manuscripts, by John Gray, *with woodcut border and decorations by Chas. Ricketts, in the boards as originally issued, one of 210 copies*   1897

1424 Of Gardens, an Essay, by Francis Bacon, *woodcut and borders, boards as originally issued, one of 226 copies*   1902

1425 Of Gardens; another copy   1902

1426 Verhaeren (Emile) Les Petits Vieux, *coloured frontispiece and initial letters in red, boards, as originally issued, one of 230 copies oblong.*   1901

1427 The Centaur, the Bacchante, translated from the French of Maurice de Guérin, by T. S. Moore, *woodcuts, buckram, uncut, one of 150 copies*   1899

1428 Hero and Leander, by Christopher Marlowe and George Chapman, *with woodcuts by C. Ricketts and C. Shannon, original vellum, uncut*   post 8vo. 1894

1429 Landor (Walter Savage) Epicurus, Leontion, and Ternissa, *the build of the book and its decoration being by Charles Ricketts, one of 210 copies, green levant morocco inlaid, with interlaced outer borders of dark olive morocco, the inner compartments filled with gold tooling of trefoils and other elaborate ornamentation, full gilt back, joints, vellum linings and fly-leaves, uncut, t. e. g. by de Sauty*   n. d.

1430 The Blessed Damozel, reprinted from the German, under the supervision of Charles Ricketts, *woodcut initials, in the boards as originally issued, one of 210 copies*   1898

1431 The Life of Benvenuto Cellini, translated from the Italian by John Addington Symonds, seen through the press by C. J. Holmes, *and decorated by C. S. Ricketts, 2 vol. uncut*   sm. folio. 1900

1432 Perrault (C.) Le Belle au Bois dormant et le petit Chaperon Rouge, *woodcut, uncut*   1899

1433 *Vincent Press.* Rasselas, Prince of Abissinia, a Tale by Dr. Samuel Johnson, *woodcut borders and initial letters, limp vellum, uncut*   *Birmingham,* 1898

END OF SALE.

DRYDEN PRESS: J. DAVY AND SONS, 137, LONG-ACRE, LONDON, W.C.

Last King's Marriage Settlement.

In the name of Allah, the Compassionate, the Merciful.

(*In Arabic*). After giving praise to Allah for the institution of marriage in order to save man from sin and for his instructions to him to increase and multiply, &c., &c.

(*In Persian*). On the night of the 23rd of Ranzan in the year 1256 of the Prophet, on whom his salutations and peace, there appeared in the Council Ghuban Nasiraldur, son of Ghuban Kubaldur (deceased) who was the representative who sat before the curtain of the curtains of the angels of purity and chastity, and the star that illumines the world, her of lofty parentage and rank, enveloped in purity, the lady the Queen of the age, the Nawab Ginat Mahil the Begum Sohelah, the daughter of Razael Nawab of exalted dignity, the jewel of the mine of liberality and manliness, the gem of the ocean of generosity and excellence, the head of the nobles possessed of dignity, the embroiderer of the coat of majesty, the lifter up of the standard of glory, the sword of the state, the noble of the Kingdom ; Amaral Mulk Nawab Ahmad Kube Khan Bahadur, victorious in battle, resembling Asaf (Solomon's vazir), son of Hisamuldur the appointed of the state ; Mayam Mulk Nawab Mohammed Abas Khan Bahadur,

the most honoured of vazirs ; Nawab Shah Vali Khan Bahadur, the pearl of pearls of the tribe. With the testimony of two just and free witnesses of ripe age, one of them Fazullah Khan, son of Karmullah Khan, and the second of them Murza Ali Khan, the aforesaid representative of the delicate person has given the aforesaid refuge of purity and chastity in consideration of a dowry of the sum of 15 lakhs of rupees of the present currency, one-third to be paid out at once, and two-thirds delayed pending the duration of the marriage, as the wife and consort of the King of Solomon's dignity in the dignity of the Court of Abuafar Sarazal Din Mohammed Bahadur Shah the Ghazi King, one prepared to die for the Faith, may Allah guard his Kingdom, and being the true son of the revered one who is at rest in Paradise, Mohammed Akbar Shah Padishah, may Allah illumine his head, the son of the venerable one who dwells in Paradise, Alan Shah, may Allah illumine his tomb, son of the Emperor, sons of the Emperors. The Bridegroom who is praised above demanded and accepted the delicate person of the aforesaid lady, with the leave of her guardian and in exchange for the aforesaid dowry, and has brought himself into the state of fixed and lawful wedlock, and the lawful demand and acceptance of them has taken place, and the knot of marriage has been tied according to firm and lawful wedlock, and it has taken place according to well-known custom and rule and in the regular way of certainty and secresy. This has taken place on the date of the month of the year above mentioned.

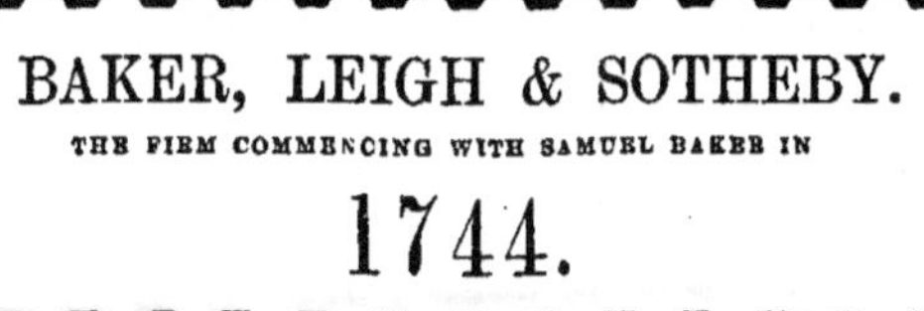

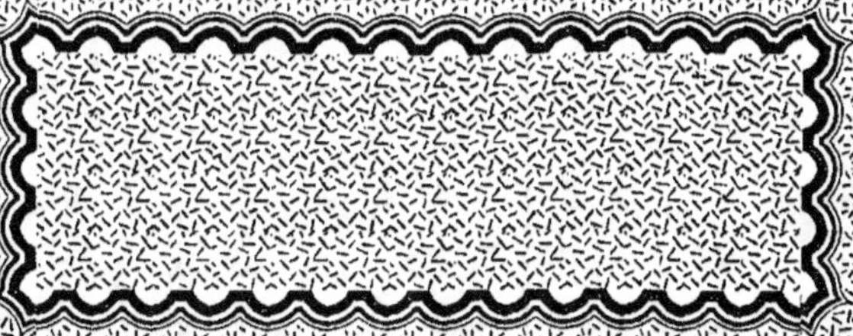

SOTHEBY, WILKINSON & HODGE.
1903.